200 241375 8

D1345483

Two week UNIVERSITY CARDIFF

ə last

Childminder

Also by Brian Jackson

Streaming: an Education System in Miniature
Working Class Community
Education and the Working Class (with Dennis Marsden)

Childminder

A study in action research

Brian Jackson and Sonia Jackson

Routledge & Kegan Paul

London, Boston and Henley

UNIVERSITY COLLEGE
LIBRARY
CARDIFF

First published in 1979
by Routledge & Kegan Paul Ltd
39 Store Street, London WC1E 7DD,
Broadway House, Newtown Road,
Henley-on-Thames, Oxon RG9 1EN and
9 Park Street, Boston, Mass. 02108, USA
Set in Baskerville 11/12 pt
and printed in Great Britain by
Lowe & Brydone Ltd
© Brian Jackson and Sonia Jackson 1979
No part of this book may be reproduced in
any form without permission from the
publisher, except for the quotation of brief
passages in criticism

British Library Cataloguing in Publication Data

Jackson, Brian, b. 1932

Childminder.
1 Day care centers — England
I Title   II. Jackson, Sonia
362.7'1   HV861.G6   79-40328

ISBN 0 7100 0272 6

Contents

Acknowledgments

This small study represents fourteen years' work with childminders. I look back with astonishment at my own innocence and ignorance to when, in the early 1960s in Birmingham, we first tried setting up small schemes — day centres, home-visiting, links with professionals, even the use of national BBC television. Many of the seeds for a more successful policy for 'other people's children' were already there. But it certainly took many succeeding phases of action, thinking, research, lobbying, research again, publicity and then transforming research conclusions into pilot projects, before something like even this modest study could be written.

I'm very conscious of how much I owe to the encouragement, stimulus and support of very many people over that time. First of all to Jenni Gunby for help long ago when we were in the midst of making the notion of an Open University practical and credible. I was immersed in that, and at the same time just discovering about childminders. These unknown areas of education — standing before and after the school system — mirrored each other. Many would have advised me to drop one. But at a desperate time (before the notion of an Open University was accepted by the politicians), it meant that we raided one frontier — a second educational chance for working adults — whilst we attempted another — a first chance for the young children of working parents. Double strikes to break the straitjacket of school-centred education, which both demanded considerable stamina from colleagues, imperfectly recognized here.

After that I don't think I could possibly have opened up the pilot work in Birmingham without the ceaseless energies of Joan Jones. I had asked her, without fully realizing what I was requesting, to help me set up some kind of community day-care system in the poorer parts of Birmingham for a thousand children under five. In the end we succeeded, and though my part diminished after the early years, Joan, at considerable risk to her health and for very meagre reward, saw it all through.

I was later to meet this same rare readiness and skill in getting things done when I asked Hazel Wigmore to help establish a National Children's Centre, along the lines of the research which Sonia, Julia and I were knitting together. What then seemed a passing invitation — a kind of community sabbatical from school teaching — was to prove an immense, almost intolerable, demand. Yet Hazel did it. And I can say just the same about my colleague Barrie Knight who would think nothing, if the need arose, of driving 500 miles in a day (unthinkable to me) to set up a Nottingham Amnesty or a Child Care Switchboard. Or just to help someone who had come unstuck in the research and action.

But behind such an interlinking chain of speculative research and risk-taking action, there must — if it is to succeed — be clear areas of stability. And at a personal level much of that has come from the executive secretary to the Trust, San Last (who also little foresaw the future demands on her life when we recruited her during one of our Education Shop projects on a Butlin's holiday camp, and lured her away from a routine post at Churchill College, Cambridge, back into innovatory work which she had last known during our halcyon days at the Advisory Centre for Education). Many other colleagues on this long road should be mentioned with thanks, especially Brian Redhead, Ruby Rae, Douglas Tilbe, Anne Goddard and Sue Owen.

This is perhaps not the place to acknowledge the different parts that Sonia and Julia have played in all this. The following pages testify to that better than I could here. But it is worth recording that this style of field research is a far cry from the tranquillity of a university library or the security of a computer. For both it meant anything from the difficulties of a 'Dawnwatch' to endless evening work in strange places seeking out mothers, fathers and minders, and occasionally some very dangerous situations.

Acknowledgments

And last of all, two special acknowledgments. First to the children: Dominic, Rebecca, Christian, Lucy, Ellen and Seth — without whose delightful demands all this would have been written up very much sooner. And to the childminders — both legal and illegal — who, quite excellently, cared for Seth and Ellen whilst we were away on this research. For us it was never a case of this being about 'other people's children', but any child of any working parent, including ourselves.

Brian Jackson
Cambridge

Authors' note

Throughout the narrative, analysis and conclusions the first person singular has been used: though, so the text declares, this frequently means different members of the team. All names are pseudonymous except for colleagues and fellow researchers, as are locations which might identify the people interviewed.

A many years ago
When I was young and charming
As some of you may know
I practised baby farming.

Buttercup's Song,
HMS Pinafore,
Gilbert and Sullivan,
first performed 25 May 1878

Part I

An investigation

1 December Dawnwatch

Boys and girls come out to play
The moon doth shine as bright as day.

Children's song

Life is like a parachute jump — you've got to get it right
first time.

Margaret Mead

Here are seven reports filed on the same December day by
seven different people who set out before dawn to watch the
first arrival of parents and small children on the city streets.

Manchester, 5.30 a.m. a week before Christmas

A dreary rubbish-strewn street on the west side. It won't be
light for a couple of hours. Cycling quickly towards me is a
young West Indian boy of about fifteen with what appears
to be a bundle of clothes perched on his cross-bar. As he
draws nearer I realize it is a three-year-old child balancing
precariously gripping the handlebars. The boy comes to a
stop at the end of the street, lifts the child off and bangs at
one of the front doors. He has to wait some time before the
door is opened by a middle-aged woman who takes the child
without a word passing between them.

A black workman with a canvas bag slung over his shoulder
slips out of a house a few doors away from where I am
standing. He has got a toddler by the hand. The child is
pitched forward on tiptoe trying to keep up with his hurrying
father. They continue like this for a good half mile through
the terraced streets, then down a flight of basement steps

3

and a hasty handover of child and small plastic food container.

I leave the back streets and talk to very young West Indian women with small babies in their arms, standing at a cold and windy bus-stop. They are on their way to work as packers in a factory on the industrial estate. Every day they break their journey halfway across town and leave their babies with an unregistered minder. It is 6.30 in the evening by the time they pick them up to make the journey back, and usually after seven before the babies reach home again.

It is 7.45 a.m. now, and the traffic has started to build up. I spot a small figure wheeling a pushchair hurrying across the road. As I draw closer I see it is a thin West Indian girl of eight or nine. The brother she is pushing must be about two, with a brightly coloured woollen hat pulled tightly down over his ears. He is clutching one of those plastic stockings filled with cheap sweets which you see in the corner shops around Christmas time.

The little girl is finding it difficult negotiating the pushchair up and down curbs, and stops to have a rest and a tickling game with the baby. Then off up the street and stops at no. 70. She can't make anyone hear by knocking on the front door, so moves on up to the top of the street, round the corner and down a row of back entries till she finds no. 70 again. This time they hear her, and both children disappear into the house.

Back of Arsenal Football Ground, London, 5.50 a.m., same day

Newsagent already open and busy. Lots of cards in the window advertising second-hand prams, wedding dresses, cookers, cots and cars. Notice one reading: 'Will mind child long hours', then another 'Do you work? Will look after baby'. Count six. One says 'registered childminder'. Must be a selling point because others don't. Last card reads 'Prisoner needs room after a very long sentence'. Anyway, off I go up Gillespie Road. Funny, mixed-up housing. Small decayed terraces, and then some very well-kept patches; not gentrified either. Dad passes me with four-year-old. Turn round and watch them disappear down Tube. Where on earth to? At this time.

Very dark, but streets already pattering with City cleaners off for the early trains. Stand outside factory gates. Lots of middle-aged women clocking on. Everyone very cheerful. Obviously I'm on the wrong patch. Go and buy paper, and now it's well after six. Then along comes a West Indian girl trundling a fat toddler in a pushchair. Then several more. I set off to note the streets and houses, but all the time I'm watching for this spectacular Comet — Kohoutek, is it? — which they say might be visible before dawn. Keep panning across the black sky.

Suddenly I've lost everybody. Made a right mess of it. Whoever thought sociology would be like this? A lot of shouting in Blackstock Road. Turn corner and creep along. Looks like a mum having a doorstep row with another woman over the child. Minder? She leaves the child and walks very quickly to the bus-stop. Can't quite screw up courage to speak to her — and here comes the bus. Wander on down Blackstock Road again. Lots of crying coming from front room. Listen very carefully. Could swear it wasn't one baby, but six or maybe seven. As I stand puzzling, young mother arrives with another. I glimpse the bottle teat (no cover on) sticking out of her bag. Feel awkward and conspicuous, so go and join bus queue. Get off near Liverpool Street. Street sign: Offord Road. Now 7.30 a.m. Lots of Asian and West Indian children on the streets. Most school-age, but many not. What are they all doing? Explore Offord Road; houses very decrepit on one side. Many empty, boarded up. On other side, lots are being poshed up. Odd. Then two children at once are delivered to one house — a West Indian and an Asian child. Takes me by surprise. I'd been looking so hard — and then it just *happened*. Anyway, I thought that house was derelict. Go behind and there's a light in the kitchen. Glimpse elderly lady. Can she be in charge? Find out later. Morale better. 8 o'clock now, and I can go back for breakfast. Join the queue and chat till the bus comes. Lady next to me says one family came home from work and found the whole front of the home gone. Like a doll's house when you lift away the facade and look at how the dollies live.

Leeds, 6.15 a.m., same day

Walk up Chapeltown Road past the synagogue, the Warsaw Delicatessen and the headquarters of Rugby League Football. Cold, huddled-up people queue at each bus stop, many West African women amongst them. Turn off into Sholebroke Avenue and the backstreets. Few street lamps working, pavement littered with sodden rubbish. Silhouette of some- one pushing a pram. Stops at corner shop for cigarettes: in the light I can see he's a young white workman, in a mac and overalls or boiler suit. Delivers baby in Grange Avenue, and half-runs to bus-stop. Five minutes later a Moslem girl, in green shalwar, emerges from the darkness. She has a pram and a toddler. Behind her a tall West Indian girl in red plat- form shoes, clacking along, roughly shouting at a three-year- old trailing behind her. All disappear in Back Grafton Street: poor dilapidated terrace houses. This one has a naked light bulb. Opposite, a bedroom window is open and three child- ren hang out and shout into the blackness. A milk float hums by, and stops at the Yam Shop.

'Yes loads of 'em,' he says, 'Y'see women taking them round minders all the time, regular. Especially these bloody blacks — and half their husbands'll be at home on Social Security.' Past us comes a Chinese lady, all furrily muffled up. A two-year-old, I'd say, walking slowly with her. They too turn down Back Grafton Street.

A pause, and it's now 7.15 a.m. and still very windy and black. Scrape dogshit off my soles for second time. Looks like the rush is over. Then at 7.30 a.m. another wave. First a fat young man, white, with one child. Then a Sikh and his child get out of a small car cram-packed with other Sikhs. And a whole bevy of Moslem ladies and their children, going in half a dozen directions. Am hard pressed to get down house numbers and streets for later calls.

Then, 8 a.m. and it must have got lighter, though the sky is still black with rain clouds. A West Indian boy with a deaf aid comes skipping out of the corner shop clutching *Beano*.

A twelve-year-old West Indian girl dances to imaginary pop music across to the cornershop.

Go and look at the bus queues. All very, very long. Guess that half of them are men and half women; half black faces and half white. I can now read the notices properly. A disfigured poster from some protest group

'Bad drains, broken street lamps, inefficient rubbish collection, not enough playgroups'

Well, I think, they're certainly right about lighting and litter — but are playgroups alone the answer to *this*? In the barber's window, it says

'Herbert's Services — Insurance, Mortgage, Loans, GCE Tuition, Hairdressing'

Very versatile man, Herbert. And a huge, vivid poster advertises a West Indian *Night of Tropical Temptation*. Only a few minutes' away, the fashionable shops in the Headrow are still an hour off opening time. And here, a score of West Indian and Asian children are already huddled in the school playground whilst many teachers in the suburbs are just stretching out of bed.

Bradford, 5.10 a.m., same day

Much too early, I grumble. Driving rain too. West Bowling is a criss-cross of back alleys, small crowded houses huddling round cobbled streets, then great stretches of devastation where council bulldozers seemingly gave up years ago. Glance at the street name — Dickens Street! The corner newsagent is opening up. Buy a *Mirror* and a KitKat, tell him what I'm doing.

'Oh yes, baby minding. There's a fair bit goes on round here. Just watch the junction, up right. Everybody passes there. Lots of Pakkies, and y'might even see some indigenous. Not that there's many indigenous left.'

Pouring rain, just *pouring*. First mum appears. Young girl

7

about nineteen if that, pushing a pram. She's white. Follow her down to a patch of waste land between a second-hand clothes shop and some house backs. Two caravans among the debris; a pile of worn out tyres, lots of rubbish, and even in this rain a whiff of smoke from last night's bonfire. Growls from a chained Alsatian inside his makeshift kennel. Past the windows of Sihail Brothers Ltd, trinkets and ear-rings winking palely in their boxes. Child handed over, and mother off to work. Then farther back an old car draws up. Indian or Pakistani father gets out with two children. Knocks on a door, waves goodbye and starts up. I walk past, curtains all drawn, jot down the number. Then two Asian mothers with toddlers and another white mum with pram. And more. A flurry of activity for ten minutes, then nothing. Must be a bus or clocking on time that they are all going for. Half an hour goes by, and nothing to report. Sikh temple — once a grimy Methodist chapel — all lit up. Wonder why?

Decide to call on the small day nursery in the district. Supervisor getting ready to receive the children.

'Why don't more of these mums come here?' I ask. 'We're full up,' she says, 'but anyway it's this terrible rise in prices — they can't afford up to £5 for a day nursery when a minder will do it for £2.50.'

Time to knock off, I think. Go back past the tinkers' caravans. Suddenly the backstreets are alive again with mums, toddlers, babies. Don't know which way to turn. Must be a later shift. None of these mums are heading to the day nursery. Take smudgy notes and console myself with the KitKat.

Huddersfield, 6 a.m., same day

Freezing morning, rain lashing my face. Already feel like going back to bed. Along the middle of Halifax Old Road come three West Indians — two men and a woman — carrying lunch bags; the cars have not yet taken over. Air full of bits of newspaper and flying sweet papers. No children at all. See newsagent's shop, go in ostensibly to buy *Mirror*, but really just for a moment's shelter. Several men, mostly black, come in and out quickly. Ask the time, just to prolong the rest. Oh God, my watch is an hour fast — Newspaperman is sympathetic,

'Oh, don't you start till eight then, love?'

Walk up the hill. See silent West Indian woman pushing pram with a chattering toddler in it. She goes at a terrific pace. I have to run to catch up. She keeps disappearing into the darkness, then coming into sight again. I scramble on. Which house is she going for? Violent gust of wind through the corner churchyard blows my scarf over my face. Run on down the hill. She's gone. I've lost her. I just stand and freeze in despair. Middle-aged West Indian, with duffle bag, turns and looks at me in astonishment. Find my way back to car and collapse in it.

Oh dear, back to it. 7.20 now, and Pakistani women on the pavement really *scurrying* to work. West Indian couple arrive in shiny car and drop off two-year-old with child-minder. In and out in thirty seconds flat. Then a Ford Capri; a man gets out and delivers a small baby. Move on, see run-over cat dying horribly in the road. At the junction of Keldregate and Sheepridge Road note a small girl — maybe three or four years — wearing a yellow traffic jacket. Can she be taking herself to the minders? Then two small Asian boys, hand in hand, and beautifully dressed in anoraks, trousers and neat little shoes. Guess the older one is four. They don't reply to me, just stare. Elder boy knocks on the door and West Indian minder pulls them quickly inside. Over to the newsagents go two beautiful Chinese girls from the take-away — maybe ten or twelve years old — they're buying tinsel for a Christmas tree. Man across the way can't start his car — plugs must be drowned. Imagine working eight hours in the mill after this!

Islington, London, 6.15 a.m., same day

Very dark. Just a scattering of dim lights in odd houses. But plenty of people out and on their way to work. Cars and trucks coming by too. Take a circuit of Kingsdown Road, Cornwallis, Alexander Road, Pallington Park, Wray Crescent,

Thorpesdale, Sussex Way. Decide to go round it three times.

Keep jottings: thus — two middle-aged women, office cleaners? West Indian youth buys paper. Two women come and fetch papers. Café open for breakfast. Lots of cats. A surviving sunflower, maybe ten feet tall. And so on.

Police calling early at a ground floor flat. Wonder why? Then see first child (with Cypriot mum) arriving at a house in Alexander Road. Then a West Indian man pushing a pram, a white woman with a pushchair and a black girl sharing a chocolate bar with two toddlers. Turn to follow, but soon spot they are on their way to Islington Day Nursery.

Eight o'clock now, and two mothers with pushchairs coming on opposite courses. Dither. Follow second one to a broken-windowed house in Tollington Road. Almost simultaneously Asian father carries in a crying two-year-old. Then a white woman with a couple of children — maybe one and two years old. Getting really busy now. Black child of around twelve months delivered by car.

The woman I first followed is at the bus stop. Go and talk to her. She's around twenty-two and works in a Tottenham factory. Picks up child around 6 p.m. and has been leaving her there since she was 16 weeks. Pays £3 a week (which includes food). Says some of the others pay £4: doesn't know why. Doesn't know whether the minder is registered or not (she isn't). Doesn't know how many other children she looks after — says there's usually half a dozen when she delivers or picks up Melanie. Bus comes.

As it pulls out I see another baby handed over and, I think, a bundle of clothes. That's the half-dozen clocked up already. Then a black mother — can't make her out better than that, arrives with her baby. Looks very harrassed. Hands over baby on doorstep and seems to have a row. Can't make out what it all is. Stay where I am, and two cars drive up — each with a black toddler. And then another car with a two-year-old. I've counted nine whilst I've been here. Give up for now and retire for breakfast.

Handsworth, Birmingham, 5.30 a.m., same day

Raining hard. Hadn't bargained for that. Must be first person in Birmingham up today. But no. Mr Nodhani, the newsagent on Soho Road already open. Pick up cigarettes, and *Mirror* to conceal my notepad. Across the road is the Indian cinema showing *Sanjihanta*, and next door is Sweet Memories — the Chinese takeaway. Dozens of faces come out of the darkness, mostly black. Decide to station myself at corner of Rookery Road; but passing the police station, call in and explain what I'm doing.

'Nothing like that round here,' says the duty officer, 'if there was, *we'd* know. Where you going first? Oh, Albert Road — West Indians down there, hundred of the buggers.'

Down Albert Road. No. 11 bus sneezes past and picks up a long queue of turbaned Sikhs. White man with corgi walks past. Corgi pees against Her Majesty's Sub Post Office. Still pouring down. Past Sidho Wine Stores (with peeling advert 'if you can't beat them . . . '), feeling very cold, and feet wet through.

Out of Albert Road comes an Asian lady, carrying one child and pulling another. Am trying to note the exact house where she hands them in when a West Indian bloke shouts at me,

'Give me a push man, this car's wet.' A yellow and black Ford Escort, all stickers and chrome. Another West Indian lad joins in and we heave into the rain:

'She's away. Thanks, man.'

Back to the job. Right away there's a West Indian girl with a child over her shoulder. Then two mums coming up Albert Road with five young children between them. Then a West Indian girl really *pulling* a small boy up Stanley Road. No good though: when she's handed him over and gets back, the No. 11 is just shunting out.

'Oh bugger it!' she shouts.

Unexpected gap. Nothing happens on the child front till 7.10. Sikh milkman drops off crates outside the café. I'm cold and starving, ready to pack it in. Resolve to give it another thirty minutes. Suddenly a flurry of Asian women — five in all and eight babies or toddlers. Make notes for later.

11

First light breaking through. If I hadn't seen it all myself, would I have believed that this was Britain now and not a hundred years ago?

Why a Dawnwatch?

This was how we began. These seven reports were filed by members of the research team a week before Christmas 1973. We put the same request to everyone.

'Get up before dawn, be in a working-class area of any city you choose in Britain, see and feel it wake up. Take notes. Above all watch for working parents, toddlers, babies and backstreet childminders.'

All tell the same story. Whilst more prosperous people (like our research workers) are normally snug and warm in bed, an unknown number of working parents are tugging their small children through city streets to spend many hours in the care of childminders who receive no support, recognition or training for their unbelievably important role in looking after small children. Is childminding a rare event or a large part of the normal life? How many minders are there who are quite unknown to the authorities? How good or bad is the care they offer? Does it affect the children's chances in school, in life? Is the childminder a key agent in the cycle of deprivation? Does she actively transmit social handicap? Or is she the special person who can break the chain? And what would she need to do that — training, money, new laws, respect?

This is the flurry of questions with which the work set off. And Dawnwatch was a way to begin. What it demonstrated for us was that the research we report here could have taken place, with similar results, in any city at all — not only in Britain but in any industrial society.

Dawnwatch (an exercise we have repeated many times since) raises a curious technical issue in empirical social science. The point was that it made the researcher cold, wet, uncomfortable, grumpy, dismayed at the early hour, the bad street lights, the gutter rubbish, and the all-demanding economic cycle driving the daily rhythms from dawn till dusk. Naturally in the social sciences one strives continually, if imperfectly, for the maximum objectivity. Yet in this stretch of the field, the data on which all is built comes from people — and people often acutely limited by the very different background that marks them off from the child-minder, the parents and the child. Perhaps by intensely involving the researchers in the place, people, relationship — not all of it comfortable — you breed fresh perception and insight which ultimately influences the whole structure that the research creates. That at least is what we have tried to do on this project.

We immediately made a public statement about what we were or were not finding through the Dawnwatch technique, and this unlocks another dimension, crucial to the way this research and argument is conducted. We have tried to conduct it as 'open research'. Open in the sense that we have done our thinking out aloud, sharing what knowledge we had every step of the way. So much expensive research — often concerned with the deprived — results in two or three years' accumulation of private knowledge, then the slow climb to publication which itself simply becomes the honeystore which the next generation of students ransack to win their certification and relatively well-paid position in the world. Again and again the 'subjects' of the research are in no way changed or better off because of it.

Nevertheless 'open research' has real dangers, principally ones of fragmentation and misinformation. This project has displayed both weaknesses; fragmentation, when people have imitated a striking research technique (the phone-in Amnesty, a market-day Play-In, the Dawnwatch itself) instead of treating it as the example of a *principle* (go public, offer pleasure, participate) which requires unique forms of expression in different situations; misinformation, when what we emphasized at one moment turns out in time to be not quite right. For example, the total emphasis on the city, or our early sense of the West Indian community as a special segment of childminding, or indeed our constant under-estimates of the total number of children involved all needed correction. Our first statement, which was a startling revelation at the time, front page news, suggested certainly 70,000 and possibly 100,000 children left with unregistered minders every day. Two years later the National Union of Public Employees independently estimated that 1,200,000 children were left daily with all minders.

Clearly there are dangers here and it is surely right to acknowledge them. And yet what do they amount to? Is it best to protect one's scholarly virginity, or to attempt public debate aimed at action with the best ideas and knowledge one has at the time? When is data ever final, research complete or knowledge secure?

The most important feature of 'open research' is its provocation to action. Classical research avoids muddying the waters. See the situation (here a childminder and her children) clearly: don't touch it: record and analyse. From the beginning of this project we have tried to provoke action by others (issuing an *Action Register*, calling national conferences, making television programmes, urging blueprints from the research, ourselves (The Children's Centre in Huddersfield, The Drop In Centre in Manchester, courses for childminders). This has the virtue of getting something done, instead of having impotently to wait for years for possible government action; and action breeds action. But it also has a crude and overlooked intellectual strength. Research is based on data, but the concluding analysis, thoughts or recommendations are untested words. They may seem to emerge logically, but do they make sense in practice? What we have tried to do here is to tackle the primary research, share findings, translate findings into action, monitor the action and thus think our way through the question which may end with a Minister for Children but begins with a damp Dawnwatch in mid-December.

2 Thinking

Just as a country gets the government it deserves, so it gets the children it deserves.   Mia Kellmer Pringle

The word 'childminder' did not until recently appear in the *Oxford English Dictionary*. Nor did it appear in any of the famous post-war British reports on education — *Early Leaving, Crowther, Newsom, Plowden, Bullock*. These have been the focus of our thinking and the ground plan of our policies on early school leaving, on untapped child abilities, on the needs of the average child, on the importance of pre-school education and on those pupils who never adequately learn to read and write.

Why has childminding — which clearly might connect with all these matters — remained invisible? There has been something odd about the way we have been looking at provision in early childhood and its possible links with the huge education system which succeeds it. Three assumptions have dominated — and blinkered — it. First a belief that education comes through *institutions*. Just as we have universities and schools, so we have thought of pre-school education in terms of expanding the institution downwards — building nursery classes. This is expensive, and therefore slow. By 1975 we had reached the situation where 33 per cent of four-year-old children were attending (usually part-time) nursery or primary classes. This does *not* mean — as successive ministers here and commentators overseas have assumed — that a third of our children begin part-time schooling on their fourth birthday. The figure includes a large proportion of children allowed to enter school at the beginning of the term in which their fifth birthday occurs —

15

only weeks away from compulsory schooling. The provision simply skims the top of the question. For example, and quite understandably, such provision only serves 1 per cent of children aged two to three years, and no children at all under that. Clearly thinking in terms of the institution has, if only because of expense, bred an educational tortoise (after all, 43 per cent of children aged three to five attended public elementary schools in 1900).[1] Such progress is difficult to win financial support for, and then — because it is not part of compulsory schooling — it is always stopped or pushed back in bleak economic years. For example, 1975 saw large numbers of authorities severely cutting back on nursery classes and eight actually sending back their grant aid to central government.[2] And as we see, this approach can never be preventative or a major force for equal opportunity. It comes too late and is too far from the formative swirl of home, family, street. Unfortunately it seems to have blinded us to the world outside the institutions — that is part of the reason why *Childminder* has not appeared in our major educational reports.

The second assumption that has curtailed our thinking has been a belief in professionals. To provide for the under-fives we have trained two cadres of professionals: nursery nurses — whose profession is health and care — to staff day nurseries; and nursery teachers — whose profession is education — to staff nursery schools. Both professions are utterly separate, and both look inwards to their institution and tend to move away from the most crucial carer and teacher of all — the parent. The Office of Population Censuses and Surveys in 1975 showed that only 16-17 per cent of mothers ever spent any time at their four-year-old child's nursery or reception class, and that 64 per cent of mothers with children at nursery school quite clearly felt that mothers were not welcome.[3]

Once again this line of thinking is costly. Professionals need two- or three-year training courses, colleges in which to house these, and more professionals to teach them. Inevitably growth is slow; so slow that following this line of thought there is no possibility of such professional attention for all young children for generations ahead. And even at the moment of writing — 1976 — which is the highest peak of nursery school provision we have seen, the ratio of child to teacher can be astonishingly poor. A National Union of Teachers' survey of twenty-six nursery schools in three areas reported teacher/pupil ratios of 1:54, 1:30 and 1:80.[4] These figures are arrived at by the somewhat artificial device of excluding nursery nurses, who largely staff these schools, from the formal definition 'teacher'. But they should be borne in mind when we later explore the number of children cared for by one childminder.

Standing against this policy that support for young children can only come by expanding the professional cadres, is the one astonishing phenomenon of the 1960s and 1970s — the rise of the entirely parent-run pre-school playgroup movement. This now claims to serve 310,000 children[5] — many times more than all the professionals look after. Of course a playgroup may be for only two hours, perhaps meeting for just one or two days a week in someone's house or a church hall. And although there are exceptions, this is — and indeed must very largely be — a service which flourishes in middle-class and some upper-working-class areas. The British Association of Social Workers summarizes the dilemma well:

'There is an important role for pre-school playgroups as part of a policy of positive discrimination. At the same time it may be difficult to ensure that they do in fact contribute to this policy. Playgroups depend on the voluntary effort of parents who know how to engage children in constructive play and who have time to do this. To have any effect on the cycle of deprivation they have to reach the children of parents who neither know how to play with their children nor have time to do so. We wonder to what extent playgroups succeed in reaching this group of children, particulary those whose mothers go out to work.'[6]

That surely is right — we have also to look for other keys, or ways of linking playgroups into other strategies of change — but the point here is that the biggest advance for the middle class (and one which, left to itself, could have the side effect of widening the gap between the haves and the have nots) has come by looking outside established professionalism and releasing neglected energies, skills and resources both in mothers and in their local community.

The third curtailing assumption that has stood behind official documents, behind our priorities and such provisions as we have made for young children, is that we are all middle class now. There is a huge gap between what we saw in 'Dawnwatch' and the last thirty years of debate about pre-school education.

One example of this would be the official disapproval (from the Department of Health and Social Security) of mothers with young children going out to work. Meanwhile, of course, other government ministries (such as Employment) have done all they can to get them to work. And the Department of Education, when short of teachers, has most positively recruited mothers of under-fives by giving local authorities funds specifically to provide nursery places for their children. It is not professional women working that is disapproved of. Nor is it middle-class mothers generally — for the last thirty years have seen a huge increase in their own private day-care system: *au pair* girls. These have in part taken over from the disappearing servant (in 1911 there were 2,100,000 women in service, now there are hardly any). But *au pair* girls have also taken over from the Victorian nanny. No one knows the scale, but probably far more middle-class children are in part looked after by this new-style nanny than ever had a nanny in the past.

No, it is the working-class mothers going out to work who are the target of disapproval, except in times of emergency. By the end of the 1939-45 war, during which huge numbers of working-class women were needed in munition works, we had rapidly built enough day nurseries for 71,806 children. But once the war was over the Ministry of Health issued a circular (221/45) saying that 'the right policy to pursue would be positively to discourage mothers of children under two from going to work.' Note the word 'discourage'. It doesn't say 'encourage them to stay at home with their baby' and suggest policies that might do that (for example, a cash bonus). Nor does it say 'pursue policies which give working mothers the maximum *choice* of whether to work or not'. The circular[7] goes on to argue and implicitly direct that day nurseries should only be seen as supplements for children with special needs; 'children whose mothers are incapable for some good reason of undertaking the full care of their children.' Clearly going to work, having to go to work, choosing to go to work, are not by themselves 'good reasons'. In 1951 the Ministry returned to the attack and in a fresh circular recommended that cost of day-nursery provision 'should not be incurred when the question of day care *arises solely from the mother's desire to supplement the family income by going out to work'*.

Similarly the academic climate was set by Dr John Bowlby's vastly influential study: *Child Care and the Growth of Love*. Two of the most widely quoted remarks from that study were uncritically repeated by generations of university lecturers and are to be found studded in shoals of minor books. The first is: 'The mother of young children is not free, or at least should not be free, to earn.' And the second: 'Young people thrive better in bad homes than in good institutions.'

It was a recipe for disaster. Society closed down day nurseries and did nothing else. By 1964, places had dropped to 21,530. In 1976 pressure at last halted the slide and the figure rose again to 23,718. Perhaps in the light of the kind of counter-arguments presented here it can be gradually but modestly increased. But there seems little chance of the money being found in the next decades to replace what has been cast away in the last ones. And at the same time as the day nurseries have been disappearing, the number of women going out to work (not only in Britain but in all industrial societies) has steadily risen, only temporarily held up by hiccups in the statistics during periods of economic recession. This leads us back to Dawnwatch, to the need for and growth of childminding as a largely unknown, self-help, working-class system; and to a sense that much of this wasteful and negative policy was essentially based on middle-class assumptions.

We have seen how that displays itself in attitudes towards the *one* form of offical provision, which is likely to be dominantly used by working-class children. The same analysis holds good if we look at the content of day nurseries and nursery schools.

Day nurseries (as we progressively explore in this research) are not educational institutions. They are run by matrons, assisted by nursery nurses, often but not always of course, in variants of hospital uniform. No one doubts their care of, and commitment to, the children in their charge, nor their achievements. But what is striking is that they serve exactly those children who (all the evidence so suggests) need the earliest and maximum *educational* stimulation. Yet day nurseries (always with exceptions) are almost exclusively concerned with care and health — screening, diet, sleep, cleanliness. Indeed our impression is that the majority of the staff (whose own training and experience may be very limited) simply do not see an educational question even when they are the major actors in it; do not know when they are holding a child back; are not aware of opportunities missed; and seldom or never operate with an educational plan for each child in mind. This is not recorded as a criticism of particular staff. How — without education and support themselves — can they be expected to have a dual professional identity as nurses and teachers? The question is how do we come to provide this institution and this profession for children many of whom must logically be at a high educational risk? It arises, I suspect, because socially we have suffered from tunnel vision[8]. These are 'other people's children'. This is what I mean by the way the middle-class perspective has dominated our thinking and our actions. Visiting a spotlessly white factory nursery in the Lancashire cotton belt, we noticed that though space was very limited (every ten children cost the floorspace of another loom) nevertheless a kind of receiving room had been screened off where mothers handed over their babies or toddlers to the nurses. They were not allowed into the main room, nor could they visit their child during the day — even though they had (admittedly brief) breaks and were working only fifty yards away. It was like watching a parcel office at a railway station. The mothers submitted. But the scene had an important invisible message. It said the mothers were inadequate (as the government circular in its polite Whitehall way also insists). The children needed a daily spell in hospital to cure them of the risks of home, family, life around. Now of course these children often *may* need a lot of loving professional attention to their well-being. One thinks again of the simple physical needs of those children in the Dawnwatch reports. But can one imagine the wife of a senior civil servant or of a parliamentary legislator docilely handing over her small child like this?

Similar tunnel vision applies with nursery schools if in a quite different way. As day nurseries have been reduced, nursery schools have become the point of official advance. But no matter how far they advance, they are never — as they stand — going to have more than partial relevance to working-class mothers with a job. A factory may start at 7.15 a.m. If you have a small child to wake, dress, feed; a childminder to take it to; a bus to catch to work — then you may well have to wake at 5.45 a.m. It is the same at the other end of the day. We begin with a Dawnwatch. We could equally end with a 'Nightwatch'. In Huddersfield (which we later explore and quantify) a job for a woman which finishes at 4 p.m. is quite commonly referred to as 'part-time work'. And of course you may work much later than that. There is overtime — suppose the foreman offers another two hours — 'there's a rush job in today'. Can you refuse? You need the money — that's why you're here: mill work is not a vocation. You may not get asked next time. And whether overtime or not, there is the bus home, a child to pick up, the walk back, and a tired toddler to undress and put to sleep. It can be a very long day indeed for mother and for child, every working day of the year.

So why have we put our major resources — and our almost exclusive argument — into nursery schools? Needless to say this is not a case against nursery schools or their work as such, but a puzzlement as to why we *think* exclusively in those terms. Nursery schools are very expensive to build and costly to run. Yet they normally operate only from 9 a.m. to around 3 p.m., for only five days of the week, and only thirty-nine or less weeks of the year. Suppose we do a sum. Let us say that there are twelve potentially usable hours each day (7 a.m. to 7 p.m.) Allow the building always to stand idle every Sunday (though one could imagine community use there). Exclude all public holidays. Exclude two weeks of the year for a complete shut down (maintenance, repairs, improvement). Leave aside the question of staff (for clearly more intensive use will imply either more staff, or rota staff, or a mixture of staff and community volunteers). Measured against this possible use of an expensive public resource, nursery schools are active only 31.6 per cent of the available time.[9] We may argue about the details here, but the answer that is always going to emerge will be of the same astonishing magnitude. (Tell those figures to someone who runs, far less importantly, a North Sea oil rig.) Of course this same analysis could be applied (often with much greater force) as one moves along the educational scale — to schools and universities. And more intensive use of the place will clearly increase some running costs.

But *why* do we tackle a situation in this way? It is, I think, because we assume a middle-class rhythm (children up at a quarter to eight), a middle-class life style, and a sense of where the woman should be (serving children's tea at four o'clock). Now there is nothing wrong in this life style, and it is of course shared by very large numbers of people who are not middle class by any definition. It is only when we hear words like 'childminders' or 'latchkey children' or 'double-shift families' that we are momentarily aware that such minimum service as we now possess does not actually match many people's needs, and particularly a large number of children who would seem to need these services as an absolute priority.

If we now look inside nursery schools we enter an Aladdin's cave of child-centred education — splashing water, sandtrays, puzzles, story time, free play. A coherent curriculum. But it is also a professional extension of the middle-class home, its perceptions of children's needs and its patterns of rearing. Again a caution. I am not criticizing such approaches (and indeed strongly share them). But this is, both in time and globally, an *unusual* way of educating very young children.[10] More immediately it is *not* the way most working-class parents look at children or behave towards children outside school. Leave aside the 'should' for a moment and consider actuality. On the whole working-class parents expect a more obvious and overt learning structure. Now in this they may be right or they may be wrong. They may be prisoners of their own restricted educational experience, or protesters that schools do not give enough of their children enough of those basic skills which can clearly transform the material basis of adult life. Or the truth may be caught somewhere in between.

The point that is relevant here is that we plan to meet the concern of most parents for their young children by offering them a strange culture. We have not, as a deliberate and practical piece of public policy, taken the trouble to be explicit and defend it. That has been left to the media and atmospherics. Consequently it is often seen by the majority as yet another educational fashion. Who knows — much of it could disappear as fast as the mini-skirt: all it needs is some influential reading — 'riting — 'rithmetic scandal. I don't offer this as forecast, and most certainly not as wish. What I do offer is the thought that the professionals have not troubled to explain themselves to their clients and pay-masters. Still less (remember those figures about parents' exclusion from nursery schools — the most 'open' part of our whole school system) have they created a cultural dia-logue with parents about how their children are, or might be, educated.

Now *why* haven't they? Isn't it because, once again, our social thinking has been innocently informed by middle-class (and often missionary) assumptions? And the immediate danger is not that it will all disappear in a puff of smoke as so many educational fashions have: where is eurythmics now; take me to the junior schools that still teach Nuffield Science; show me the vast forests being chopped up into Cuisenaire rods. The hazard is that the parents will not use the service. And the more 'we' define 'them' as most needing it for their children, the less in practice we will find them taking up such slender opportunities as exist. Quite apart from the fact that the siting of nursery schools (in developing rather than derelict areas) is in itself an unaware but powerful act of discrimination, we will also find that the unknown, unbelievable or unexplained content means that many working-class parents actually do not see why they should prefer it for their child (especially if it is inconvenient, official, and very part-time) instead of the (to us) unstimulating care offered by auntie in the next street or the paid childminder over the road or a harassed mother at home by herself.

Put them together and these three exclusive and under-questioned beliefs — in institutions, in professionals, in middle-class styles and attitudes — at least go some way to explaining the astonishing absence of childminding not only from the accepted university dictionary of the language (even though one hears the word in every corner shop) but from the vast and very concerned literature on the needs of pre-school children.

Before trying to think to the next stage, perhaps I should underline (because in seminars and meetings I find this is sometimes a tripwire) that though this may be an analytical critique, it is not an attack on institutions, professionalism, middle-class styles of living — and most certainly not on pre-school playgroups, day nurseries or nursery schools.

I am quite ready to be open about all those. I was one of the earliest supporters and members of the pre-school playgroup movement. I have always been associated with campaigns for nursery education. The first article of any effect at all I wrote in *The Times*, 'Forget-me-not', was a documented plea, at a moment of possibility, for a real government plan for nursery schools instead of the fragmented situation we had then. Perhaps more to the point, we send our own children to nursery schools and playgroups and have set up many of both from scratch.

Nor am I against institutions. Indeed I use the word in a very simple sense: bricks-and-mortar which then tends both to include and exclude and help create a whole internal network of behaviour. I am certainly not for abandoning schools tomorrow in search of suddenly richer ground. Though I very much respect and have learned a good deal from that American school whose epicentre is probably the writings of Ivan Illich, I suspect that to translate it into these terms will in time leave one with the educational equivalent of fool's gold.

Some essential forms of education can *only* happen in institutions or through professionals, but it may also be that much if not most education — in broad motivational or experimental terms — clearly takes place, and will take place, far outside them.

It is only the narrowness, inflexibility, and waste with both institutions and professionals that is germane here. And finally I considerably admire middle-class patterns of child-rearing and child-centred schools which, ultimately, I think, are a professionalization of them. What I am concerned about is that without more explicability, more readiness to give and take, more preparedness to recognize and meet with other styles of life, then our present viewpoint on pre-school children will simply widen the educational gorge. Christopher Jencks says 'variations in what children learn at school depend largely on variations in what they bring to school'. He ends, I think wrongly, 'not on variations in what schools offer them'. Dawnwatch shows us some of the variations in the early morning streets. A look at policies and provision shows us the often unexpected and unplanned variations there that may change a child's whole life. But a look inside a day nursery or a nursery school — or if we get behind those childminder's doors — also suggests that those internal variations could be part of that mysterious, serviceable and delphic phrase: the cycle of disadvantage. Slowly, one begins to see why the street word 'childminder' has been missing so long from the *Oxford English Dictionary*.

3 Exploring

One doesn't discover new lands without consenting to
lose sight of the shore for a very long time.

André Gide

Childminder — that missing word in the academic vocabulary
— could open up, if not a new avenue, then an unexpected
alleyway to some of the needs of many young children who
have the odds stacked against them. Just possibly it could
allow us to do more than that. Maybe here is a way of re-
defining the pre-school question, asking it afresh and therefore spotlighting new and hopeful ways forward. And *if* it
did so, then since these very early years are, on all the evidence, the time when so much human potential is often
critically galvanized or curtailed, then .... But this is the
eternal Castle of If. Is it made of playing cards or stone? We
need to look at the evidence so far.

First of all, we know the number of registered childminders in England and Wales. It is 30,333 licensed for
91,878 children. Partly because of this 'open research' and
the public way in which some of it has been conducted, the
number of registered minders is rising rapidly. So we have a
substantial base number which on the official evidence has
shown a consistent *upward* trend. Whether this is a real
figure or not we must doubt. Clearly very few, if any, of the
children seen on dawnwatch would end up as government
statistics. The true figure is going to be higher, but how high
we can't yet tell.

Nevertheless, let's take the base figure and compare it
with other forms of day care. Local authorities offer this,
through day nurseries, for up to 25,700 children. There are

also day nurseries offered by employers.[1] These give another 2,400 places. We can be very confident about this figure, since employers commonly count this provision against tax. But we should record that voluntary nurseries provided by employers tend either to be where there is a specialist labour shortage (as with the excellent nursery at Gannex Mills, Elland, Yorkshire, which helps to attract and hold trained collar, pocket and button women); or else they are where an educated, professional workforce demands it. For instance, the Inland Revenue, some hospitals and many universities provide this service. So this figure may be highly socially selective or include many children who enjoy excellent educational support.

There are also 22,000 at private establishments. Some of these are clearly there to provide a useful service for ordinary working mothers, like the corner shop. Others are really extended kindergarten: a preliminary part of the private education system. We simply do not know the proportions, but the fact that they must make profits suggests many are really part of the pre-prep scene rather than the major world of working-class childminders that we are exploring here.

Nevertheless if we total these figures, we end up with 50,100 children as very much an arithmetical and social maximum provided for by the state, employers and private enterprise together; compared with 91,878 children as very much an arithmetical and social minimum provided for by known registered childminders. Clearly childminders are the major form of day care. And the clues are that more information about the real numbers and who their clients generally are may lead towards an increasing sense of their critical role.

We can note four other preliminary points about childminders. First they are not only looking after four-year-olds as a nursery school might. They are looking after very young babies and toddlers ('with what appears to be a bundle of clothes perched on his crossbar') as we sensed in Dawnwatch. They are receiving children from early hours and may keep them late. They are offering — in terms of time — a form of care which far outstrips what any later teacher (or often their own parents) can give. Then clearly the demand for their services is the highest in poorer areas where mothers are under pressure to work, where state provision is often weakest and where most costly forms of private nursery do not normally exist. Last, and this could prove to be important, there is no significant cost to the ratepayer or taxpayer (as there is with day nurseries or nursery schools). This is a private financial transaction, and that must imply both strengths and weaknesses.

Serving more children than the state, taking them from a very young stage, caring for them over very long hours, working chiefly in areas of great need, and at negligible direct cost to society, could childminding be a clue towards breaking the cycle of deprivation?

That is not, of course, how Parliament has seen it. Childminders have twice come to parliamentary notice. In the late 1940s several tragic fires in which children died whilst the minder was out shopping led to a newspaper campaign, which resulted partly in the drafting of the 1948 *Nurseries and Childminders Regulation Act*. This, for the first time, required minimum standards for people caring for other people's children and being paid for it. The Act is overwhelmingly concerned with children's health, and inspection of childminders is delegated to local health authorities. There is no sense at all of childminders having an educational role, nor indeed of their having any possibilities. The implicit image of the childminder, as reflected in the law, is of a tiny backstreet industry where children have lice in their hair and are left alone with unguarded paraffin heaters. The Act empowers health visitors and fire officers, if not to stamp out childminding, then to limit, inspect and control it. Up to three children could be looked after without registration. Clearly civil servants and parliament were legislating on the basis of a now-forgotten newspaper campaign and literary memories of Victorian baby-farms. There was no trace of any research. No sign that anyone ever visited a childminder or asked them for their opinion.

Twenty years later the whole scene was re-run. Again there were prominent reports of children burned to death. The paraffin heater was blamed. So was the shopping childminder. Working-class children die every week, of course, in areas where everyone's house is a fire hazard. It happens whether parents are there or not. But a second newspaper took up the issue (one can almost see a journalist flicking through the back files) and turned it into a campaign — with the childminder as target. This led to a committee, and a very good independent report.[2] The result, filtered through Whitehall and Westminster, was the childminding section of the 1968 *Health Services and Public Health Act.*

This is the law now in force. The law requires that anyone who looks after a child, other than a relative, for more than two hours a day — and gets paid for it — must register with the local authority. This was at first the health authority, and then became the new social services department. The penalty for not doing so is £50 fine or three months in prison.

Conditions of registration may be interpreted locally in varying ways. But the standard procedure is that the prospective minder must make a declaration of health and has usually to attend a hospital for a chest X-ray. She must also sign a statement saying that she has never been convicted of an offence against a child or young person, and has never had a child taken into care. There is a question about 'nervous or other similar illness'.

Afterwards the minder's home is normally visited 'to check on health facilities'. This means measuring the cubic airspace per child; the number, height and condition of toilets; hot and cold water, sinks and baths. There may also be a visit from the fire officer who will look for unguarded wires, heaters, fires, extinguishers, escape routes (chutes, fireproof doors etc.). There will certainly be a report and recommendation on other hazards — steep stairs, stone floors, stairgates, first aid kits, window guards.

If these conditions are met, the local authority may then register the applicant for a stated number of children. There may be other conditions added. The prospective minder is sent a copy and has fourteen days in which to object. If there is no objection, the registration will be confirmed by successive committees and then the full council. After that a certificate is granted, specifying the number of children; the hours and days on which they can be minded; whether helpers can be employed and if so, how many; and there may be other stipulations.

All this may take two or three months. It is quite common for it to take six months or more. With some of the minders we have interviewed it has taken eighteen months. (Where, meanwhile, one wonders are the children supposed to be?)

Naturally some authorities have interpreted this as liberally as they could. But as we begin this research it is clear that most local bureaucracies have actually increased and complicated the legislation. Glamorgan, (which is a long way from being an unimaginative or unconcerned authority) can be taken as a median example. Its application form required, in addition to the above, full details of 'any serious mental or physical illnesses' experienced by anyone helping the childminder (and underlines that the minder 'is responsible for notifying the social services department of all changes'). You then have specifically to declare that you have never murdered a child, helped a child to commit suicide or killed one of your own babies.

It is finally pointed out that if you now sign this wrongly, the penalty moves up to a £100 fine *and/or* six months in prison. The law is entirely negative, hugely time-consuming, most intrusive, implicitly insulting, and a million light-years away from the streets of *Dawnwatch*. I am astonished that we have any registered childminders at all.

Inevitably it becomes a law which does not work. In 1972, probing the question, we discovered that even in a progressive London borough like Haringey, three out of four applicants withdrew before the registration process was complete. (But clearly the children needing minders did not suddenly drop by 75 per cent). With considerable difficulty we obtained figures of prosecutions under these Acts for 1964-69:

1964	3 prosecutions
1965	5 prosecutions
1966	1 prosecution
1967	2 prosecutions
1968	2 prosecutions
1969	0 prosecutions

One may argue that this is the kind of law — the social worker as policeman — which almost never *should* be enforced. The fact is that it almost never *is* enforced. It harasses, devalues and finally drives the childminders in the neighbourhoods of most need underground.

Now research often seems to begin with a problem. And to call it that is already to give it a shape, edges, and value which thereafter stop you thinking freely, protect you against new, unexpected or contrary data. But, given the problem, you then seem — by a series of logical enquiries and analyses — to move towards a 'solution'. Almost always we project this white-coated sense of social scientists statically testing and thinking in that queer laboratory which is all of us together. This is of course a display of inferiority and mimesis to the physical scientists. It is also a misunderstanding of what actually happens in an innovative laboratory. Almost always there are moments when you seize the question like a dog with a bone, but other moments when you hibernate with it like a squirrel hoping the nuts will hatch in the spring. Times too when you toy with it all — and indeed those can often be the apparently illogical ones when you glimpse the dilemma or the possibility from a stange new angle. And more queer forces — time or luck — intrude, hinder or suddenly start doing some of your work for you.

In a much smaller way it has been like that with childminding. Growing up in a working-class street, I've always known the word 'childminder' — something you overheard listening to the mothers' conversation in the fish-and-chip shop queue, something you saw among the little white cards advertising second hand prams, old fur coats or wedding dresses ('only worn once') in the Post Office. But I can't say that it focused for me until the middle 1960s. I was working with Joan Jones in Balsall Heath, a huge, poor, dismal, derelict and ignored stretch of Birmingham. The only time the nation noticed that area was when an eight-year-old boy (whose father was dead and whose mother died of cancer) lived rough, flitting from empty house to empty house, until the authorities decided to hunt and capture him. That, by some accident, made headlines. At the time, we were trying to set up a string of playgroups and day centres for a thousand children under five in that area.

We created the play centre out of almost nothing. But then — the children — except the few better-off white children — didn't come. What we were encountering at that time was an Asian or Caribbean population who simply did not see why their child needed to go to a nursery, or why the child should play. What was the point of this alien provision and behaviour? Huge cross-cultural questions hit us every minute with every child or parent we talked to.

After two or three years (not only because of our own, often despairing efforts but also — I now think — because the new migrants were beginning to recognize that they were always going to live in Britain, and that was where, for better or worse, their child's future lay) the children began to flow in. A good period, and yet as one greeted the green-turbaned Sikhs, the Pakistani ladies who had never worked, the young English scaffolder in his metal hat, one wondered where other children were? Where were the children of all those unmarried West Indian girls around? That was the question we saw first.

Having created an interlinking chain of playgroups in a very deprived area, we began to grow out of triumph and think again. It was my colleague, Gill Southwell, who casually opened a new door. At St Paul's in Balsall Heath, we had set up a day nursery for thirty children. Gill was in charge and we took them in from just after seven in the morning.

There was a small baby girl, with huge blistering sores around her lips, and what looked like incipient abcesses adjacent to both ears. I picked her up and asked Gill.

'Yes — that'll be the childminder — I think she props the bottle in their carrycots and leaves them. Sometimes the milk runs round the side, and of course they're all by themselves. I think that's what causes the sores.'

Childminder, I thought. That's where they are. I see, of course, that the dribbly milk bottle may not and perhaps cannot explain that little girl's sores. But at that moment it seemed credible. What seemed more possible was that, idiotically, I wasn't reading one of the simplest features of the social landscape.

It took five years of laborious, time-consuming discussion with government departments, local authorities, private trusts and foundations to raise the very modest money to take a small but systematic look at childminding. I've written that application so often that I could write it in the sand at Blackpool with my left big toe whilst reading the football results. And then the Social Science Research Council agreed to back it. Into action.

At this moment I was the Simon Fellow at Manchester University. With the usual horror of a Yorkshireman I shuddered every time I crossed the Pennines and met that metropolitan hunk of stone on the M62 with the red rose engraved and painted on it: the ancient rose of blood, Tudor treachery, and of too many undeserved Lancashire victories at Old Trafford. Really I knew nothing about Manchester. Even the most obvious features of its social structure were invisible to me. Like Rochdale, it was one of the seven forbidden cities. Certainly in Manchester University childminding was the strangest of concerns. I looked blankly out from my oil-heated cell in the tower-block university at the rotting streets around, slowly ripening for the corporation bulldozer. Along the corridor PhDs flitted to and fro.

Still, everyone agreed that childminding went on in Manchester, and that it was important to know more about it. So we decided that this enquiry would be a local study — midway perhaps between sociology and anthropology — in some selected ward of Greater Manchester.

Then we thought about a control situation. And that's where Huddersfield came in. It was accessible, I'd done two previous studies there, and when we consulted the officials they assured us (this was before Huddersfield became Kirklees) that childminding was very minor, not a problem at all and that unregistered minding did not exist. We double-checked on these soundings. The most distinguished educationalist in Huddersfield was Trevor Burgin who had in *Spring Grove* written one of the pioneer books on multi-racial education. He arranged a seminar in Huddersfield at which twenty-five of the most likely teachers, social workers, parents and officials could pool their sense of childminding. It was agreed at the end of the seminar that the official view

33

was broadly right.

So there we had our control. What was different in employment, housing, pre-school provision and attitudes to the young child that led to childminding in Manchester on that side of the Pennines but not to childminding in Huddersfield on this side? It was on this basis that we received backing for the research and on this basis that we conceptualized and planned it.

The idea of Dawnwatch had not then crossed my mind. I was instead concerned to seek out any previous research which could yield any clues. The educational and social service shelves proved a blank.

But fugitive medical literature was much more promising. It was clear that a number of eminent doctors, paediatricians and psychiatrists like Eric Stroud and G. Stewart Prince were particularly concerned about West Indian mothers, whom they saw as patients, and their young children. There wasn't very much, it was all narrowly specialist and unrelated but it was research of high professional quality and considerable human caring.

Only one enquiry focused specifically on childminding in the West Indian community. It was carried out by Eva Gregory as part of a wider study of child-care practices in a group of West Indian families. Her sample consisted of eighty-seven mothers in Paddington who had given birth to children between 1 January and 30 September 1964. She found that 56 per cent of these mothers were working, a figure nearly three times the national average, and that the majority of the others had worked at some time during the two and a half years since the child's birth. For most this was a matter of economic necessity. Either they were supporting the family on their own, or their husbands were in poorly paid manual occupations. Two-thirds of the sample had left other children behind in the West Indies, and contributions towards their keep were a further drain on the meagre wage packet. Many of the non-working mothers would have worked if they could have found someone to look after the children.

Four mothers simply left their children uncared for during part of the day, but most of the others found a solution in the unregistered childminder. This was not necessarily because no local authority day nursery was available, though only the unsupported mothers would have had much chance of getting places there. Three-quarters of the working mothers had not even considered a day nursery. They were deterred by the distance to the nursery — time taken in getting the child there had to be added to each end of a long working day — and by the idea of being assessed for payment on a sliding scale. A childminder was likely to be nearer and cheaper.

Mothers who used illegal childminders had usually found them through shop-window advertisements or personal recommendation. They seem to have been quite willing to give the names and addresses of their minders to the research workers, which suggests that the regulations were not well known or effectively enforced. When the unofficial minders were asked why they had not applied for registration, most were either unaware of the law or had simply not bothered.

The seventeen illegal childminders who were contacted in this way were compared with the thirty-nine registered minders in the district. Eva Gregory found it was impossible to draw any clear demarcation line between the two groups. The unofficial minders tended to be cheaper and to look after more children so as to make the work financially worthwhile. Three of them lived in one room, each looking after nine or ten children with ages ranging from a few months to five years. Overcrowding was the main characteristic which distinguished illegal from registered minders. Otherwise there was no guarantee that the children would get better care from official minders. No doubt, Eva Gregory comments, the local health authority was unwilling to enforce too stringent standards in an area where need so far outstripped provision.

The frequently casual nature of the arrangements was brought home by the finding that many childminders were unsure of the childrens' names and addresses. Nine of the unofficial minders and five of the registered ones had no idea where to contact the mother during the day in case of emergency.

What quality of care do the children get during their mothers' long working days? The report offers a few alarming glimpses. Heating is chiefly by oil stoves. None of the illegal childminders had taken any safety measures. A third of them said they would leave the children alone if they wanted to go shopping. In seven homes there were no toys or play equipment at all, and ten minders (three of them registered) admitted to having neither time nor inclination to play with the children. A large number of children were confined all day to the one room used by the minder, even if there was a garden or yard where they could have played.

These findings have been confirmed by two other London studies. Dr Eric Stroud of King's College Hospital in a survey of one hundred consecutive admissions of West Indian mothers found that 63 per cent of the mothers went out to work and nearly all left their children with a childminder. Only three had found places in an official day nursery. Half the children had been cared for by more than one minder, and a quarter had been minded by at least three different women.

Later, the Institute of Race Relations published a study of one-year-old West Indian children in Paddington. This describes a very thorough medical and social survey of a representative sample of West Indian babies — all those in a chosen area whose birthdays fall between certain dates. The authors were mainly interested in the children's physical condition and in the extent to which their mothers were aware of and made use of available health services, but they did also collect evidence on the mothers' work experience and childminding arrangements. Over half the West Indian mothers went out to work, as compared with 18 per cent of the non-West Indian control group; 14 per cent of the babies were in local authority day nurseries and the remainder went to relatives or baby minders, most of them unregistered. For many of the children this had begun in the earliest months of their lives, and some had already had two or three different minders; thirty-nine of the children spent at least nine hours a day away from their mothers. Most of the private caretaking arrangements were considered by the research team to be 'grossly inadequate'. There seemed to be little interaction of any kind between children and minders.

The general conclusions of the study were reassuring. The

majority of West Indian mothers appeared to be making good use of the medical services, there was no evidence of physical neglect, disease or deformity among the 101 children examined, and nearly all came within normal limits on tests of development. The report concludes however[3]

We were concerned by the lack of day nursery places and by the apparent lack of enforcement of adequate child-minding standards. In this one area the medical services seemed very far from meeting the needs of the immigrant population, and it was felt that this was an area deserving further, more detailed study.

The research evidence, though sparse, is remarkably consistent. It shows that between one-half and two-thirds of West Indian women with young children go out to work, that most of the children are left with childminders, and that local authority supervision is powerless to enforce even minimum standards.

The effect of this was to confirm our sense of being on an important new trail. But just as we were beginning to escape — with difficulty — from the 'Dickensian baby-farm' viewpoint so we now slipped almost unawares into a new perspective: the plight of the West Indian child.

Thinking about the West Indian migrant's situation in Britain, and especially that of the young mother and child, two dominant thoughts began to emerge. The first was that childminding experiences were particularly damaging to West Indian children when they later went to school. We noticed that West Indian children were not, as a group, very successful in class. Why? Of course there was always the genetic explanation, but we didn't believe that. Anyone who has worked in social science knows the astounding selective differences that the interplay and mirror-back quality (self-images, self-fulfilling prophecies etc.) of complex environmental forces can produce. To be this kind of social scientist is of course to be an optimist — you are always thinking how these environmental forces can be located, analysed and changed. At that moment of every thousand children in England and Wales, seven attended schools for the educationally subnormal. This was implicitly an extreme measure of educational difficulty. When we looked at Pakistani children, only four in a thousand went to such schools. With Indian children the figure was even less — three in a thousand. Now on closer enquiry, there is considerable local variation, and many other factors beside ethnic grouping are in play (different forms of assessment, different kinds of provision, different attitudes of teachers in referring particular children for assessment). But there was no baulking the West Indian figure — twenty three in a thousand. Surely childminding could be a factor in that — and one that could be changed? It wouldn't account for all of it maybe, but one could imagine childminding could have a negative influence on language development. And if West Indian children with minders were noticeably passive then one might expect them to burst out, in the freedom and stimulation of a child-centred school, and be sometimes exactly that uncontrollable and even destructive child who drives teacher to pick up the phone and ask for an educational psychologist — and the ultimate shunted-off solution of the separate ESN school. We were able to get at least a starting figure in Huddersfield, but this wasn't available in Manchester. In Huddersfield at that moment the proportion of immigrants in ordinary schools was 15 per cent. In educationally subnormal schools it was 19.7 per cent — and both our own eyes and the teachers confirmed that this was mainly made up of West Indian children. There was no doubt about the stigma ('all those bloody black nippers down on the laughing farm') nor of the cost (£400 p.a. for a place at an ESN school compared to £90 p.a. then at an ordinary school).

So now the task was to look at part of Manchester with all its obvious problems and at part of our control city, Huddersfield.

4 Childminding in Huddersfield

In Odersfelt, Godwin had six caracutes of land to be
taxed but it is waste.   *Domesday Book*, 1086

I rode over the mountains to Huddersfield. A wilder
people I never saw in England.   John Wesley
Diary, 1757

Huddersfield — the handsomest by far of all the factory
towns of Yorkshire and Lancashire.   Friedrich Engels,
*The Condition of the Working Class
in England*, 1844

Huddersfield men and women go for quality in cloth,
in engineering, in chemicals, in anything we produce.
We expect quality in music, in sport and in the other
things we enjoy.   Harold Wilson writing as
Prime Minister in *The Story of Huddersfield*, 1968

Huddersfield is plainly in a dark and pagan condition
George Bernard Shaw after the indifferent
reception of *Back to Methuselah*, Theatre Royal
Huddersfield, 1930

Huddersfield was the control city. A handsome woollen
town, permeated by a vivid sense of place, a criss-cross of
small communities. The city hangs together. It has none of
the anomie and vast dereliction which blights larger industrial
cities. You feel at once that people here would know all
about their neighbour's child. Yes, it looked a perfect contrast to the Old Trafford or Moss Side districts of Manchester

39

which we were considering on the other side of the Pennines.

Best to start with an official call, and enquire about the list of registered minders.[1] Clearly, visiting a sample of them would tell us much of what we wanted to know — and as for any unregistered minders — who was more likely to know of their existence than these, their business rivals?

After some uncertainty in the front office we were directed to the court officer.

'Childminders? We know there's illegal ones but we don't go out of our way to look for them. We just administer the 1948 Act. This job was inflicted on us under the new regulations. There were ten health visitors and a doctor to do it, now there's just me, one man. . . . The educational side doesn't come into it at all — that's not in the Act.'

The assistant court officer, a solid grey-haired former police officer, was hostile: he could tell us nothing without the authority of the director of social services, and we'd certainly never get that as he was far too busy interviewing applicants for jobs in the new local authority. Local government was being reorganised and Huddersfield was to become part of the new metropolitan district of Kirklees.

'What do I do about childminders? I know the Act and I carry it out.'

At this time he had been doing the job for fifteen months, essentially on the same lines as the health department which previously had this responsibility, but without their specialist knowledge. The main job as he saw it was to register applicants, which he did with impressive speed and efficiency. The average waiting time for registration was only two weeks.

He took up references — police, health, personal, inspected premises for fire risk, measured rooms in cubic feet, told the applicant to get rid of the oil heater and buy a fireguard and that was it. If they wanted advice he couldn't really help them. With children of their own they probably knew far more about it than he did. Sometimes they asked what they should charge or how many hours they should offer. The answer? 'That's nothing to do with me.'

Supervision, with his caseload of 120 and all his court work to fit in as well, could only be minimal. 'I try to get round them every three or four months. It only takes about five minutes each. I pop in, count heads, check the fires and I'm away again'. Unlike the court officer, he knew exactly how many minders were on the register — forty-eight English, Irish, West African, West Indian. He thought the one Indian might have given up. He tried to help everyone who came looking for a minder. It's a problem sometimes because they are so unevenly distributed — only one minder in the whole of Milnsbridge for instance (a densely populated industrial area of over 6,000 people). Some parents have to travel miles every day because they can't find a minder nearby.

He tried to match up children and minders by race and class:

'After all if you were a childminder, you wouldn't want a scruffy child would you? And I've had women say "I don't want any black children". Fair enough, it's their house, they can take who they like.'

What sort of people make the best childminders, I asked?

'All our minders are best. The houses have been passed as suitable. I've never had a complaint from a parent. We're not really bothered about education. Most of the children are very young — 18 months to 3½ years. After that the mothers seem to go for playgroups. Anyway, some of the childminders teach them as much as playgroups. After all if they've got their own children, they're not going to be doing nothing all day; they'll be teaching them and the others at the same time.

'You wouldn't get a woman sitting a child in a chair all day doing nothing, would you? Of course if I did hear of anything like that, I'd go and see to it. But you couldn't imagine a woman doing that to a child, could you?'

Yes we could. It was a scene we had seen often in our pilot

41

research, and were to see over and over again among the very childminders registered here. Otherwise his confidence might have been convincing.

When we asked for a list of registered childminders, the atmosphere froze. They don't have a list, only a card index because the situation changes daily. And why did we want it anyway? 'To quiz them like you've been quizzing me? Oh no, we couldn't supply a list to anybody.'

It was to take us three years to obtain that list. We were to meet a similar response in other authorities. We approached every local authority in England and Wales, asked them to nominate someone to liaise with us, and besides some baseline information, asked for their views on childminding. Of course there were many exceptions — especially amongst the London boroughs — but it was clear that Huddersfield had quite typical officials, with fairly standard views.

This surely was the effect of the law. Childminding was seen as something to be policed — not as a major part (with all the influence and resource that implied) of the pre-school system. Similarly the list of registered childminders was not felt to be a public service which, for instance, a working mother could consult at a clinic, library, post office. There is nothing in the Act which says that this is private information. But the court officer — like many of his colleagues elsewhere — had extended the negative view of parliament and transformed that list of names and addresses which mothers were anxiously seeking into secret and inert information in city hall.

Still the question was how to proceed. The popular image of social science is of white-coated technocrats feeding inky questionnaires into winking computers. The truth is quite different. The discipline is quite different, more demanding and suddenly varied; not easily planned. One moment it is cautious and calculating, the next it is theatrical and risk-taking, then suddenly it is a matter of scent, clues, classical detective work — and maybe last a matter of sheer play with the evidence as the dispassionate mind seeks for patterns and resolutions.

We had our sample cities. And — as in a Royal Commission Report — a fair sense of formal opinion. But with the

Dawnwatch exercise, we had acted, felt and thought in a more dramatic way. And what Dawnwatch suggested was that there was a social underbelly to all our cities not articulated in official statements or recorded in academic reports.

But where to go now? We decided the next step was to check out the accepted official provision for a working parent with a very small child – the day nursery. As we have already recorded, day nurseries – never large in number – have dwindled until recent years because the controlling policy imagination simply did not understand the notion of mothers working.

Waiting for a place

We decided to interview all applicants for day-nursery places because it seemed likely that some at least would have looked for a childminder when they found no place immediately available.

The emerging Kirklees social services department allowed us access to the file of applications, from which we compiled a list of those outstanding on 10 February 1974. At that time there were on their books 61 families with 78 children waiting for a place in one of the four Huddersfield day nurseries. A third of these were classified as 'priority' cases, including six single-parent families. Some parents had already been waiting as long as two years, and the average waiting time for the top priority category was five months.

Most of the families on the list were interviewed during the following two months, March and April 1974, but because other lines of enquiry intervened, several applicants more difficult to trace or living in outlying parts of the area were interviewed up to twelve months later. Despite this, *only four* of the forty-eight families interviewed had a child attending a day nursery at the time we interviewed them. One more had been offered a place at the most distant nursery, and after three months of dragging right across town with him (two buses at 6.30 on a dark morning) and then back to the mill where she worked, decided to give it up.

None of the Fartown parents (the area we decided to put under the social microscope) had even received an offer.

By the time we interviewed them most of the single parents had received at least one offer, though not necessarily one that suited their needs and current circumstances; two-parent families with medical or social work recommendations had been waiting seven months, and the average waiting time for non-priority cases had risen to fourteen months. No one in this category had heard anything more from the social services department since their initial application. *In practice, then, this was a dead file.* There was no moving up the queue because whenever a vacancy occurred in a day nursery it was immediately taken up by a new child whose need was urgent. The clerk in charge of processing applications admitted that no two-parent cases had been accepted for at least a year unless they were recommended by the health visitor or social worker on suspicion of neglect or battering. Even single top-priority parents sometimes had to be 'sent upstairs' to be given names of registered childminders, because no place was available. A marked difference was evident in the attitude of both office and nursery staff to single parents 'struggling to bring up a family alone' and married women 'just doing it for the money'. This black and white distinction − so clearly reflecting the official thinking we analysed − bore no relation to the varied problems and pressures on the fifty-four two-parent families. This explains the low number of single parents on the waiting list by comparison with the high proportion actually in the day nurseries.

The day nursery waiting list almost certainly bears little relation to the demand for day care in Huddersfield − as probably elsewhere. Whatever governments say, people must know from the experiences of relatives, friends and neighbours that there is little chance of anyone, however acute their need, getting a place to start next Monday or next month, and that very few married couples are offered places at all. So most mothers of pre-school children who want to go out to work never bother to apply. Official 'waiting lists' are documents of illusion and despair.

Those who do apply need to be very highly motivated, to have considerable drive and confidence, to find their way to the fourth floor of the council offices, to identify the right person and make their application (which had to be done standing up in the passage because the office is so over-crowded).

Later interviews confirmed that these were people espe-cially concerned for their children's welfare and future success. For most of them a day nursery was not just a con-venient place to stow children while mother worked, but a place which would actively encourage the child's develop-ment: 'give him a better start'. To the question 'Have you ever considered using a childminder?' the answer was often a very emphatic 'no', and the reason given that childminders couldn't or didn't give children enough attention — 'they don't learn them enough'.

On the other hand, many of the applicants seemed to be rather isolated people with few links outside their own families, and often having moved from another part of the country or town to their present home. For Asian women the very idea of working outside the home was a recent development, and it was partly for these reasons, perhaps, that they did not share the common knowledge that apply-ing for a day-nursery place was a pretty pointless exercise.

One of them, Margaret Marsden, summed up the experience of most applicants 'I went to see this woman in the council — it were up ever so many stairs — and I told her all about it and said we'd be willing to pay the full price, thinking it'd be quicker, and she said "you'll hear from us", but we never did!'

Did they know, we wondered, how small the actual chances were? We asked everyone. 'When do you think you will get a place in a day nursery?' Aware as we now were that the non-priority file had lain untouched for over a year, it was saddening to hear the patiently optimistic answers 'Any day now'; 'Hopefully, we'll get a place soon'; 'Event-ually'; 'It can take a year, you know'.

Our main concern was to find out what happened to these children when their parents failed to obtain a day-nursery place for them. This was the picture we found. (Table 4.1)

Just over a third of the mothers were not working at the time we interviewed them. Some were still waiting hopefully

or lived in depressed apathy on social security. Several had
tried to work for short periods but their childminding arrangements had broken down. Others had decided to wait till the
child started school if necessary, rather than accept any kind
of day care less satisfactory than a nursery.

*Table 4.1 48 children on Huddersfield Day Nursery waiting
list February 1974*

At time of interview	*White	Black	Asian	Total
now attending day nursery	3	1	—	4
with relative	6	1	1	8
with registered minder	2	1	1	4
with unregistered minder	5	1	2	7
parents alternating shifts .	6	2	—	8
mother takes child to work	2	—	—	2
mother not working	6	3	5	15
Total	30	9	9	48
childminder used during previous year	6	3	1	9

*This classification is, of course, a transient convention.

In nine families the parents worked alternating shifts. Four
nights a week at the biscuit factory or the five-hour shift
from 4.45 to 9.45. The money on the night shift was very
attractive — £31 for four nights, well outside the normal
wage rates for unskilled women. But for mothers of young
children the routine is hard because they can get no sleep
during the day. Most find they can only stick it for a few
months at a time. The evening shift sounds better but also
has its problems. Work times were often glibly recounted —
'We don't both work together. My husband does 7 a.m. to
4.30 and I work 4.45 to 10 p.m.' But then an evasive note
would creep into the conversation. How long does it take to
get home, and does he never stop on the way, even for an

instant? And to catch the work bus to Halifax for the 4.45 shift must mean leaving home up to an hour earlier. What happened to the child at the cross-over point?

None of this group of parents admitted to leaving babies and toddlers alone or in the care of only slightly older brothers and sisters, as did many later in our area study.

Eight children were left with relatives. Sometimes this was a temporary expedient — just 'helping out' until the still-hoped for day-nursery place materialized. For other families the arrangement was more formal, indistinguishable from childminding except in the legal sense, with parents paying a regular weekly sum — ranging from 50p to £4.50. Most related minders were grandmothers or aunts, but in one case a married daughter stayed at home to look after her young stepsister while her mother went out to work because 'my husband didn't like it when I used to work in a factory and come home with dirty hands'.

Only two of the day-nursery applicants, both single parents, had been positively advised to look for a child-minder. Three more had tried unsuccessfully, asking neighbours and phoning round the numbers suggested by the social services. Dawn Patterson, now reluctantly working on the night shift at the biscuit factory, didn't give up lightly.

> I rang loads of childminders, but they were all full,
> except one and she asked £7.50 a week when I were only
> going to bring home £16. I went to see her though and
> I weren't right keen — she didn't look too clean to me.
> Then I went to one in Trinity Street — she had about
> twelve. I wouldn't let Kelly go there anyway, but she said
> "I only take coloured kiddies". There is another lady
> down Bradford Road, she knocks hell out of them — I've
> seen her.'

Not unexpectedly, the nine families who had sent children to minders but had given up by the time they were interviewed were mostly unhappy about the experience. An Indian father said: 'It was just so awful I would prefer not to talk about it. Never will we send Sanjay to another child-minder.'

Others found it hard to articulate their dissatisfaction, obvious enough from their tone of voice. 'She were all right but . . . . ' Often they could only express it by praising the day nursery (which they had usually never seen). 'They've everything to play with there'. 'Them nurses are dedicated to their work — there's plenty to look after the children. Not like having ten with one person that just gets on with the housework and pays no attention.'

Angela Morton was 'very unhappy' about her childminder 'but when you're pushed you can't be too fussy.' Mrs Morton was very pushed, with her previously married husband bringing home £32 a week, of which £14 had to go to his first wife and children. She paid £4 a week for Mrs Nelson, an unregistered childminder, to look after two-year-old Dominic. That included food — she had no idea what food, but he was always starving when he came home. ('Nobbut chips', intervened twelve-year-old Sara at this point). Mrs Nelson had 'a lot of patience with kiddies' or she wouldn't have left Dominic there as long as four months — but when he came home with lice in his hair that was too much.

Mrs Morton was in the last stages of pregnancy when we interviewed her, but was planning to go back to work as a hospital orderly when the baby was two months. 'They must take them at day nursery then, they must, they must. They wouldn't give me an abortion on the National Health so what can we do? We're desperate.'

Parents using childminders

Talking to the eleven parents who were currently using childminders, words like 'desperate' came up often. Money was the most usual reason, predictably for single parents. 'I don't think they will ever give you enough at the social security so that you can live decent and save a bit.' 'I like to have my own money, then no one can tell you what to do with it'. The married women, too, were very hard-pressed. Like Mrs Scargill: after eight years of marriage she and her husband had given up all hope of ever having a child. They had scraped together every penny to escape from their decayed terraced house in 'a right sleazy area' to their present immaculately furnished semi-detached unit on a neat middle-class estate. Then 'the minute we moved in I got pregnant'. To meet the high mortgage repayments from Mr Scargill's earnings as a joiner seemed impossible; to give up the dream house unthinkable. Mrs Scargill has a high opinion of her minder, who for £4 a week provides breakfast and a cooked dinner, has 'bags of patience, a sense of humour and always makes time to play with the kids, no matter how much other work she has to do.' But she feels at once guilty and resentful that she must go out to work when the longed-for baby is still so young. 'Mothers should have a chance to enjoy their children, at least till they're three years old.'

Only one Asian mother was working at the time of our survey. Most reluctantly, after waiting a year for a day-nursery place, she had been forced to take a £15 a week job, for the same reason as Mrs Scargill, to help with mortgage repayments. Her husband already worked shifts, seven days a week, and they had to send money back to aged relatives in India. The children, Hardeu and Purvinder, went to what their father euphemistically described as 'a private nursery': it was, in fact, a West Indian childminder looking after five other children. Their mother, tongue-tied in English, became passionately articulate in Hindi. Given that she must work outside the home — and she would certainly stop at once if they had even a little more money — she wanted the children to go to the nursery where they would have plenty of space and toys to play with, be properly looked after and learn English to give them a good start at school. The childminder was cheap at £4 a week for the two children, but otherwise gave them nothing — no room to play, no toys, nothing. Mrs Shabhir was just waiting for a day-nursery place in order to take them away at once.

Her misgivings were only too well justified. The contrast between the two children seen at home and at their childminder's was striking. At home they were normal, lively, mischievous children, chattering non-stop like most toddlers. When we saw them at the childminder's house they almost always sat silent and withdrawn, unable to communicate either with the minder, the other children or each other.

49

Purvinder spent long hours lying in an upstairs cot staring at the blank ceiling and bare walls. At twenty months she was still fed exclusively on the tinned food her mother took to the childminder each week. Hardeu sat quietly and obediently on the sofa all day long. Only if a visitor brought toys would he come to life and fall on them like a starving man, usually provoking a sharp rebuke from the minder. Three years of this and his parents' hopes that he would do very well at school seem unlikely to be realized.

Mrs Fife, a resilient West Indian mother of three, went out to work after a protracted and violent break up with her husband left her with a heap of unpaid bills. Back home in Jamaica she was on the point of going to college when her father sent for her, promising untold opportunities in England. But after a period as barmaid in pubs and discos, and as a winder in the mill, she had become pregnant, and now all her ambitions were projected on to her children: Vivian, Graham and Charlotte. The two girls were staying with their grandmother in another part of town while Mrs Fife 'got back on her feet'. As soon as she got a day-nursery place they would all be together again.

Meanwhile Graham went each morning at 6.15 to Mrs Forster, half an hour's walk up the hill from where they lived, in the bleakest, most neglected pocket of council housing in Huddersfield. Mrs Fife had clear views about children's needs in general and what she wanted for her own.

> 'It's got to be someone like a mother so the kid is broken like you want him to be broke. There should be some discipline but love and understanding is very necessary. They need two parents who love them and care about them and spend time with them. Before they goes to school they should have colour learning, should be starting to read and count. Graham's got a right quick brain. He'll be OK once he gets a bit less rowdy. Certainly brainwise he'll be good'.

Despite her own experience she feels there is 'more equal opportunity for children here than there is back home' and thinks it very important to do well at school.

Undiscouraged by her unpromising situation and dismal surroundings Mrs Fife glowed with optimism — 'something good is around the corner'. She spoke very warmly of Mrs Forster:

'She isn't organized, but the kids are happy. She cares about children. Every child is treated the same — if one gets a lolly they all do. She's a really nice woman. She lets them play and then clears up after they've gone home — well, you can't clean with young kids around, can you?'

Either she did not see or did not want to know the other side of the picture — the long hours aimlessly sitting while Mrs Foster bustled about the endless task of caring for ten other children; hours, days and weeks lost for learning. Like Hardeu Singh, Graham was a different boy at home from at the childminder's.

Most families can do with a bit of extra money, but for several mothers this was not their most important motive for choosing to work. Some simply could not stand being in the house alone with a small child all day.

One such was Mrs Spivy. 'If you stay at home day in and day out you get dull and bored.' With her unnaturally black hair dressed in elaborate coils, heavy eye make-up, clothes and jewellery matched like a glossy picture from a women's magazine, Mrs Spivy looked too smart for a Sunday afternoon at home. Thick turquoise carpeting covered every inch of floor. Lynne, aged two, sprawled sucking a dinky feeder on a squashy leather sofa, half-watching the colour television. There were no toys or playthings to be seen, no sign of a child in the house, except the child herself.

Mrs Spivy went back to work filling bottles for a firm of medical suppliers when Lynne was six months old, and hadn't regretted it. She was the only parent using a childminder who no longer wanted a day-nursery place. 'As long as Mrs Snow is looking after her I'll leave her there because she looks after her pretty well.'

Like most parents using childminders, Mrs Spivy was very vague about what happened after she delivered Lynne to Mrs Snow at 7.20 a.m. until her father picked her up at 5 in the afternoon. What did Mrs Snow give her to eat for instance? 'I don't really know. She gets a cooked meal.' She had heard of Mrs Snow through a friend, never thought to ask if she was registered with the social services department. It was enough that she seemed to look after the other kids all right. The best — the only thing — she could say about Mrs Snow as a minder was that she had trained Lynne to sit on a potty, and that the little girl had learnt a lot from being with other children. Questions about children's needs, learning, school, left her quite blank, either because she had never given them any thought or from a general inability to express herself. Finally her husband intervened. 'Go and see Mrs Snow yourself' he said, 'you'll understand then. She's just the right sort of person to look after children'.

Rather sceptically I visited Mrs Snow. It would be hard to find a better description of her than Mr Spivy's.

At first glance rather severe-looking, with tightly set dark hair and a middle-aged style of dressing, Mrs Snow turned out to be a childminder of exceptional ability, combining a natural warmth and love of children with a keen interest in their emotional and intellectual development. She had been minding for ten years, and currently looked after another little girl the same age as Lynne and her own three-year-old, Sandra. In contrast to Lynne's mother, she talked constantly to the children, asking questions, listening, explaining. The room was full of toys, well-used but neatly stored, a shelf bursting with books; paper and crayons on the table. When Mrs Snow's two boys came home from school at dinner time they whisked the little girls off to play on swings and pedal cars in the securely fenced garden while she finished preparing a substantial cooked meal.

What the waiting list tells us

In practice day nurseries no longer offer a service to working mothers as such, only to some single-parent families and those in acute social need. And not even to all of those. Two unsupported mothers on our list were never offered a place. We came to know of many others who were discouraged from applying at all, either because of the long period of uncertainty while waiting for a place or because they had heard there was no chance. Among these was a group of prisoners' wives, surely amongst the most disadvantaged of all mothers. Thanks to the local probation officer we were able to join the group for several sessions and interview the women, and later to establish the group on a more secure basis at the Children's Centre. All but one of the fifteen with pre-school children said she would go out to work if she had somewhere to leave the child. Nearly all these women were living in poor housing: unmodernized council houses — plagued by money worries, ostracized by neighbours, with the doubtful pleasure of the monthly prison visit their only relief in a monotonous existence. In such a life, a demanding toddler is simply another burden to be borne, and too often the mother's justified depression and hostility is projected on to the child. 'He's a terror', 'I could kill her sometimes', 'I'll cut your little willie off!'

The probation officers agreed that for these women to go out to work would be pure gain, both for them and their children. More money, less stress, company and variety for the mother; for the child a more stimulating relationship with an adult, cheerful, good-tempered conversation and the sand-water-paint-building constellation of activities they have little chance of experiencing at home.

One could perhaps point to other specially disadvantaged groups. The National Health Service Act of 1946 (with subsequent amendments) gives local authorities powers to make arrangements for the care of pre-school children. Subsequent bulletins from the Department of Health and Social Security have stressed that priority should be given to children with a special need — children with working lone parents, children with mental or physical handicap, children from socially impoverished homes, or homes under strain, or children whose parents are so ill or handicapped that they cannot look after them during the day.

Even were there day-nursery places for all such children, this would still be a thoroughly undesirable form of provision — an educational ghetto confined to the disadvantaged. Such children may be far better off in the more homely atmosphere of a really good childminder, like Mrs Snow, mixing with more fortunate boys and girls.

But the day-nursery provision does not exist. In January 1975 the DHSS informed us that they estimated there were 12,000 'priority' children still without a place, and those are children specifically known and so classified by their local authority. But as we see, even in this miniature study many parents who ought to be regarded as priorities are not known to the authority, or don't see the need for professional day care, or are not articulate enough to press their case. So the real figure must be many times greater than 12,000.

Yet what can the local authority do, except fruitlessly add their names to these static waiting lists which can be uncovered in any industrial town? Huddersfield, it must be remembered, is not a very deprived city, has great communal strength and has an above-average number of day-nursery places. Perhaps one thing we should do is to see how these waiting parents helped themselves.

On the list we have just explored, thirty-three of the children had mothers who were working at the time of our interview. Four children were now in a day nursery — private, state or factory. Of the remaining twenty-nine, eight were being looked after by relatives (often in the same formal paid way as with a childminder). Another eight had parents on split shifts which in practice often means they were left alone in the interval, or in the care of a young child, or simply spent most of the day, as well as most of the night, in bed — since whichever parent was at home usually wanted to sleep. Finally eleven children were formally with childminders — seven with illegal ones. A further nine children whose mothers were temporarily not working on the interview date had been with a childminder in the previous twelve months.

I think we could regard all this as a childminding system and its extensions, variants, penumbra. We get a fresh glimpse of it as that large but little-known network which lies around the day nursery and serves so many children in great need.

Three-quarters of the mothers had found their childminder on the grapevine, and not by consulting officials. Only four knew whether the childminder they used was registered or not, and eighteen out of twenty said it was of no importance to them.

Once again we see the effects in real life of social ignorance in high places. For clearly these unsupported and unvalued childminders were likely to have a considerable influence, for good or ill, on the children in their care. It was sadly unlikely that Purvinder or Graham would fulfill their parents' ambitions for them after three or four years of blank days without conversation, activity or toys. On the other hand Lynne, with Mrs Snow, was actually getting a better start in that child-centred home, than she would have done beached in her own house with a bored and resentful mother.

Why couldn't all these children — including the ones caught in the split-shift vice — have their own Mrs Snow? Clearly in this case childminders were not seen as a major part of the pre-school system ('the educational side doesn't come into it at all — that's not in the Act'). But surely childminders can be recruited? Trained? Linked with playgroups? Backed up with books, toys, visits?

It was already clear that our control city was turning out to be no such thing. Even a buoyant neighbourly place like Huddersfield had this dark side to it for many underprivileged children in their early, formative years. But we still knew too little about it.

We'd been through Dawnwatch, listened to officials, traced the children who were waiting for a place, met others like the prisoners' children who never even got on the list, unravelled something of how people created their own system of childminding, met childminders, some who were legal, some who were not, some who were very good, some who were very bad.

Now we changed our tactic and decided to take one area of Huddersfield, knock on the doors and find out what was happening to every child under five. It would be a long, exhausting task. But at the end we should have solid ground to work from.

The 1971 census divides Huddersfield into fifteen wards. Using the census, the Huddersfield Polytechnic has produced a *Social Atlas of Kirklees*[2]. In this they combine six social indicators to rank the wards in terms of social priority. The indicators are housing tenure (whether rented or owned); housing amenities (lack of hot water, inside WC, fixed bath); demographic structure (population change, birth-rate index, old people); socio-economic status (qualified workers, professional workers, semi-skilled and unskilled, unemployment, car ownership); household occupancy (persons per room, overcrowding, large households); immigrant settlement.

We would not entirely agree with such a model which combines several unlike features. And in particular we don't feel happy about immigrant settlement as an index. Nevertheless, it does give us as objective a measure as we are likely to find. On this scale we can identify three wards which most typify the inner city working-class areas. Of these we chose Fartown: a name always associated with the famous claret and gold of Huddersfield Rugby League Club.

5 Under five in Fartown

Laws that only threaten and are not kept, become like
the log that was given to the frogs to be their king —
which they feared at first, but soon scorned and
trampled on.   Cervantes, *Don Quixote*

In this hotel at an historic meeting on August 29,
1895, was founded the Northern Rugby Football
Union known since 1923 as the Rugby Football League.
plaque in the George Hotel, Huddersfield marking
the creation of an international working-class game

Play is the exultation of the possible   Martin Buber

'It was a nice suburb at one time, and now it's full of
Pakistanis. I can walk down Willow Lane and feel I'm not
in my own country. It's a twilight area — there's a feeling
of decay and unlooked-afterness. The housewives would be
out every Friday morning to sweep and donkey stone the
steps. You'll not see that now.'

In fact, Fartown has always been a mixed area, a social
step down from neighbouring Birkby. In old days the more
aspiring residents would advise visiting friends to take the
Birkby tram in preference to the Fartown one: 'Its a nicer
approach'. And it was already declining in the 1930s when
those who could afford it began to move up into the cleaner
air of the surrounding hills to Cowcliffe, Fixby or Beaumont
Park.

This is now reflected in the age structure of the population,
with whole streets occupied by retired couples, or elderly

single people, many of whom have lived forty or fifty years in the same house. In this part of Fartown the houses are solid, stone-built with doorcases that seem designed for grander buildings altogether, crowned with stone wreaths and pediments, suddenly visible now that sand blasting has removed the hundred-year encrustation of soot. Among the Victorian terraces, square windows, curly roof lines and narrow-cut stones reveal the survival of what were isolated farmhouses or weavers' cottages before the Industrial Revolution washed over them. All the houses have neat-hedged front gardens, many of them brilliant with roses or chrysanthemums. There were strong feelings about the newcomer who cut down his hedge, concreted the flower-fringed patch of grass and ran his car on to it.

The sense of decline and decay so strongly expressed by old people in the area is not obvious to an outsider. Even in Bradford Road houses are well kept and neatly fenced. The shops look prosperous; traditional butchers, newsagents and high-class shoe repairers rubbing shoulders with the Muslim Commercial Bank and the Aslam Food Store. In the side streets whose name immortalize the builder's daughters — Clara, Eleanor, Honoria — the hedges are higher, and the trees unpoisoned by diesel fumes. Next to the red-brick Working Men's Club, heaped round with empty beer barrels, stands the new Health Centre, built at a time when public money ran freely. The elaborately cobbled forecourt gives way to plate glass, carpeted corridors and doors neatly labelled with doctors' names.

If the working men's clubs still flourish — there are three in Fartown — their old rivals, the churches, have gone down to heavy defeat. Fartown never had a parish church of its own. People either had to trudge up the long hill to Woodhouse or go to St John's, Birkby, designed by the great Victorian architect, Butterfield. Now they seldom bother to do either. The churches still stand, kept in decent order by dedicated churchwardens, their nineteenth-century grimness softened by the devotion of the flower-rota ladies. But the once numerous Nonconformist chapels crumble and decay until at last safety demands their demolition.

Woodhouse Hill is the nearest Fartown approaches to a

middle-class area. Several large detached Victorian houses, still lived in by local business families and a well-wooded inter-war private estate. Here it's a point of honour for every house to be different from its neighbour — grey pebbledash, red brick, concrete, traditional stone, doorways arched, pointed, porticoed. Some owners have replaced their windows with 'Georgian' bow fronts and bulls' eyes panes. The children coming up this hill after school are all white.

Down the other end of Bradford Road, where it runs under the railway into the city centre, the scene is very different. Cattle market and tramway depot still stand against a backdrop of cooling towers, gasworks and the council garbage disposer. On Mondays the street market is thronged with bargain hunters turning over seconds, bolts of substandard cloth, smudged china, tangled trimmings, off-cuts of foam rubber and carpet. There's usually a fast-talking salesman with a miraculous new paint or a household gadget. People come from all over Huddersfield to the Monday market, and for the Asian women who live in the tight-packed triangle of houses between Calton and Alder Street this is their major shopping expedition of the week.

'The Terraces' as they are always called — Orange, Holly, Rose, Hawthorn — are 'unadopted', which means the council doesn't clean or mend the paths. Once they must have been very drab places, with the high walls blocking out what little light could squeeze between the narrow houses. But now they are painted green, purple, turquoise and yellow, and brilliantly coloured washing blows in the damp air. Little dark faces peep out between the blackened stone gateposts — the gates have long vanished. The few white people who still live here are nearly all old.

In one of these tiny cottages lives the first Asian child-minder we met in Huddersfield. In India she had her own bungalow and many servants. Her husband sticks his credentials on the doorpost — *BSc (Eng)* and meanwhile works nights at the mill. She suffers Hawthorn Terrace uncomplainingly in the hope of her children's education.

In the Terraces one senses a new community growing. Houses may be cramped but they are well kept and children can play safely in the car-free passages. Hillhouse Lane, fifty yards away, has slipped down to hopeless decay and dereliction. Gardens full of rubble, broken fences – no sandblasting here. Children's faces, half seen behind drawn curtains, imprisoned by the lorries that thunder down from Bradford to the huge complex of factories and workshops on Leeds Road.

Leeds Road is the industrial heart of Huddersfield. Here cluster most of the council houses in the ward, the oldest that survive. As with all unpopular municipal housing, the poorest, least competent, most unlucky families have gravitated here and suffer from their proximity to each other as well as from their own problems. It's a place to escape from, pervaded by an atmosphere of defeatism, depression and gloom. The playground, grimy and vandalized, is overshadowed by mammoth cooling towers, the air perfumed on one side by the gasworks, on the other by the giant ICI complex. The streets seem full of police cars. On the doorsteps, men in pyjamas shouting to other men hurrying to work with lunch boxes. A poor place to bring up children. Some families try to shut them in the house, others give up, and you see tiny ones clutching dolls and teddies trotting unaccompanied along the broken pavement whilst intercontinental juggernauts blast past them.

Leeds Road can never have been a desirable area, but it must once have had a certain style. Lea Royd Mill has the classical proportions of an eighteenth-century stately home, its graceful bell-tower framed by delicate wrought-iron tracery. Behind the floodlights of Huddersfield Town Football Ground rises Kilner Bank, grimy scrubland transformed by an imaginative parks superintendent into a mass of autumn colours with a few houses dramatically breaking the skyline. Somewhere up there, Charlotte Brontë once lived and taught.

Yet there is no shortage of open space even here. Across Leeds Road beside the day nursery, down the neglected lane by the cement works, and you're in a different, older, slower-moving world. Here the Calder and Hebble Navigation runs into the Huddersfield Broad Canal, Sir John Ramsden's Canal. Hawthorn and elder, chestnut and sycamore, blot out the rubbish tips. Opposite, cabbages and onions grow up the side of the embankment, a railway built and never used. Beyond, nature and the parks department have rescued the long bank devastated by fire-clay works in the last century and over the other side acres of playing fields have been reclaimed from mine workings only remembered when, as happened during this survey, a corner of the cricket field fell down an old mineshaft.

None of this institutional open space is of much use to housebound under-fives. Older Fartown and Sheepridge children play among the scrub, brambles and broken brick of Hall Bank, and every year or so a young life ends in the canal.

Fartown in figures

Unlike most parts of Huddersfield, Fartown has been little affected by clearance and redevelopment. A few of the worst back terraces and yards have been pulled down or bricked up, but the only substantial new building is the council's garbage disposal works, yet another source of noise and smells for the unfortunate inhabitants of Hillhouse Lane.

So the population remained more or less stable in the ten years between the 1961 and 1971 Censuses and it can probably be assumed that the 1971 census figures give an accurate picture of the ward as it now is. (Table 5.1)

From Table 5.1 it can be seen that Fartown is statistically typical of inner city areas. It has a high proportion of residents born in the New Commonwealth: 18 per cent, more than twice as high as in Huddersfield as a whole. Among children under five the percentage shoots up to nearly half. Economically, it is a poor area, with home ownership below the average for Huddersfield, and much below the neighbouring ward of Birkby, where 78 per cent of householders own their home. A quarter of the inhabitants live in rented accommodation as compared with the 16 per cent overall figure for the town. 30 per cent lack one of three basic amenities: inside toilet, bath and hot water supply. Fewer than one household in three owns a car; in neighbouring Birkby nearly half do, and even in Deighton, Fartown's other neighbour, where 69 per cent live in council houses,

Table 5.1 Statistical profile of Fartown (1971 census)

Total population	8020	

	No	%
Number of children aged 0-4	847	10·5
Residents born in New Commonwealth	1,446	18
All residents with both parents born in NC	2,048	25·54
Children aged 0-4 with both parents born in New Commonwealth	403	47·6

Number of households	2,783	

	No	%
Owner occupied	1,474	53
Council	635	23
Private unfurnished	519	19
Private furnished	154	5
With inside toilet, bath and hot water supply	1,955	70
With car	743	27

Per cent of married women aged 20-45 who are economically active	44·3
Number of married women with children under five working more than 8 hours per week	110

the level of car ownership is higher.

But for the crucial question of working women we are on shaky ground. In the first place the census figures absurdly do not include single, widowed or divorced women. Second, the figures are derived from the 10 per cent sample, the numbers involved are sometimes very small and the probability of sampling error correspondingly large. Third, it is our experience that working mothers with young children often understate their hours. Lastly, some may not give the information for tax reasons.

The proportion of married women aged twenty to forty-five (that is of child-rearing years) who are 'economically active' in Fartown is 44·3 per cent, rather less than in Huddersfield as a whole. The probable explanation is the large number of Asian women, who have only recently begun to go out to work even when they have no young children. This is one figure that may have changed significantly since the census was taken.

When we look only at married women with children under five, however, even in 1971 Fartown had a relatively large number; 110 worked for more than eight hours a week. Assuming that on average these mothers had 1·3 children each aged under five this would mean a *minimum* of 143 children, or 16·8 per cent of under-fives had working mothers.

Of course all these figures are far too low, excluding as they do those very mothers who are most likely to choose, or be forced to go out to work while their children are still very young: the unmarried, divorced and widowed. The very way the Census data has been collected enshrines unexamined and unhelpful attitudes towards working mothers with small children.

This ward then gives us 843 children under five. Some 44 per cent of married women of child-rearing age are out at work, 110 mothers with around 140 children under five are certainly working more than eight hours a week. Data on the crucial group of working mothers who are unmarried, divorced or widowed are not available. Similarly, any lone fathers bringing up very small children are not recorded.

So our baseline is around 17 per cent of the under-fives in Fartown, though the real figure may be 25 per cent or more.

We decided to look at what provision was in theory available for these children, and what it was like. We visited every playgroup, day nursery and infant school in the ward and every one outside it to which they could reasonably be taken.

Provision for under-fives in Fartown

There is only one playgroup for the 800 pre-school children

of Fartown, 9.30 to 11.30, two mornings a week. The building, an untidy collection of wooden huts down a dirt track by the paper tube factory, is also used for discos, weddings and old people's dinners, so part of each session must be spent packing everything neatly away behind the stage.

With only one toilet, which the supervisor usually has to clean up before the children come in, and no washing facilities, the council had to stretch a point to allow thirty children. Another forty wait hopefully for a vacancy and with luck some may get a term or two there before they start school.

The playgroup supports itself on the modest fee of 20p a morning, paid monthly in advance, supplemented by termly fund-raising efforts and occasional grants from charity.

The supervisor works part-time for the Community Relations Council and spends one afternoon a week visiting immigrant families in the neighbourhood. The racial mix of the playgroup testifies to her energy and powers of persuasion, with twelve Asian children and five West Indians on the register, though some only attend intermittently. Three unregistered childminders use the playgroup for their own and minded children, two of them paying the fees themselves out of two or three pounds a week they charge the parents. Again one glimpses people trying to create their own alternative pre-school system.

Even two hours' escape from the dark, cramped little houses in which most of these children live must be good. Freedom to run about and shout, a foretaste of the rough and tumble of the school playground. But the Fartown playgroup sadly echoes the poverty of the neighbourhood. Parental participation is limited to the formal rota of mother helpers — a bewildered Asian lady sitting against the wall giving her beautifully dressed child little pushes in the direction of the battered toys.

The style of leadership is authoritarian. Milk and biscuits consume a large slice of the short session. Every child sits quiet and still while the snack is served. Apart from this there is little structure to the morning, no sense of anything thought out or planned. Confident children rush around on tricycles and pedal cars, knocking over anyone in their way, timid ones cry a lot and are left to get on with it.

With two paid assistants and a mother helper in addition to the supervisor, there is no shortage of adults, but they adopt a passive role, preventing accidents, sorting out squabbles, rarely initiating any kind of play or engaging the children in conversation. Even conversation between the children, imaginative or co-operative play is not much encouraged. The playgroup can make very little contribution to the language development which many of these children so urgently need.

St Chad's Playgroup in neighbouring Birkby, which takes a sprinkling of Fartown children, presents a very different scene. The gloomy church hall has been transformed with blue, yellow and silver paint. The dominant sound is a quiet, purposeful hum, in contrast to the deafening uproar or fidgety silence of Fartown. In the body of the hall, swings hang from the ceiling. Climbing frame, slide, sandtray can stay permanently in place. On the platform the book corner is comfortably furnished with chairs and carpet, children play with jigsaws and dough; they paste, cut out and stick.

The playgroup leader, 'just an ordinary mum' before she started five years ago, attends courses at the technical college, reads *Contact*, (the playgroups magazine), and visits other groups and schools. Each week she plans some special adult-supervised activity — it might be potato-printing one day, pasta-collage another, or making woolly lambs for Easter. All standard playgroup activities, but chosen to help the children acquire new skills and offer an occasion for conversation. Biscuits and milk at 11 o'clock are the signal for story time and more deliberate attempts at language development. Most of these three- and four-year-olds respond fluently as the supervisor draws them out to talk of their families and homes, the activities of the day, the story she has just read. All too soon, it seems, mothers are arriving at the door.

After Fartown the room seems full of fair heads and pink faces. The forty-six children on the register (each attending two of the four sessions) include only nine from Asian families and two West Indians. One black childminder sends her own child but not the others she looks after.

Very few of the twenty children on the playgroup waiting list can hope for a place because the turnover is so slow. The children who do get places are unlikely to be those most in need, since the onus is on parents to apply early enough to obtain a high place on the list and there is no home-visiting programme.

For the two hundred working mothers of children under five in Birkby and Fartown, the playgroups are of course largely irrelevant. But if they get priority ranking, are fortunate and not in too much of a hurry perhaps the child may go to a day nursery.

One of these, Riding Road Day Nursery, is in Fartown ward, but because of the way the buses run, many Fartown mothers prefer the city centre nurseries, Church Place and King's Crescent. Officially parents applying for day care must accept any vacancy that arises or sink to the bottom of the queue. In practice bureaucracy is moderated by common sense.

And surprisingly, each of these council-run nurseries has its own distinctive character.

Riding Road Nursery is a cheerful friendly place, full of colour and activity. Hours, as in all the Huddersfield nurseries are 7 a.m. to 5.45 p.m., still not quite long enough for the many mothers who start work on the 7 a.m. shift but more than enough for the staff who are usually shorthanded, and often have to skip rest breaks or work overtime.

The building, a hastily erected cluster of wartime huts, is tucked in among the mills, cement works and garages of Huddersfield's industrial centre. The children eat, sleep and play against a backdrop of roaring lorries, screeching brakes, the rumble of drills and crash of hammers. Inside, the barn-like structure has been humanized with makeshift partitions, festooned with children's artwork, so that the nursery can be organized in family groups. Each group includes a baby over nine months and toddlers of assorted ages with a nurse and a student in charge of them. So far as any institution can be informal, this one is. Children wander into the kitchen and matron's room, play in the corridors, sleep or watch television with unusual freedom. Drop-side cots have been transformed into comfortable, gaily-coloured sofas where a tired child can put his head down when he feels like it. Toys and play equipment come out straight after breakfast at

8.30 a.m. and after that the scene is much what you would see in any good nursery school or playgroup, sand, water, clay, dough, paint, jigsaws, dressing-up.

Sixteen of the forty-two children attending have at least one immigrant parent. Nearly all come from the large, West Indian-dominated council estates over the hill. Several, previously with childminders, had been brought by dissatisfied parents, even though they now had to pay much higher nursery charges. A two-year-old cheerfully playing was pointed out. At fourteen months this little boy could not sit himself up. 'He lay against a cushion and never smiled. The childminder just kept him in a corner all day.'

A chronic shortage of equipment and materials — the council allocation for play things hardly covers the cost of paint — is not allowed to limit the children's activities. Nothing is ever thrown away that can be re-used. Matron's room is piled with milk-bottle caps, grocery boxes, wallpaper books, scraps of material, mostly supplied by mothers. Parents move easily about this nursery, coming right inside for a chat with the nurses, making confidently for the coat hooks or toilet, in no hurry to rush away.

But the contribution it makes to this desperately deprived area is limited. Most working mothers have no chance of a place. The lucky ones, once their children reach school age, must either give up work, or leave them to fend for themselves before and after school. Many do. And at five those lovingly cared for babies and toddlers become the enemy. They are 'outside children' who climb the padlocked gate on summer evenings and at weekends to play on the swings and roundabout — and sometimes break them. There is nowhere else.

Kings' Crescent Day Nursery between the ring road and the swimming pool has none of the homeliness of Riding Road. A hospital-like hush strikes as you pass through the locked inner door. The trough of plants in the hall only reinforces the clinical impression made by the bare walls and highly polished floors. Most activity seems geared to the beautiful new builidng; cleaning windows, wiping down paintwork, washing the already spotless floors. Babies lay in cots with plastic rattles tied to the rungs. When a

67

toddler came in to see his baby sister, Matron smartly dismissed him to his own 'family group' room. Children played listlessly with standard toys, rarely speaking. None were reading, drawing, painting or cutting out, no stories or singing broke the silence. The architects included a 'Wendy room' with an elaborate toy shop and dressing up clothes, but it was not used.

None of the nurses could tell me anything about the children's background or previous history. Some clearly had problems. In one group, five of the seven children were black, none of them speaking. Jill, in a red tartan dress and tight little plaits all over her head, slipped a hand into mine and silently asked to be picked up.

Loreen, aged two, kept hitting me and making strange noises. Matron assured me:

'There's nothing wrong with her, she just copies her
brother. We used to think he was deaf but that's now been
excluded. He became very attached to one of the nurses.
She was inclined to favour him, cuddle him and so on. It
wasn't doing him any good — he needs a firm hand — so
I had to move him into another room.'

Half of the fifty children on the roll have parents from Commonwealth countries, only six have both parents at home. Matron has a low view of the mostly unsupported mothers 'They just hand the children over and don't want to be bothered with them'.

She doesn't have a parents' association 'because of staffing difficulties'. She doesn't encourage parents to bring children into the nursery — 'they settle down quicker with mothers out of the way'. Mothers can see their children play 'by arrangement' but they must look through the glass windows — 'they start showing off if they see their mothers'. Nurses dress the children ready for collection at the door — 'West Indian children always play their mothers up when they come to fetch them'.

Rules are strict. Babies must be collected by five at the latest. If the mother has a day off for whatever reason her child cannot come to the nursery. Older boys and girls who call for their younger brothers or sisters on the way home from school are never invited in. Both geographically and humanly this very expensive public provision is isolated from the community it serves.

Church Place Nursery right in the middle of the city, near to the magnificent new sports centre, is not so lavish as King's Crescent Road nor so ramshackle as the wartime day nurseries. Clean, but not clinically so, the walls not too precious to be covered with children's paintings, the cheerful sound of young voices mingled with those of adults coming from every room.

The social composition is very similar to that at King's Crescent; half the children come from immigrant homes, most of them West Indian, not quite half are from single-parent families. Mothers work in mills, hospitals, factories, shops and offices.

Matron does not confine her role to caring for the forty-eight children on the register. She expects to spend many hours listening to parents' worries and problems — usually when she collects the money. By definition, since only priority cases are accepted all these parents have troubles, and too often nowhere else to turn for help.

The main problem among the children, she felt, was slow speech development. She recently referred two boys, both West Indian, for audiometric tests because they weren't speaking at three, but neither had any hearing loss. One was thought to be 'autistic'. She did not know where he had been before he came to the nursery as no records were kept at the social services department and no information about the child's previous experience is passed on to matron.

The fourth Huddersfield day nursery, Milnsbridge, is far over the other side of town, and serves almost exclusively mothers who live and work in that tight-knit concentration of mills and factories.

Where the schools fit in

Two of the infant schools which serve Fartown — Ashbrow and Woodhouse — have nursery classes. The third, Birkby, not only has no nursery class, or any prospect of one, but is so overcrowded that it can only accept children in the *term after* they become five. So the accident of living on the wrong side of Bradford Road can deprive a child of at least a year's schooling. Let's start with that.

With nearly 450 on the register, Birkby school is by far the largest of the three. To see these enormous numbers of tiny children hustled through the two dinner sittings makes you wonder how they ever survive their first day; the clamour and the pushing and shoving even with the best of discipline must be so overwhelming to a child straight from a quiet home.

The population of the school is very mixed, with many children coming by bus from middle-class Fixby and the more prosperous parts of Birkby. Nearly a quarter of the pupils are Asian and many start school with little or no English. A language teacher from the education department comes to teach them four-and-a-half days a week. The headmistress is aware that West Indian children also have language difficulties, particularly if they come from a home where Creole dialect is normally spoken, but they receive no special help.

Social problems arise chiefly among one-parent families, of which there are many. They account for most of the 10 per cent of children entitled to free school dinners — a surprisingly low proportion which reflects the relative prosperity of the area. The children look well-dressed and well cared for; when they strip for PE their underclothes are dazzling white — the child with a grubby vest or torn pants stands out as the exception. Physically the school is typical of its period: classrooms opening off the large central hall, forbiddingly walled playground, high windows. Inside it is full of life and colour, with every inch of precious space, even the roof beams, used to display children's work, store equipment or provide a corner for some special activity.

Parents are in and out of the school all day, helping to relieve the hard-pressed teachers of routine tasks. They are specially invited to Friday assembly, and they have coffee afterwards with the staff, a time when many family worries are brought to the surface. West Indian mothers often come straight to school after the night shift for the Friday morning sessions. This is a school where all the teachers convey concern. All the more strange, then, that this concern does not seem to stretch back into the pre-school years which so largely limit the teacher's chance of success or failure. These decisive years remain unknown, unpenetrated by their work.

At Ashbrow, the new infants school at the top edge of Fartown, the importance of the earliest years is fully acknowledged. The headmistress makes active attempts to recruit for the nursery class children she feels to be in need. 'If parents come to register older children and they look poor, I ask if there are any younger ones who could come to the nursery'. She spends much of her time visiting the childrens' homes, some of which she finds 'indescribably barren'.

Ashbrow draws some of its pupils from Fartown, but far more from the Brackenhall council estate, in which are concentrated the most severe social problems in Huddersfield. Forty per cent of the children have free dinners, usually because their families are on social security. The district nurse now comes every Tuesday to delouse heads; before this started some children would miss two or three weeks at the start of every term because they were excluded from school. When they hold a school jumble sale, Mrs Macdonald takes out all the underclothes, coats and boots to distribute later to children in need: 'we give out loads of wellies'.

Child care in this district tends to be haphazard. Very young children are left to fend for themselves while mothers work in the mills or biscuit factory. Often they return too tired to do more than fall into bed, and the child turns up to school half-clothed and breakfastless. Mrs Macdonald keeps unofficial supplies for them.

One problem the school does not have is truancy. School — warm, bright and welcoming — is a much pleasanter place for many of these children than their own homes.

In such a school population West Indian children (23 per cent) stand out as healthier, better fed and clothed, just as teachable as others. 'Their values are material', the headmistress told us, 'but at least they have values.'

Their main problem, according to her, is linguistic. They don't talk because they are not used to conversation. They don't have the words they need for everyday school activities — the most conspicuous example is ignorance of colour names.

The nursery class tries to counter this disadvantage. The headmistress actively supervises and directs a highly structured language programme. Playgroup-type activities take second place. So though it is staffed by nursery nurses, not qualified teachers, the Ashbrow class may make a greater educational contribution than many more favoured nursery groups.

The third school, Woodhouse, is old like Birkby, but much smaller, and as at Ashbrow, most of the immigrant children (about 30 per cent) come from West Indian or mixed homes. One does not feel here the acute consciousness of social problems so striking at Ashbrow, even though the catchment area is rather similar. Since a West Indian boy was killed by a bus three years ago the staff have organized a rota to look after children left behind at home time, but otherwise they simply note and regret that too often the child's home pulls against and not with them. They know that children are left alone, locked in their houses, that they come to school with little experience of play or conversation and do their best in school to make up for it.

The nursery class, run on conventional lines, has a waiting list of forty. Only a handful of three-year-olds squeeze in, usually in the less-popular afternoon sessions.

The number of nursery class places is of course tiny in relation to the need: eighty-eight for the 1,163 Fartown, Birkby and Deighton children aged three and four. As with playgroups, it depends largely on the parent's initiative which children get those scarce places. Head teachers will give priority to children recommended by health visitors and social workers, but this does not seem to happen as often as might be expected. Where so many children must overcome barriers of poverty and cultural difference before they can begin to benefit from what the infant school has to offer, it is a matter of fine judgment to decide whose need is greatest. Failing any more systematic method of selection, it is the children from homes with some sense of the importance of education, with better organized, more resourceful parents, who get that precious extra experience of school which makes life so much easier for them once they start full-time. Those children whose parents apply are admitted in birth-date order, introducing a further arbitrary factor — a child born earlier in the school year has more chance of a place. And Asian children face a special obstacle. According to one headmistress the medical examination they are required to undergo takes so long that they seldom get into the nursery classes at all.

And of course the other large group of children barred from nursery classes are those with working mothers. Nursery sessions are 9-11.30 and 1-3.30, so unless the parents can find a minder willing to take and fetch the child (and we came across *none* that were — how could they, with three or four other children to care for?) the present pattern of nursery education is useless to them.

Who are these children with mothers, who, contrary to the custom of the neighbourhood, go out to work before the children reach school age? We can guess that some types of family will be disproportionately common among them: single parents for whom the choice is work or social security, West Indians whose cultural tradition sends mothers back to work as soon as possible after the birth of a child, and families under severe economic pressure where one wage is not enough to cover necessary expenses. In other words, the poorest children, and those most liable to be linguistically handicapped, with the greatest need for an extra boost before they start school, are precisely those with least chance of gaining any advantage from the nursery programme or from playgroups.

This shows up clearly in the figures for Huddersfield as a whole and for the nursery class at Woodhouse Infants School. Although this school is on the edge of a council estate in which well over half the houses are lived in by West Indian families, and the proportion of children in the catchment area with both parents born in the New Commonwealth is at least 40 per cent, there were only seven West Indian children in the nursery class at the time of our survey, and no Asians. The picture is similar at Ashbrow, where only a hand-ful of black children are to be seen in the nursery class, in contrast to the main school with 43 per cent coming from black or racially mixed families.

In all three schools we were able to meet and talk to reception class teachers and sit in on some of their lessons. We asked them all if they had special problems with any of the children coming into their classes. We found — perhaps it was naive of us to be surprised — that reception-class teachers in Huddersfield are not routinely informed of the pre-school experience of new pupils. Some heads did not even obtain this information at the time of registration. Without this knowledge it must be easy for a teacher to mistake unfamiliarity with school procedures and expectations for naughtiness or lack of ability.

Nevertheless, in all three schools, reception-class teachers, little aware of the subject of our research, spontaneously recalled children with special difficulties who had spent some of their pre-school years in the care of childminders.

Two quite distinct types of problem emerged. There is the child who in an often-repeated phrase 'goes wild' when confronted with the rich variety of an English infant classroom.

'They don't know how to play, some of them, because they've never played at all. They're bewildered — they go wild rushing from one thing to another.'
'Charles is a real trouble. He hits and intimidates other children, throws things, shouts all the time. I don't know what to do with him. Perhaps they'll put him in a special school.'

Hard to recognize in this description the Charles we had seen more than once crouched silently under the kitchen table of his illegal childminder.

Even more worrying to most teachers was the child who continued to sit in passive silence, not joining in class activities, unwilling or unable to communicate. Language problems they are accustomed to; children for whom English is a foreign language or grammatically different from their own dialect, children unused to carrying on a conversation. But what can you do with a little girl like Regina who hasn't said a single word to her teacher for a term and a half, though she seems to chatter to other children in the playground? Or Tony, with his dozen hardly comprehensible words, who otherwise behaves like a child of normal intelligence? 'Very stubborn', 'difficult to get through to him', 'he just clams up', said their teachers. Sometimes the teacher knew something of the child's background. Tony, for example, 'was just passed from one childminder to another; his mother's worked since he was tiny.' Sometimes we could make the connection through previous contact with the family or minder while the teacher was working in the dark.

Like the day nurseries, schools often referred particularly unresponsive children for hearing tests or psychological assessments. None could remember any case where the child was found to suffer from hearing loss but in three cases a diagnosis was made of elective mutism or autism. All three children were West Indian, a fact which strongly suggests that the schools were observing the syndrome described by Dr G. Stewart Prince in his paper on pseudo-autism among children of depressed and overworked West Indian mothers.[1]

A one-year project did not allow time to follow up these children and find out what happened to them. But among so many children whose difficulties might look more remediable, it was hard to imagine overtaxed teachers finding enough time or determination to undo the damage of those early years. Some teachers frankly looked forward to the time when the child would be assessed as maladjusted or educationally subnormal and whisked away to what the children call 'the silly school'.

The childminders

Most of the official and semi-official provision for under-fives in Fartown is, as we have seen, reserved for those with a parent who can stay at home to look after them and arrange his or her day to fit in with two-hour playgroup or nursery-class sessions.

Working mothers, unless lucky enough to be offered a day-nursery place, must go to a childminder.

At the time we began our survey Fartown had three registered childminders: Mrs Prem, the only registered Asian, a very elderly lady on Leeds Road and Mrs Daley. Halfway through the year Mrs Daley, who had combined minding up to six children with working nights at the biscuit factory, decided to go on an extended holiday in Jamaica, her home country. A month later the elderly minder died. Mrs Daley's place was taken by Mrs Joan Robson, a minder who had been previously registered in another part of town. At the time we interviewed her she was expecting her third child in a few weeks and planned to give up minding while the baby was young.

So by the time we completed our survey there was only one registered minder in Fartown, Mrs Prem. Her service was strictly limited. She looked after four Indian children aged one to four and insisted that they came from 'good' families. She appeared to mean 'high caste'.

We do not claim to have located the *illegal* childminders in Fartown. Our information came from all sources — older brothers and sisters, playgroup leaders, shopkeepers, mothers and fathers. Often it proved unreliable — the woman just helped out a neighbour occasionally in return for the odd packet of cigarettes. Or the children were related to her and the arrangement therefore fell outside the terms of the Act.

But we found twenty-one unofficial childminders looking after two to six children each in one small quarter of the ward. It was the part where Asian families had most thickly settled. And altogether we were told of twenty-eight women and two men looking after children for pay, unknown to the social services department in this tiny net of criss-crossing streets.

The childminders, official and illegal, are described and discussed in detail later in this report. The point here is simply to record that on the most conservative estimate at least ten times as many Fartown children with working mothers were being looked after by illegal minders as by day nurseries and official childminders combined. And this is a typical inner city ward.

We now have a fairly clear picture of the likely pre-school

experience of children in Fartown. (Table 5.2)

We found that only 14 per cent of Fartown children had *any* kind of group or organized play experience before they started school at the age of five — one child in seven.

Table 5.2 Pre-school provision in Fartown

Number of children aged 0-4	847

Provision for children of non-working mothers:

Official (nursery classes)	88 places
Semi-official (playgroups)[a]	34
Total	122

Provision for children of working mothers:

Official (day nurseries)[b]	15
Semi-official (registered childminders)	8
Total	23

a. Including one-third of places at St John's playgroup which also serves Birkby.
b. Number of places calculated in same ratio as population of Fartown to Huddersfield.

For children of working mothers the position was even worse. Places in day nurseries and with registered childminders are available for only one child in thirty-six — and this is based on the census data which, as we have seen, seriously under-records the number of children actually concerned and at risk.

It is quite clear, then, that the official provision of day care was grossly inadequate to meet their needs.

Where were these hundred or so children whilst their parents worked? Were they, as some optimists would like to believe, lovingly cared for by aunts and grandmothers? Or as health visitors and teachers often suggested, locked up alone in upstairs bedrooms? Were they supervised by sleepy fathers just off the night shift? Or were many of them as our pilot research had led us to expect, looked after by illegal childminders in the back streets and alleys with which Fartown is honeycombed?

The picture was now building up quite strongly. Fartown was in many ways a deprived area, but by no means the worst in Huddersfield. And deprivation in Huddersfield is not as intense or extensive as it is in most British cities.

We had elicited the minimum number of children whose parents went out to work. A careful look at the playgroups, day nurseries, nursery and infant schools showed that they could not meet the need. And confirmed our earlier thinking that the whole pre-school concept and structure was wrong — and would never as it stood (even if expanded) help many of those children who most urgently needed it. Sadly we were patrolling the early frontier of our huge education system. Looking in from outside it was clear that very few teachers were aware of the world without, or saw it as a responsibility of education to penetrate these early years. Yet it was here that the decisive dice were often tossed, the game frequently won or lost before the child entered school.

Now we needed one more stretch of basic evidence. It was time to go and knock on all the doors.

6 Where have all the children gone?

Children used to be brought up by their parents.

Urie Bronfenbrenner

We planned to interview every family with a child who was under five in Fartown, to find out if both parents were working, and if so, who looked after the child. The first problem was how to find the families.

Fortunately we had established very good relations with the health visitors based at Fartown Health Centre. They supplied from their records a list of addresses: every household in Fartown with a child under school age, a total of 474. The records were believed to be comprehensive, accurate and up to date.

Twelve students from Huddersfield Polytechnic, as part of a special course on Urban Education, were trained as interviewers. With their help, we visited every house on the health visitors' lists, some of them up to five times, until a contact was made or found to be impossible. We were able to complete 368 interviews with fathers or mothers of 535 children under school age.

The 474 addresses supplied by the Health Centre could at best have been expected to tell us the whereabouts of 663 children. But the 1971 census gives a figure of 847 children aged 0-4 in Fartown. Since there is no reason to suppose that the population had dropped substantially in the following three years, then approximately 200 children had been 'lost' from the health department records. Seven young children had reached school age in the interval between compiling the lists and carrying out the interviews. The remaining thirty-two families either had only older children, or the

79

address was clearly mistaken.

Language difficulties might have proved a far greater obstacle in an area where so many mothers had arrived fairly recently from India or Pakistan and spoke almost no English. The policy of repeated visits paid off here as nearly always we eventually managed to strike a time when the man of the house was at home and we could talk to both parents together. We also had the invaluable help of an Indian psychologist, Kum Kum Bhavnani, who was able to interview some Asian mothers in their own language. In five cases the language barrier proved insurmountable and we could obtain no usable information. Only 3 families out of the 447 addresses refused to talk to us. They thought we were officials, and in some way would harm them.

This left a further fifty-nine addresses, where we might have expected to find eighty-three children. Instead we found empty houses, bricked-up windows and vacant sites. Adding these to the hundred we have already estimated to be missing from the records, we note that the health department had lost or failed to establish or maintain contact with around 300 children under five in Fartown, more than a third of the total.

Unfortunately, all the evidence from previous research suggests that it is precisely the most vulnerable section of the population, families or single parents on the move, with poor communication skills and low appreciation of their children's health needs, who are most likely to slip out of the records in this way. The possibly tragic consequences when health visitors 'lose' a child are well illustrated in the account of the death of a minded baby later in this report.

We have no way of knowing if the families we were unable to contact differed significantly from those we did interview, except that we were able to check one obviously important variable — that of race. (Table 6.1)

From this table it can be seen that we or the health department had 'lost' a slightly higher proportion of children from immigrant families, but oddly enough exactly the same actual number — 156 — from each group.

The census table showing how many residents have parents both born in the New Commonwealth does not identify the parents' country of origin, so we cannot tell directly if black or Asian families are less well represented among our interviews. However, it is possible to estimate the number of Fartown residents born in the West Indies (called 'America' in the census) and Asia. This is 529 and 921 or a ratio of approximately 3 to 7. Among the families we interviewed fifty-five had both parents born in the West Indies and 109 had both parents born in India or Pakistan: 1 to 2. It looks, then, as if health visitors find it rather more difficult to keep track of Asian children than of white or black ones, something we soon found very easy to understand. Like social workers and teachers, health visitors were often defeated by the unfamiliar complexity of Asian forms of address and especially by extended families in which no two people shared a common name. On the working lists supplied by the health centre, Asian families were usually listed simply as 'immigrants'.

Table 6.1 Families interviewed in Fartown survey

	White and mixed	Both parents born in New Commonwealth	Total
1 No of families	204	164	368
2 No of children 0-4	288	247	535
3 No of children 0-4 according to 1971 census	444	403	847
4 (2) as percentage of (3)	64	61	63

Apart from this slight under-representation of families from India and Pakistan, the above figures indicate that our area survey fairly accurately reflects the racial composition of Fartown.

This evidence now led us to three interim conclusions. First of all, we had the maximum number of names and addresses. Persistence and a varied team had reduced the refusal rate and the language barrier to its probable minimum. Second, a third of the children — due to rehousing or shifting addresses — had been 'lost' by the authorities: in this case a good, concerned team of health visitors. It seemed all too probable that the same situation prevailed elsewhere, and probably much more so. This is a very serious and perhaps characteristic break in the chain of service. Third, all the preliminary signs were that the 'lost' children were that third most likely to have working parents, not to be using state day care, and very probably to be drawing heavily on unregistered minders. Whatever our findings were to be, they were likely to *underestimate* the importance of childminding.

Do Fartown mothers go out to work?

There is massive discouragement for mothers working outside the home while they have children under school age. Leaving aside the absence of day-care facilities, doctors and health visitors, schools, social workers, newspapers, radio, television and neighbours all look with disapproval on a woman with small children who goes out to work. Nevertheless national census figures indicate that very large numbers defy received opinion, either from choice or economic necessity. Was this true in Fartown?

We asked every family 'Do both parents (or the mother if single) go out to work? If so, for what hours? And who looks after the child?

The answer we had been told to expect was that no Asian women and few white ones with young children went out to work. The handful who did could draw on family resources — grandmothers and aunts — to care for the child if it was very young. Older children would be at playgroup or in nursery classes. West Indian mothers were moving towards the Huddersfield pattern — staying at home with small children — or if they did work it would be on the evening or night shift. Childminding was thought to play a negligible role. It was for this reason of course that we had selected Huddersfield as a control to Greater Manchester, where day care and a low standard of childminding were generally acknowledged to present an urgent social problem.

Our previous study of families on the Huddersfield day

nursery waiting list, together with the survey of facilities —
or lack of them — for children under five in Fartown had
already made us sceptical of the official picture. It had, of
course, some basis in truth, and in particular the sharp distinction between racial groups was fully confirmed by our
survey, as Table 6.2 shows.

Table 6.2 Fartown families with children under five

	White No.	%*	Asian No.	%*	Black No.	%*	Total No.	%*
1 Mother not working	132	68	85	77·9	11	20	228	63·7
2 Mother or both parents working	62	32	24	22·1	44	80	130	36·3
3 Full-time days	27	43·6	15	62·5	23	52·3	65	50
4 Nights	1	1·6	2	8·3	12	27·2	15	11·6
5 Evenings	17	27·4	6	25	8	18·2	31	23·8
6 Part-time day	12	19·3	—	—	1	2·3	13	10
7 Other (e.g. shop)	5	8·1	1	4·2	—	—	6	4·6
Total families	194		109		55		358	

* From 3 onwards, percentages are of all those working.

We found no families where the mother went out to work
while the father stayed at home, though in two cases the
father had to play both roles because of the mother's illness.
The norm is for black mothers to go out to work (eight
out of ten in our survey did so) and for white and Asian
mothers to stay at home, but there were substantial minorities of nonconformers. The common assumption that Asian
women never go out to work is nonsense. Even with such
young children, over 20 per cent were in outside employment. The mother was working in just under a third of the
white families interviewed. The lowest proportion of working mothers was found among racially mixed families — white
mothers and black fathers. Although they were probably the
poorest families we visited, only one mother was working,

and then only mornings.

The pattern of work also differed strikingly between racial groups. Over half the white mothers only worked part-time, either a four-hour evening shift, mornings, or a couple of hours a day — school crossing keeper or dinner lady. Both black and Asian mothers were much more likely to work full-time. Over a quarter of the West Indians put the children to bed and then set off for the night shift. Evening work seemed less attractive to them than to white or Asian mothers, and there was only one part-time day worker among them.

On the whole, mothers prefer not to work until their children are at least two years old, and women with two or more under-fives are much less likely to work than those with only one.

But five white mothers, three black and one Indian mother with babies less than a year old were working. Several of these were single-parent families. The youngest of all, a baby boy only three months old was the child of a sixteen-year-old unmarried girl living with her own mother.

Hours and type of work

The two major employers of working mothers in Fartown are the textile industry and the United Biscuits factory in Halifax. United Biscuits runs a free bus service from Huddersfield for the evening and night shifts; and many of the mills also run evening shifts, usually from 5.30 to 9.30 p.m. Mills are so thickly clustered around Fartown that women who want to work can easily find a job within reasonable walking distance. Nearly all the mothers in our survey worked in low-paid, unskilled jobs. Only one working mother could be classified as middle-class: married to the managing director of a small engineering firm, she helped him with the accounts in the morning while her little boy was at playgroup. There were five nurses: an Irish woman working mornings only, and two black and two Indian mothers all working permanent nights. Other mothers were cleaners, shop assistants, hospital domestics, barmaids and factory workers. One mother of two was reluctant to specify her night job. Neighbours claimed she was a prostitute.

Black and Asian mothers, as we have said, tended to work much longer hours than white ones. Over half the white mothers worked part-time, either mornings or evenings, rarely more than 20 hours a week or 3·5 hours a day. Day workers averaged just under seven hours, and the average number of hours worked by all white mothers was 5·2.

Asian mothers worked on average 8·5 hours a day. Two of them put in a 10-hour day, and the average for day work was 9·4 hours. The six evening workers all did 4- or 4·5-hour shifts.

Nearly all the black mothers worked an 8-9 hour day, except for the few who worked evenings and one whose regular overtime took her working day to eleven hours. Night shifts were longer; 10·25 hours at the biscuit factory, 12 hours in hospitals, but normally for only four nights a week. The overall average for black mothers was just under 8 hours.

These differences in working hours reflect a marked difference between the three racial groups in motivation and attitudes to work. White mothers were much more likely to work 'to get out of the house'; to earn a little money that they could call their own; or 'to buy a few extras', not because the family was under severe economic pressure. Most had gone to some trouble to fit their working hours to family commitments and would give up work if they were dissatisfied with their child-care arrangements.

Indian and Pakistani mothers, once having taken what must have been a very daunting step into the working world, wanted to earn as much as they possibly could — perhaps in the hope of retreating into their homes again once immediate financial needs had been met. This accounts for the very long hours they all worked; *the shortest factory day was 8·5 hours and nine out of ten worked over 9 hours a day.*

For West Indian mothers too, economic motives were paramount, and though they did not work quite such long hours as the Asians, they were of course much more likely to be working in the first place. All were full time.

85

An investigation

But who looks after the child?

All the parents we interviewed chose, if they possibly could, to have their children cared for within the family, and a fair number succeeded. The next choice was a day nursery — but only twelve families were lucky enough to get a place. After that they fell back on friends, neighbours and most often, childminders.

Family care has the great advantage of cheapness — in most cases only token sums of money changed hands. But it would be very unsafe to conclude that it is necessarily good care, or good for the family. The very common expedient of parents alternating shifts, for example, often left awkward gaps about which some of our respondents were evasive and others despairing. Babies and toddlers were left alone with neighbours 'listening' or minded by other children scarcely older than themselves, and obviously quite incapable of coping should anything go wrong. Some husbands and wives hardly saw each other for weeks on end: 'I go out when he comes in'. Tired fathers or mothers coming off the night shift were left to care for lively three-year-olds just out of bed. Some shut them in a room and hoped for the best, others dozed on the sofa, irritable through exhaustion, certainly in no mood for games and conversation.

Table 6.3 shows what happened to the 535 children whose families we visited, while both parents were at work.

Table 6.3 Care of children under five with working mothers

	White	Asian	Black	Total
Day nursery	8	3	1	12
Childminder	9	4	16	29
Relative	9	10	14	33
Parents alternating shifts	22	3	11	36
Children minding	3	2		5
Other	9	2	2	13

From this we can see there were three broad bands of care. First of all, childminders or children acting as childminders looked after thirty-four of the children. Relatives cared for thirty-three children. And the unsatisfactory alternating shift system — one of the least desirable arrangements — but one which avoided expense or recognized that there was no relative, childminder or state provision available — covered thirty-six children.

These then, in an area like Fartown, are the three main forms of day care. Nurseries come a long way behind, and nursery schools, reception classes or playgroups hardly appear at all.

The figures do not easily add up because some families used more than one form of care — for example, a grandmother on two days and a childminder for the other three. Or other relatives helped out when mother's and father's shifts overlapped.

Arrangements for child care, like other aspects of work, differed between racial groups, but another important factor was the mother's working hours. Nearly all the evening workers, for example, relied on the children's father to look after them, supplemented if there was a gap by older children coming home from school.

It can be seen, what had now become familiar, that only a handful of children, three-quarters of them white, were served by the official form of substitute care — day nurseries, even

Table 6.4 Type of care by hours of work

	Part-time day	Full-time day	Evening	Night	Total
Day nursery	1	11			12
Childminder	1	22		6	29
Relative	2	21	7	3	33
Parents alternating shifts	4	9	18	5	36
Other children		2	3		5
Other or none	5	3	4	1	13

though many of these parents had a strong claim for priority attention.

John Allan's mother developed a puerperal psychosis soon after he was born and has been in hospital ever since. His father suffers from epilepsy. For a time the baby was looked after by a friendly but elderly neighbour. When she became too poorly to carry on, Mr Allan started to work nights so that he could be with the child during the day. Later, fearing that exhaustion would bring on his fits again, he accepted an offer of help from an illegal childminder, Mrs Aspley, who lived in a back alley off Bradford Road.

'He started coming home as though he hadn't been changed all day. Then he came home with a bruise. And then another bruise. I wasn't quite satisfied with what Mrs Aspley said, so I took him to the hospital. It were the doctor there that got him to the day nursery in the end — I thought it weren't worth applying. We waited a year as it was.'

Three mothers alone, including one with a husband in prison, had also waited several months for places, and one mother who had applied for a place unsuccessfully had to fall back variously on a sick grandmother, on the father when his shift worked out right, and on an unregistered childminder. The child appeared bewildered and backward.

Three families had stopped using day nurseries. One mother found going out early on winter mornings brought on her little boy's bronchitis. Two decided it cost too much. In both these families the father was intermittently and unpredictably incapacitated by severe depression. It seemed that the method of calculating parental contributions was not flexible enough to allow for this. The mothers both now went out to work hoping that the fathers would cope somehow. 'I'm a bit stuck when he's bad,' remarked one.

For families with other primary-age children, getting a day nursery place was not the end of their troubles. One suddenly-deserted wife was given an emergency place but still had to leave her six-year-old at 7 a.m. when she went to work. The child had to get his own breakfast and cross the busy main road to school. The nursery is half empty at that time of the morning, but say they can't make any exceptions or 'they'll all want to come'. His mother worries constantly but can't face the idea of sitting at home on social security. 'It's all asking neighbours for favours, which I don't like, but what else can you do?'

'What else can you do?' asks another mother, who 'goes sick' for half-term and all the school holidays. A houseproud Scottish woman, she spends her evenings writing to MPs and councillors in a vain attempt to escape from the mouldering, wood-lice infested council house where she has lived for three years.

'It's shocking down here. No playgroup. Swings all broken. The river's unfenced. The Council don't bother with these houses. They won't do any repairs. They were modernizing them but they only did one and never came back. You lose heart. I'd go mad if I couldn't go out to work. It was all right when both boys were at day nursery but since David started school I just don't know what to do.'

The contribution of the day nurseries was limited in two ways. First, by their inflexibility. They did not see it as their role to provide a family service. Their concern, sincerely felt, began and ended with the child whose name appeared on the register. And, as always, by the very small number of places available. Only 15 out of the 180 children of working mothers in our survey had *ever* attended a day nursery; only 12 were doing so at the time of the interview.

Of the rest, the largest group of those whose mothers worked full-time during the day were cared for by child-minders, and this is discussed in more detail below. The next most important group, disregarding alternating shiftworkers, is relatives.

Children looked after by relatives

Among white children, six were cared for by grandmothers, two by aunts and two by an elder brother and sister. aged fifteen and nine. Most of the parents were satisfied with these arrangements and very definite that it was the only possible one for them. 'I wouldn't leave him with anyone but Mum.' One woman shared both her job and the care of her child with her mother who lived down the road.

But another mother had switched to a childminder when the grandmother began to find two lively toddlers a bit much to cope with. And one grandmother, who told us emphatically 'I believe in looking after my own,' we accidentally overheard a few minutes later telling someone on the telephone that she was looking out for a childminder.

Asian working mothers also relied heavily on grandparents, with the cultural difference that in every case this was the father's mother and not the mother's. Three children were looked after by the mother's sister along with her own babies. And two by the father's brother after his night shift.

Very young children had to bear heavy responsibilities. Ranjit (2) and Jasbinder (4) were 'looked after' every evening from 4.30 to 7.30 p.m. by their six-year-old sister. In another family four children aged one to ten years have to fend for themselves for several hours after their mother goes to work. Jasbia at twelve does all the housework, takes and fetches her baby brother from his childminder, gives three younger children their tea, and looks after them in the school holidays.

Only three black women could turn to their own mothers for help — most grandmothers were working too, or far far back in the West Indies. Three children were minded by their great-grandmother — or at least she sat in the house with them — one by a paternal aunt, and two by teenage uncles.

Eight children were asked to mind their younger brothers and sister, sometimes just to 'fill in', sometimes for several hours on a regular basis.

Two cot-bound babies and a little boy of three were regularly left entirely alone between the time their fathers set off to work at 7.30 a.m. and when their mothers arrived back from the night shift sometimes after 8.30 a.m.

Families with experience of using childminders

Thirty families used a childminder at the time of our survey and a further eleven had done so in the recent past.

Of those with a child currently with a childminder, eleven used registered and nineteen illegal childminders. The parents very seldom mentioned registration spontaneously, and most did not even know if their minder was registered or not. We were able to check this from our own records.

Table 6.5 Fartown families using childminders

	White	Asian	Black	Total
Registered	5	1	5	11
Unregistered	5	3	11	19
Average weekly cost	£5.40	£3.15	£2.00	

Registered minders

Five different minders cared for the eleven children. Four of the black families used the same registered childminder: Mrs Jolly of Elland Old Road. The fifth, and one of the white children went to Mrs Daley, who worked nights and minded during the day. The Pakistani boy attended Mr Evans's small private day nursery once a week — which he had developed out of childminding.

The other four white families used registered minders in another part of town, explaining that they had to put up with the bus journey because they could find nobody closer.

The nineteen illegal minders nearly all became known to us in the course of our research and some are described later in this report. Only two minders came into the category of 'friends helping out', and only looked after one child. They were both white. One Irish boy was taken across town every morning at 7 a.m. to 'a friend's husband', a Jamaican night-shift worker, who unofficially minded children during the day.

The black children, as Table 6.5 shows, were looked after for the lowest rates — £2 a week on average, sometimes even including food of a kind — and predictably got the worst care. In no case did their minders approach minimum regis-tration standards; several children were in physical danger or suffering positive neglect and ill-treatment.

Two of the three unregistered Asian minders who appear in this survey offered an acceptable standard of physical care, but not much else. The third, a Sikh lady (paid £1.50 a week,) took the minded child along with her own to Fartown playgroup, an effort not much appreciated by his mother who refused to pay the 20p playgroup fee.

The eleven families who no longer used childminders had mostly had unfortunate experiences.

'She smacked him when he were naughty so we took
him away.'
'They don't look after them properly.'
'We tried a childminder once but he cried all day.'
'She wasn't looking after him right so I stopped working.'

There was no doubt that childminders had a poor image in the neighbourhood. We base this claim on first-hand knowledge, not on press publicity. The question 'Have you ever used a childminder?' often produced a strong reaction:

'Certainly not. We believe in caring for us own children.'
'I don't believe in childminders.'
'My husband wouldn't consider the idea.'
'I don't think childminders are reliable — and I know a
few round here.'
'No one will ever look after my children except me.'
'We wouldn't trust her to anyone but a proper nurse, she's
too precious. That's why I work nights.'

On the other hand, several non-working mothers said they had tried unsuccessfully to find a childminder and asked if we could help them. And among black families there was a striking absence of prejudice against childminders. Only one had any objection to them in principle. This was a Grenadan couple, living in a run-down council house, but with impressively high standards of child care. The father explained that they had preferred to wait two years for a day-nursery place because 'I think they teach them something there. A childminder doesn't have time. She's too busy looking after them.'

Conclusion

By putting this small part of Huddersfield under the microscope we have tried to find out what is the daily experience
of a pre-school child in an inner area of an industrial town.
Taken as a whole, Fartown is not — as we have seen — a place
of acute social deprivation, but an ordinary working-class
district which has absorbed a number of newcomers and now
again settled back into some kind of equilibrium. At the time
of our survey there was not much obvious poverty to be seen,
and a remarkable absence of racial tension. But can we feel
happy about our findings?

In the first place, the chances of a baby born in Fartown
slipping unnoticed from the surveillance of the health department appear disturbingly high — one in three. The chances of
that child being offered any kind of pre-school play
experience are much smaller, perhaps one in seven.

When we looked at the playgroup and nursery-class provision for the area we found it grossly insufficient in quantity
and variable in quality. Very large areas of the ward, including the decaying council estates, are not served by any playgroups at all. Selection and admission procedures tend to
favour better-organized families with some idea of the importance of pre-school education. So having eliminated by their
physical location the most needy children, play and nursery
facilities within those more fortunate areas are primarily
used by better-off families.

A sense of social purpose and the ability to do the job
effectively did not always go together. For many of these
children the play experience they did get was too brief and
unfocussed to make much impression on the disadvantages
they would take with them to school. But they were lucky
compared with the much larger group of three- and four-year-
olds in Fartown who had no chance of going to a playgroup
or nursery. Nearly half of these children, it must be remembered, lived in homes where the language spoken was not
standard English, if it was English at all, and in families
where toys and playthings, drawing, painting and reading
were not part of the cultural tradition.

Not surprisingly then, the schools to which they would go

expected to face an uphill task and were all too well prepared for the probability of failure.

When we looked specifically at the children of working mothers, the picture was bleak. We identified 130 families in Fartown in which a mother on her own or both parents went out to work for more than eight hours a week. This is twenty more than the census estimate, but almost certainly much fewer than actually exist. Our respondents included hardly any unmarried mothers, for example. Only one child of these 130 families went to a playgroup, none to a nursery class.

Grandmothers, who loom large in local mythology, turn out to play a relatively minor role in enabling mothers to work. The total number of families in which children were looked after by grandmothers was only fourteen.

A much more common form of in-family care was parents alternating shifts. We are not aware of any research on shift work which considers its implications for children, though its destructive effect on emotional stability and marital relationships is well known. Not realizing when we began our research what an important feature of family life in Fartown it would turn out to be, we had not planned any close enquiry on the subject. In later interviews we began to ask more detailed questions of shiftworking parents, and our impression was that this group of children may be especially disadvantaged. They were more likely than any others to be left alone in the house, either when the parents' shifts over-lapped or when both parents were temporarily on nights. Of course very few parents would openly admit to leaving their children alone, but we had plenty of reason to think this happened much more often than we were told. Hardly better off were the children left in the care of very young brothers and sisters: one of these child childminders was only six years old herself.

For many children whose parents said complacently, 'They're never left', it might seem rather that the parents were never there. Mothers who worked the evening shift rarely saw their husbands and often seemed to drift through the day in an exhausted daze. Night workers, expected to look after small children during the day, either shut them up in a room with a few toys (if they were lucky) and hoped for the best; or tried to snatch a few hours of sleep on the sofa, waking up to shout bad temperedly at the children from time to time. Some children were put back to bed almost as soon as they'd got up. Others were kept up till midnight in the hope that they might sleep through the morning. These parents' lives rarely left time or energy to play or talk to children, and especially in winter, weeks might go by without the children leaving the house.

Of course our major interest at this point was in the numbers of children looked after by childminders. It was far, far more than we had been led to expect, considering the tiny number of registered childminders in Fartown. More than twice as many children were with illegal minders as with registered ones, but when we looked at the quality of care they were actually receiving, registration turned out to be quite irrelevant. The disturbing truth was that no more than half a dozen of these children were looked after in safe and comfortable conditions with the kind of care that might help them to develop physically and mentally. At least an equal number suffered serious neglect and harsh treatment, if not actual cruelty. And most of the rest spent their days in the typical emptiness of life with childminders who work for a pittance, without support or supervision. Day after day they sat passively on a sofa, without conversation, toys, books, visits or stimulation of any kind.

Given that this was what childminding meant in Fartown, it was easy to understand those families who preferred to work alternating shifts or resorted to haphazard care by relatives, neighbours and older children. As things were, Fartown children whose mothers worked and sent them to childminders were very likely to grow up in conditions positively harmful to their emotional and intellectual development. But paradoxically the survey also showed the key potential role of childminders in an area like this.

Despite all we had been told in advance, childminding played a crucial part in the human potentiality and economy of Fartown.

Our control had crumbled in our hands. All lines of investigation locked in on one point. Myth after myth had melted away in front of us — myths about every-ready grandmas in the next street, myths about getting into a day nursery, myths about Asian mothers always staying at home to look after the young family, myths about warm Yorkshire parents never leaving their babies alone in the house. And above all, myths that childminders were marginal, and illegal ones as rare as tigers in this neighbourly northern town.

We were faced with a whole array of problems: the economic pressures on these families; a cultural inheritance which often had within it a very weak sense of a child's needs; the lack of education for parenthood; the tiny amount and varied quality of state provision; the innocent indifference of schools to these deciding years.

We often felt that we were asking for the moon, the new Jerusalem, or an overnight change in the human heart. But more reflectively there *was* a way of probing forward. Broadly our sense was stiffened that all these years we had been asking the wrong questions about pre-school education — and that was why, nationally or in Fartown, we were ending up with the wrong answers. The history of provision or intervention in early childhood showed that questions were always asked, as from the top. That was how we had ended up by investing almost solely in physical institutions, why we had ended up with dual responsibilities (education and social service) and disconnected professions. We needed to ask the questions the other way round — to start with people as they actually were, and see what provision could or should be developed from their situation, their sense of needs, their resources.

And second, in the short term, childminders were a quite specific and very major key. They could be identified. Their standards *could* be vastly improved. And this in itself gave some hope of breaking the cycle of disadvantage as it so rapidly gathered these very young children into its viciously multiplying circles of failure.

Our thinking had been unexpectedly tested. It was time to cross the Pennines and explore a contrasting working-class area in the vast sprawling city of Manchester.

7 Cornflake kids

*Non contemnenda quasi parva sine quibus magna
constare non possunt.*

(The apparently small details should not be ignored
for it is only through them that large designs are
possible.)   Saint Jerome

Every morning at 6.30 a.m., an orange and cream No. 98 bus
leaves Deansgate, Manchester. The bus stops opposite the
sophisticated department store of Kendal Milne, where the
dark windows glint with furs, perfumes, rare foods. The
destination is the Trafford Park industrial estate. The bus is
packed with women. Many of them young West Indian
mothers. 'Any more for the African Queen?' shouts the conductor. Another bus pulls in, fills up, and away to the largest
industrial estate in the world outside Japan. A whole convoy
streams out of Deansgate for an hour. You get the impression
that there are more black faces on the earliest buses, but
mostly white ones on the later ones.
   The Trafford industrial estate is huge — 1,400 acres —
encircling a tiny little community of terraced houses. These
streets, with their Lancashire corner shops (and now a tiny
mosque) all have American-style names: First Street, Second
Street, Third Street. The roads are jammed with huge intercontinental transporter lorries, and criss-crossed by busy
railway lines: an old fashioned green engine chugs unexpectedly across the road in front of you. This massive industrial
city, with its scores of chimneys, virulent and coloured
smoke, constant clanging, whistling, thumping and screeching, employs a huge number of women — almost all on

routine production-line tasks — from dawn to dusk, making the packaged food, soap, household cleaners, beer and cosmetics that are part of the daily life of most British households.

Instead of at once repeating the dense area survey we were doing in Huddersfield, we decided to begin by asking a new question. How did the situation of the child look, if one began with the women on the production belt? Did industry itself recognize or carry any responsibility towards their young children left behind that dark, wet morning?

At first we considered trying to interview mothers with young children on those winter dawn buses from the centre of Manchester: a new kind of mobile survey. But a few pilot trips showed that, attractive as the idea was, it was probably impractical. We doubted if — in all the rush, stops, jocularity, tiredness and public position — we would uncover data about the toddler left behind, data which so often would be guilt-edged.

We then approached the most famous household name on the estate — Kelloggs, makers of cornflakes, of daily sunshine breakfasts enjoyed by small children everywhere. What could the mothers on the Rice Krispie packing line tell us about their own children?[1]

Kelloggs employ just under 600 women. Of these 250 are on the shop floor. There is no crèche or nursery. Indeed there is nothing like this for the many thousands of other women who work on the estate. During the brief lunch-breaks, there is nowhere at all to go. No open spaces, nothing. Just the chance of a quick fag in the yard. Wherever their children are they must be many miles and many hours away.

We began by asking the personnel department how many of their employees had children under five. Personnel tried to help us, but in the end confessed that they did not know — and did not know how to obtain such information.

We switched our tactics and approached the foreladies. At first we met with a good deal of reluctance. Who were we — standing there with our ballpoints and notebooks, whilst everyone else — in their white paper hats (hygiene control is severe) — were chained to the endless packing line? Some thought we were efficiency experts in disguise who — given a scrap of information — would increase the work and lower the pay rates. When, after long repetitive explanations, that fear was calmed, a bigger one reared its head. Many women knew perfectly well that the personnel department did not know whether they had children under five or not. And they didn't want them to know. They felt it could only do them harm — possibly they would never be asked to do any of the scarce overtime, or possibly they would be the first to be laid off if there were redundancies. So the babies and toddlers back somewhere in the streets of Manchester were a locked-up secret. Personnel did not know, the mothers did not speak of it, and felt that the less said about their children, the better.

A very hard problem, not made easier by the deafening noise everywhere. In the end we took just one section of the shop-floor — women packing Rice Krispies. It was a patient matter of talking to foreladies and packers — in the midst of busy, tied-down work — and trying to find some who would admit to being mothers of small children, and who might then say how their child was being cared for that day.

On the production line we studied,[2] twenty-seven women finally admitted they had children under five and told us about them. This is certainly an underestimate. And we would assume that the ones who did not tell us, probably had even worse day-care arrangements for their children than those who finally spoke.

The women work 7 a.m. to 3 p.m. and 3 p.m. to 10 p.m. alternate weeks. The starting wage is approximately £23 a week, rising to about £27. There is little opportunity for overtime. The work is monotonous and fairly exhausting. A woman will be in charge of a section of the production line — pulling and pushing levers and packing the cartons into huge cardboard containers that she then has to manipulate across to the collection point. Conversation is virtually impossible, the noise level is extremely high and women are spaced in such a way along the lines that in order to exchange words they have to leave their position and shout directly in each other's ears. The women have frequent five-minute breaks, but no proper rest facilities — just two old battered armchairs in the locker room.

The staggered shift system is dreadful for a mother of small children. One week she has to find someone prepared to take her child in at perhaps 6.15 in the morning, and then the following week keep the child until 10.45 or so at night.

Some mums said that they felt these working hours did have the advantage that every week they could spend a fair percentage of time with their children. But others admitted to being so exhausted after their early start that they often didn't pick up their children immediately they returned home. And of course when they were on the late shift they slept on in the mornings. We noticed a couple of the mothers regularly arrived at the factory at midday when they were on the late shift. This was partly in order to take advantage of the subsidized canteen, but mainly to meet and chat with workmates before work started.

Of the twenty-seven women we interviewed, twenty-two left their children in the care of illegal childminders. One had her child fostered privately for a week at a time. The remaining four left them with close relatives; one with her own mother, one with her sister, one with her sister-in-law and one with an aunt. Not one woman was using day-nursery provision or a registered minder. Between them they had thirty-three children, the youngest six months old. (Table 7.1)

This table spotlights another factor. We began by looking at the size of the question using official figures, but increasingly felt that these were serious understatements. At least three of these packers, for instance, would not show up in the census tables, and none of the twenty-two childminders would appear in *Social Trends* or DHSS statistics. Possibly we have all been a little over-awed by the statistic-makers, and not always asked them the simple, but useful, questions. Then we probed a day-nursery waiting list. That suggested that childminding was a wider practice than we had previously thought, but we were aware that less-articulate and less-informed mothers in serious need often did not get as far as these near-static waiting lists. We then went over Fartown with a social toothcomb. Again the dimensions and importance of childminding seemed to grow, with illegal child-minders now beginning to appear in a substantial way, as

Table 7.1 Twenty-seven packers at Kelloggs with thirty-three children under five

Name	Status	Country of birth	Child's sex	Age	Day-care Provision
Pamela Shaw	M	GB	b & g	2 and 3 years	Illegal minder
Stephanie Gordon	S	WI	g	4 yrs	Illegal minder
Sylvia Collier	M	GB	b	8 months	Illegal minder
Lakshmi Gopal	M	Pakistan	b	4 yrs	Illegal minder
Josie Davies	M	GB	b	2 yrs	Illegal minder
Barbara Phillips	Divorced	GB	g	6 months	Illegal minder
Sue Hanley	M	GB	g & b	4 yrs	Illegal minder
Rosalie Cox	S	WI	g	2 and 4 yrs	Illegal minder
Charleen Harris	S	WI	twin girls	2 yrs	Illegal minder
Joyce West	M	GB	b	1 yr	Illegal minder
Audrey Dent	M	WI	b	2 yrs	Illegal minder
Mary Brown	M	GB	g	3 yrs	Illegal minder
Phyllis Martin	S	WI	b	9 yrs	Illegal minder
Marcia Lovemore	S	WI	b	3 yrs	Illegal minder
Thelma Mackintosh	M	WI	g	1 yr	Aunt
Mavis Hyde	M	GB	g	2 yrs	Illegal minder
Deanne Abbott	S	WI	b	17 months	Illegal minder
Pearl Mulligan	M	WI	2 gs	3 and 4 yrs	Illegal minder
Peggy Kaka	M	Nigeria	g	3½ yrs	Illegal minder
Aldeane Jones	S	Nigeria	g	3 yrs	Privately weekly fostered
Elizabeth Egbu	M	Nigeria	2 gs	2 and 3 yrs	Illegal minder
Shirley Giles	M	GB	g	4 yrs	Illegal minder
Jennifer Grey	S	GB	g	4 yrs	Illegal minder
Janice Kirk	Divorced	WI	g	3 yrs	Sister-in-law
Olive Ramsbotham	Divorced	GB	b	4 yrs	Illegal minder
Wendy Johnston	S	GB	g	4 yrs	Mother
Jacky Elliott	M	GB	b & g	2 and 3½ yrs	Sister

* These are not, of course, the women's real names.

101

UNIVERSITY COLLEGE LIBRARY CARDIFF

even more important in a working-class area than registered childminders. Yet, we knew there were parents and children we were not picking up — the strange third that officialdom had lost. And meanwhile our other probes — the seven-city Dawnwatch or the backstreets of Balsall Heath — were all pointing to the severe problems of working mothers in deprived areas, and the paramountcy of the illegal childminder.

Now, by turning the question on its head, and tackling the mothers on the production line, we had confirmed — even if very modestly — the pattern that was almost etching itself, so long as we kept alert and moving. Perhaps we will never have a total detailed map of childminding. Possibly we don't need one. At this stage it was like mapping out the shape of a new social continent. And the cornflake kids had given us at least a rough sense of a missing stretch.

It was not possible, under the conditions, to press on any further at Kelloggs. But we wanted to get just a bit more sense of depth before retiring. After immense difficulty, we made the journey home ('first stop the Khyber Pass', shouts the conductor, indifferent to the deckful of wholly white or Caribbean faces. No one minds. The cornflake day is over, and ritual jokes like wallpaper music in the factories ease tedious life along). Seven of the packers with small children agreed to see us in their homes. More might have done but, like them, by now we simply did not have the energy to cope with more. Still it was worth mining a little more evidence. It could be a long time before anyone else followed us down this road.

Pearl Mulligan

Pearl is a lively chatty girl of twenty-two or twenty-three, born in this country of a Jewish mother and a Jamaican father. She lived in the very area we next chose to research.

She has two daughters, Lorelle, aged two, by her husband, and Delia, three, from a previous relationship. Both children had been minded by June Hawes (one of the two registered minders in the district) for about a year. But at the time June had temporarily given up and taken a job in a boutique. Pearl discovered an alternative unregistered minder with whom she was quite happy to leave the girls.

Pearl's husband has a permanent but not very well-paid job and spends a large proportion of his earnings on gambling. Their financial situation is worsened by the fact that they have Pearl's twenty-five-year-old unmarried sister living with them. Zena has an eleven-year-old son (conceived when she was fourteen) and is now training to be a nurse, so is greatly dependent on the Mulligans.

Before she discovered June Hawes, Pearl had a succession of bad minders. Her usual complaint was that she felt the girls 'weren't happy' with the women. But she's more specific about one woman who she maintained never changed the children and made them play around the house and garden without shoes and socks.

'I used to wonder why their feet were so filthy. Their socks would be as spotless as when I'd put them on in the morning. But their feet — ugh! Anyway one day I was dressing Delia and she says to me, "Don't want shoes on", and when I asked why she said, "Nanny takes shoes off". So next time I picked them up I asked her about it and she said at first that it was nonsense and then admitted that she did take them off them so they wouldn't damage the furniture. Well, that's all very well if it's warm, but this was winter and she had an outside lav. Her house was spotless, I admit that. But it makes you think, doesn't it? If it was more important her house was clean than my babies warm — what else was she doing?'

Pearl has always used white minders. Never West Indian.

'Oh! I'd never let them near a West Indian minder. When me and my brothers were tiny my mum used to leave us with this Jamaican woman. She kept us in the cellar *all day*. We never came out. We used to go home and tell our mum we was in the dark all day. But she wouldn't believe us. It wasn't until our dad turned up early one day and found us down there that we were taken away. I've never

forgotten that. Neither have my brothers. The smell was
terrible. All musty and damp. So I'd never dream of
leaving mine with a West Indian. All our friends are
coloured. But a coloured minder for my kids? Never.'

Phyllis Martin

Phyllis is West Indian, about thirty-five years old, unmarried
and has four children. Of the four, only Tommy, the youngest — now nine — was born in this country. He was minded
from the age of three months until he went to school.

'That boy's too lively. Can't keep still for one moment.
Some time he just run and bang his head on wall. Bang,
bang. He's going to special school next month. I thought
that sounded real good — "special school". But they said
he's backward that's why he's got to go. So I suppose
it's right. It's going to be real strange not having him here.
But they said he'd be able to come home for the holidays.'

Tommy was with a succession of minders during his first
five years. Some good. Some bad. Phyllis describes mornings
when, at 5 o'clock, she's stood on a minder's doorstep with
Tommy in her arms, trying to wake her.

'I've been that scared. Not wanting to ring and ring in case
she'd be cross and not take Tommy in. And there was my
bus going in five minutes! That was always happening.'
    And then there was the minder that never changed him.
'You know what that woman did — she just dipped those
clean nappies I sent in water. I know that because I
marked a nappy one day and put it on him at five in the
morning. He had that same nappy on him when I collected
him at five at night. She made him ill too. Had to go to
hospital with a bad stomach. I don't know what that
woman did, but I used to send him with a flask of real
good porridge. She must have given him bad food.'

The next minder was better. Tommy was happy. 'There

were lots of other children there for him to play with.' He stayed there for twelve months. Then disaster struck. One evening the minder opened the door to Phyllis with the news that she was being threatened with prosecution for illegal minding. She'd have to give up. 'I was so worried. It was a Thursday. I *had* to go into work the next day.' (When asked why she couldn't just explain her position to her employers she said she'd have lost her job altogether if she'd told them she had a child under five that she couldn't cope with.) 'But I had this real good man then. He was on nights so he kept Tommy with him for a week.' Then she was really desperate. Determined not to 'go on the state' she spent afternoons on her early shift weeks walking the streets with Tommy. Knocking on doors where she saw children playing. Begging them to take him. 'You know, those weeks, *I just had to leave him in the house*. I'd walk out of that door, and pray to God he'd be all right till I came back. I used to think about him all day at work.'

'I was walking past the newsagents on Ayres Road one day. I know this is wicked but I was thinking if I can't find no way for Tommy I'll do away with him. And then I saw this woman. She was English but she had three coloured children with her. I just went up to her there and then and asked her to take him. She said yes, and he stayed there till he went to school.'

Mary Brown

Mary is white, just nineteen and very pretty. She flirts continually with the men in the factory and isn't popular with the other women. She's married to a young man who also works at Kelloggs. They have one daughter, Sharon, aged three.

'I couldn't imagine not working. I had Sharon when I was just sixteen. So we were able to get married before she was born. Two weeks before, actually. I couldn't stand being stuck out here all day. Send me mad. I suppose I'm lucky Dick doesn't mind. I know some men kick up if their wives want to work. But Dick doesn't. Anyhow you just have to look round this house to see what me working has done. We'd never have a nice place like this on Dick's money.'

They live in Worsley, a good eight miles from Trafford Park. A neat little modern terraced house, elaborately furnished.

Mary had a bad experience with her previous minder. They were living in Salford then.

'I thought she was OK at first. The house was quite neat. I paid her £4 a week. There were about five other children there so she wasn't doing too badly. It used to worry me sometimes that Sharon cried so whenever I got near her house. But I thought it was because she didn't want to leave me. Well, one day she came home with this awful mark on her face. At first you couldn't tell what had done it. It was so swollen up and red. But next morning you could see it was a cigarette burn. I went straight round with her. The woman said her own child had done it because she was giving too much attention to Sharon. But I never believed that. What would a tiny kid be doing with a cigarette anyhow?'

Mary gave up work for a short while after this incident.

'But I hated it. I suppose it's OK when you're older. But I'm young. I don't want to be stuck at home. Actually I minded for a while. Just one kid. A Jamaican. Didn't do it for long though. The neighbours used to shout lousy things at me when I took him out with Sharon.'

Then they moved to Worsley and because of the mortgage and other additional expenses it became necessary for Mary to work again. Kelloggs was an obvious choice as her husband worked there. They deliberately work the same shifts, although this makes for worse problems with Sharon. They prefer it this way though because they can travel backwards and forwards together.

Mary was very lucky to find Betty — her present minder.

'I was out shopping in the Precinct one day and I saw this girl. I thought I recognized her. Well, it turned out we'd been to the same school together in Salford. Only she was a year or two above me. Anyway, she's got a couple of kids and said she'd love to take Sharon in. I pay her £5 a week. In fact her house is always full of kids. Not just ones she minds but neighbours' kids that just come in to play like. Betty seems to love it. Wouldn't do for me.'

A snag had recently occurred in this arrangement. Betty had decided to take a job in a pub in the evenings. So this meant that every other week Sharon would be left alone in the house from six until eleven.

'I don't worry too much though. I know Betty settles her down well, and always leaves a drink by her bed so she doesn't have to go downstairs. And the toilet's right next door to her room.'

Peggy Kaka

Peggy and her husband are Nigerian and have only one child, a girl of three and a half. Peggy has to work. Her husband has been off work for two years with a back injury. We do not know why he did not look after the child himself.

Peggy now leaves her daughter with a minder in Cheetham. Right over the other side of the city. She pays her £2 a week and packs up sandwiches and a drink for her child every day. She's had her name down on the local day-nursery waiting list for two years, but now says she won't bother even if she gets a place because the hours wouldn't fit in with her working day anyway.

She had her daughter fostered with an ex-nurse for a while. One day Peggy went to visit her but no one came to the door.

'I walked round the back and looked through the kitchen window. I could see my child lying on the sofa. There was some food on the table. I waited, thinking the lady had just gone round to the shops. This was at 2 p.m. When it got to three, I called on the people next door, but they didn't know anything about the lady. I didn't look through the window much because I didn't want my girl to see me. You see, I couldn't get in. And it would upset her if she saw me outside. The lady came back at 6.30 in the evening. *She'd been to Blackpool.* I took my girl away with me that night.'

Shirley Giles

Shirley is white, about thirty, married with three children, Alison, eleven, Clint, nine and Audrey, four.

She's only been at Kelloggs for a couple of months. She has Audrey minded by a friend, Elsie, further down the road.

'At least Elsie has her when I'm on earlys. When its lates she leaves her with one of her friends while she works in the Co-op. I pick her up from there when I get back at eleven. No I don't know who the friend is. Audrey calls her Maggie. I think she's about two streets away.'

The eleven-year-old, Alison, is at a special boarding school.

'I had to have her sent there. I just couldn't handle her. She'd rage around the place all the time. There's no kid down this street she hasn't had a fight with. And when Alison fights it isn't just a slap round the face!'

Shirley appears to resent her marriage and, to an extent, her children. 'He's nothing but a layabout' she says of her husband.

'Look out of that window. See those two cars. They're both ours but none of them bloody well work. He spent a fortune on buying them. He earns good money mind. I didn't have to go back to work for that. It was the doctor that said I should. I told him I was going bloody mad in this place. Do you know what I did? Well, you can see. There should be a wall dividing that bit of the room, shouldn't there? Well, one day I just rings up this builder fellow I know and asks him to come round and knock it down. He did it in a day. Looks bloody awful doesn't it? You should have seen my old man's face when he got home from work that night.'

She's worried that Audrey isn't talking properly yet. 'You listen to this. Say "my name is Audrey".' Audrey stares blankly at her mother. 'Come on — say it, stupid. There! I bet you couldn't understand a word of that could you?' Audrey wanders out of the room and walks slowly upstairs. 'I'll be glad when she's at school. Someone else can worry about her then.'

I asked Shirley about her minder. 'Oh, Elsie's all right. A bit soft in the head. But she's good with Audrey. Audrey goes down there even when I'm around.'

Later, very worried, we called on Elsie. She is a gentle woman who welcomed us. She couldn't have any children of her own. She loved having Audrey. 'She can speak, you know. I've taught her. She's starting to read as well. I've bought all these books. And paints. And when the weather's nice, we go for walks. She's a lovely child. I wish she was mine.'

Olive Ramsbotham

Olive is a pathetically frail and lonely white woman in her mid-forties. She has three grown-up children by her husband who walked out on her ten years ago. Four years ago she bore a child by a West Indian neighbour.

At Kelloggs she denied having a young child. But as the other women were insistent that she had one, we later called on her at home. She had her son with her.

Marco is a lovely, extrovert four-year-old, very bright and chatty. Olive has him minded by a West Indian woman a few streets away, and is happy with the arrangement. She pays her minder £2 a week and provides pre-cooked meals.

Olive hates having to work.

'I've no real friends there. I suppose it's because I'm not

one for fooling around. I'd love to be home here all day with Marco, but I don't think I could manage on the Social Security. I like to buy him lots of things.' (The house was crammed with toys, books and games.) 'He's bright, isn't he? Would you like to hear him read? Do you know what really worries me? Having to wake him up at night and bring him home. I'm sure it's not good for him. And he is a weight now, but I have to carry him. He's that sleepy. Sometimes when he's more awake we have a game and a read when we get in. And then I look at the clock and it's gone midnight. It's not right for a little boy is it?'

Suddenly Olive was let down by her minder. At that early stage in our research we knew of no one else suitable in the neighbourhood to whom she could turn. The only person that she could think of was a friend in Wythenshawe. She got on the bus with Marco and arrived at her friend's house by midday. The friend was sympathetic but unable to help: she'd just taken a part-time job. She told Olive of a foster-mother living nearby. She walked round there with Marco. Yes, the woman would take him in — but for three weeks only. Olive couldn't bear the idea of being separated from Marco for so long. A compromise was reached. Olive camped out at night on her friend's sofa; grabbed the odd hour or so with her son, and commuted daily to Trafford Park.

'It's difficult having a kid when you're on your own. His father doesn't help, even though he's only just down the road. My other children have done well for themselves. They've all got good jobs. They never used to come over much — but since I had Marco they never come near. But I wouldn't be without him now.'

So these were the cornflake kids. Almost certainly something like this would hold true in any industry employing women. We now had the outline map in our hands. But how should we be thinking of changing it?

Of course you could create financial incentives to keep mothers of young children at home. And yes, we would support that. But it was obvious, now that we knew the streets and factories, that many would still choose work. Some children might be better off in good day care than trapped at home with a reluctant mum. But, beyond that, it would have to be a very big financial incentive indeed — possibly a socially unacceptable one — that would have any effect. For the foreseeable future, most of the cornflake mothers will seek work, will leave toddlers with untrained minders like the lady who went to Blackpool, or total strangers as happens to Audrey; or sometimes, as with Sharon, all alone for several hours.

We had already begun to think ways forward here. But wasn't there another one? Surely if the price of the mother's labour could be the educational future of her child, then industry, too, carried *some* responsibility.

There was no day-nursery provision on this huge mother-employing industrial estate. We explored further afield and looked at day nurseries set up, by private enterprise, in the Lancashire cotton-belt for employees. They were not satisfactory. Clinical, commercial, keeping mother at a distance (we watched handovers of babies in a white sealed off room between mill and crèche in the Rochdale area), above all, never disturbing the mill rhythms.

We also looked, in the Yorkshire woollen area, at crèches set up by concerned, benevolent employers. These were much better, but were still under-resourced. Above all in not having skilled, independent educational staff. And they depended on two factors. First, the personal concern of a mill-owner (on which you couldn't rely — and indeed could not hope for with an international, anonymous company). Second, their scarcity of places had to be rationed out. Almost always these ended up as carrots for specialist forms of skill in shortage (such as pocket-makers), and they excluded women who were available in abundance (menders, cleaners, typists). It looked to us as if it could all too easily develop into a variant of the 'tied cottage' system.

A social audit

No, if it was reasonable for industry to carry a responsibility, it had to be seen in more general and equitable terms. We began to wonder whether firms, besides submitting to an annual *financial audit* (against which there was originally such fierce objection), should not — by law — have to file a *social audit*. Why should companies not be obliged to render some independent account of what they were putting into society — and what they were taking out?

Or, to look further, surely there should be a legal obligation to offer a crèche on any factory site where more than a minimum number of mothers were employed? Of course, by itself that could be a disincentive to employ them at all — the Rice Krispie ladies scented that at once. But suppose it was financed by a tiny levy across all industry (like the training levy), whether they employed women or not, whether those women were mothers or not? Wouldn't that have the opposite effect — and make them want to have value for their tax, to have a state-supported crèche if their women employees could use it?

New thoughts. But it was time to press on. Time to choose an area in Manchester, look at the day-nursery lists as in Huddersfield, and check out what was happening in those streets too when mother was out at work.

8 Old Trafford

Over 500,000 people gathered around City Square,
Manchester to welcome home the Old Trafford team
that beat Liverpool in the Cup Final at Wembley
Stadium last Saturday — a sure signal that community
spirit is alive and living in the North of England.

Newspaper report, May 1977

Old Trafford is the red-and-white home of Manchester United. Almost everyone here treasures that night in the Iberian Stadium of Light when they became the first English team to win the European Cup. No team in Britain has such massive and loyal support. But to visit Old Trafford is to step into a vast — and at first featureless — working-class stretch of Greater Manchester. It was part of this area that we chose for our balancing study.

At first we had been fascinated by the island community of First, Second, Third Street enfolded in the middle of Trafford Park industrial estate. But we rejected that partly because it had such a high proportion of Asians living there, and far too many people at this time were inclined to regard childminding as 'an immigrant problem', and partly because of the odd situation of this community — and we wanted a very ordinary section of working-class Manchester. We looked at Cheetham Hill, and were able to do some small research into the probable extent of childminding there, which in part led to the setting up of a centre for childminders. We explored Hulme — a huge, working-class community rehoused largely in flats. Even an official Manchester report speaks of its 'jungle-like conditions' and 'the almost wanton human disregard that pervades the whole of the Hulme environment'.[1]

113

So many human problems had been dumped and magnified there that we thought this again was too extreme a case. We then half-settled on Moss Side, and began by calling on the schools. The teachers had plenty to say:

'We've officially got 60 per cent immigrants here' said the head of one remedial department. '*Their* figures of course. In fact it's a much higher percentage. The majority are West Indian. They always think they're going to get on, at least the parents do. But they *never* achieve anything!'

Some teachers, in their despair, attributed often unreal wealth to their pupil's families. But almost always this came from a teacher who never visited a single home in Moss Side:

'All the coloured kids in our worst class have got colour telly and telephones and cars. So you see they're not all that deprived. According to a West Indian schoolteacher I know we only get the dregs here in England. All the West Indians with any brains or go about them go to Canada or the States.'

Other teachers were more sympathetic:

'Yes, childminding is going on all round here. I sometimes give the girls a lift home in my car, and of course pop in with them to say hello to whichever parent is home. Well the moment that girl enters the house she'll tie on an apron and start peeling the vegetables. Girls are sometimes kept home to look after younger brothers and sisters, and their home responsibilities are enormous. I've seen this happen time and time again.'

Moss Side has 4,000 children under five. In this and the surrounding middle-class areas there were officially twenty-eight registered minders. We found that the list was well out of date and that ten of them no longer minded or had left the district. In Clarendon Road, for example, we were told by the woman who came to the door: 'I'm fed up with people calling for that Mrs Laxton, I can tell you. Nearly every day there's a woman with a kid in her arms knocking for her.' We called and interviewed eighteen registered minders.

These varied from Mrs Theakston, minding three Irish toddlers in a truly filthy back room with no toys, to Mrs Hall, a trained Montessori teacher with her upstairs front bedroom used as a classroom in well-heeled Chorlton-cum-Hardy. But there was something in common to all eighteen minders. *Every one of them* said they almost daily had to turn away often desperate, sometimes crying mothers, who needed immediate day care for their child.

On the days we called we saw fifty-two children being minded. By far the majority of them were black. And this — despite all the spade work we had done — made us decide to conduct the research elsewhere. To base it in Moss Side would be to focus too much on the West Indian population. It was also an area that was being swept off the map. Whole streets were crumbling under the attack of corporation bull-dozers.

So it was this trial and error process (in the absence of any social maps as we had in Kirklees) that led us to choose part of Trafford. We wanted a plain, working-class area. An area with problems perhaps, but not those different extremes we had seen in Hulme, the planners' nightmare, or Moss Side, the decaying black ghetto. And we wanted an area that was not going to be destroyed. Official forecasts for Trafford actually envisaged a population increase of 11,000 within the next decade. This is contrary to the situation in many inner-city areas which are generally losing population to out-of-town council estates.

So Trafford it was. And within that we selected the wards of Cornbrook and Clifford. The last census population was 7,079 with 794 children under five. The immigrant popula-tion from the New Commonwealth was then 1,320. As we've pointed out earlier we can't get a reliable figure for working mothers from the census data because of the exclusion of single, divorced or widowed women of childbearing years. But one could quickly see that most of the working women found employment in the Trafford Park industrial estate where we had already looked for the cornflake kids. What happened here to the children? Let's begin with a walk around the ward.

The two churches are the first things you notice approach-

ing Old Trafford from Brooks Bar. The United Reform —
squat, ugly and blackened. The Polish one — tall, slender and
newly cleaned. They stand close together: one on each of the
roads that form part of the boundary of the area.

Walking along Shrewsbury Street you can still imagine what
it was like fifty, sixty years ago. ('My dad was a milkman and
before he'd let me help him deliver the milk as a kid, he'd
give me lessons on how to knock at the posh houses.') Large,
once-grand Victorian terraces. Three storeys high with short
flights of substantial stone steps leading up to the front doors.
Now the front gardens are rubbish tips and the windows are
broken and boarded-up. All turned into bedsitters and small
flats. There's never much sign of life along here. Windows
closely curtained.

The contrast is very striking as you take the first turning
to the left. Now you're in the network of backstreets that
make up the heart of the area. Cobbled roads, the very first
electric street lamps, converted directly from gas. Lots of
front doors open to the pavement. And kids everywhere.
Whatever the time of day there are always school-age children
playing in the roads. And babies too. Parked in prams on the
pavement. Toddlers plonked down on front doorsteps.

There's a park nearby, but rarely any children playing in it.
Mothers say they'd never let their children go in there. 'Too
many funny types roaming around.' It's usually patrolled by
a couple of policemen.

Many of these little early-Victorian terrace houses are
being modernized. The tenants get very little warning from
the landlord that they're going to be re-housed. Sometimes
only a month. The builders move in and make smart new
front windows and proper kitchens. Then the houses are
bought up by younger West Indian or Asian families.

Small shops still stand on most of these street corners.
Newsagents mostly. Making their profits from children's
penny sweets and mum's cigarettes. Some tiny butchers'
shops too. All selling tripe and cow heels, mince and cheap
cuts of lamb. Smelly greengrocers offering very inferior fruit
and vegetables. And always those stiff wedges of salt fish for
the West Indian customers. The only smart places are the
launderettes and betting shops. There must be at least five of

each in the small area.

A visitor walking down Ayres Road mid-morning would imagine that this was largely a white area. Hardly any black faces about. By four in the afternoon the scene has changed completely. Masses of West Indian and Asian children surge on to the street from Seymour Park School at the end of the road. Sikh turbans and plaited top-knots everywhere. And the early shift of mothers are starting to turn up. Collecting their babies from Mrs Hain at the corner house and their washing from the launderette opposite. Sleepy-looking West Indian men coming out of houses, on their way to night shift at Trafford Park.

There's another wave of mums on the street at about six-thirty in the evening. Rushing through the rain with toddlers in pushchairs.

Down at the Sharon Church with its mauve front door the lights are on in preparation for the evening prayer meeting and sing-song. The old caretaker at the United Reform Church says this smallish church was erected a hundred years ago especially for the servants of the grand people in the area. Built to seat fifteen hundred. Now only a little ante-room is used for services. The rest is derelict.

Within reach of the area are two day nurseries which between them were looking after sixty children. All the children are priority cases and more than half of them come from outside the ward.

There's a marked difference between the nurseries. One is situated in a large Victorian house at the south-west corner of the survey area. Normal house-size rooms which are used for family grouping. Masses of children everywhere. Lots of noise and bustle, and a young and happy staff. The matron is well aware of childminding and concerned about it. She has several children in the nursery that were originally with minders and describes vividly how these children react when they enter the nursery. Very quiet and immobile for a week to ten days, then a complete reversal to wild and anti-social behaviour for another couple of weeks before finally settling down. She has a child of three at the moment who won't speak although he's been at the nursery for six months. There appears to be nothing wrong with his hearing (he has been tested) and the matron feels inclined to connect this with the fact that he was with a very bad minder before he came to her.

She has an impressive knowledge of the home background of virtually any child you mention, and she welcomes parents into the nursery at any time.

The second is a purpose-built nursery on the northern boundary of the area. The staff on the whole are much older than at the first day nursery. There are three large rooms. No family grouping. Not a very happy atmosphere, with lots of crying children. When asked whether they had any children who had been previously with minders they said they didn't ask mothers about *that* sort of thing.

It was noticeable in both nurseries that there were very few West Indian children.

The area has a school which is fortunate in being able to take around twenty children under five in its nursery class, and there are two playgroups. These meet from 10 a.m. to 12 noon in church halls. Oddly both were short of children. Naturally they couldn't be of much service to working parents, but possibly the very notion of a child-centred playgroup as an educational activity was only partly accepted either by the old working class or the newer migrant cultures of the neighbourhood.

This was the provision — day- nursery places for perhaps twenty of the 794 under the age of five. All twenty were priority cases (not necessarily with working parents) decided largely by the social services department. Another twenty or so could attend the nursery class during school hours, and a further twenty the playgroups for a couple of hours a day.

Finally there were two registered childminders. Mrs Owen, who is fifty-five, is registered for seven children. Normally during the day she has five or six, but this number increases dramatically from 7.30 a.m. to 8.45 a.m. in the morning, and from 4 p.m. to 7.30 p.m. in the evening. She then takes in large numbers of young school-age children. She has no proper space for any of the children. They all cram into a tiny back kitchen, together with her elderly paralysed mother.

Mrs Montgomery is twenty-three, with two under-fives of her own. She has been minding for a couple of years, but has only just registered. She's registered for one child, but normally takes in four or five. There are always lots of good toys about. The children are given plenty of space, and frequent trips, in good weather, to the nearby park.

When we first called on them, neither knew of the other's existence.

We now had the official map, as it were, together with some unofficial edges. At this stage, we read a statement by a local official in one of the professional journals,[2] 'Today wholesale childminding by unregistered people has probably largely died out.'

We now had developed several techniques for testing this. First we tried Dawnwatch. This led us to six illegal minders, three of whom were in the ward area, and three just outside it. We then looked at cards in shop windows. This led us to two illegal minders who regularly used the post office to advertise their service. Third, we had checked on one production line at Kelloggs. Not all the children minded there were in the ward, but again it confirmed a pattern of unregistered minding.

Fourth, we took the waiting list of the first day nursery. This carried forty names. Of these, six were untraceable: the house was demolished or they had left Manchester. We traced and interviewed the remaining thirty-four. Of these, fourteen were not working at the time we saw them. Four had been on the waiting list so long that their children were now old enough to go to school. This left sixteen mothers with twenty children under five.

The picture we found, was very similar to what we had seen in Huddersfield, the mixed pattern of life that is often lost in official statistics. There children are usually grouped as being either at home, or at a nursery, or at a playgroup and so on. In reality people are often stitching together different forms of provision, and shifting from one to another — under pressures of work, time, money and quality.

But childminders (and almost certainly every minder referred to here is unregistered) emerge as a kingpin. Five of the mothers were using a minder the day we interviewed them. Two others had done so in the very recent past, and one was looking for one. Taken together that is half the mothers on the list.

And then how is one to interpret those who say 'a friend' is looking after their child.? Consider Mrs Catlin, who is paying her friend exactly as she would a minder, and is not happy about the child being left alone. We see too how using a relative can be indistinguishable from using a minder. Mrs Bowden makes a formal payment and actually refers to her sister-in-law as 'minding'.

Close fieldwork begins to show a series of concentric rings. In the middle is the registered minder — but, as with Mrs Owen, she may *also* be caring for large numbers of 'latchkey' children in addition to under-fives. Then there are the unregistered minders, who in this area outnumber the registered ones. A further ring still are 'friends' who may prove to be simply unregistered minders whom you know personally or who only mind for you, or perhaps you and other friends. And then there are varying degrees of paid relatives (indeed sometimes almost everyone in the local Asian or West Indian sub-community is described as a relation).

Fifth, we then tried to trace women in the ward with a child under five. This was extremely difficult because we did not have the resources to employ a team of interviewers, and all area surveys, even of the most modest kind, are heavily time-consuming and demand constant evening work.

In the end we located 408 mothers with children under five. Of these, 204 — exactly 50 per cent were working. This suggests a very important point which has increasingly become plainer in our fieldwork. That is that all discussion of working mothers with under-fives is based on national figures. These (in the 1971 census) give a national figure of 18 per cent. This is probably rising, and a 1974 Office of Population Censuses and Surveys study placed it then at 26 per cent. But the key point here is that in more prosperous middle-class areas the figure may well be much less and in inner-city working-class areas it is (as in Trafford and Fartown) certainly much higher. These are, of course, just the very areas with the least day-care provision. One begins to see the inevitable pattern which produces this previously little-known network of backstreet minding.

We then asked the 204 mothers (they had 241 children under five) who looked after their child that day. It was the

same criss-crossed picture as that thrown up by the day-
nursery waiting list — relatives, friends, taking the child to
work, older brothers and sisters, and all the combinations
between them. The family in the broadest sense was clearly
the main provider. But we were positively able to say that
eight of the children were with a registered minder that day,
and that fifty-one were with an unregistered minder. This is
probably a considerable underestimate, since many of the
answers one gets: 'me friend in the next street', 'a lady I
know', 'well, there's a lady down Byron Street', 'it's a relation of my husband's really,' probably also, on investigation,
would mean an unregistered minder.

Finally we took one last investigatory step before our
research time ran out. We chose the criss-cross of streets
around the Sharon Church, and tried in this one small section
of the ward to locate as many childminders as we could. This
was not a specially deprived area. These were and are traditional Lancastrian working-class streets in which nowadays
one in every eight families comes from the Irish Republic,
and one in every seven families from Asia or the Caribbean: a
normal inner-city scene. We chose this focus because when
the research ended we hoped it might be possible to set up a
drop-in centre for childminders either in a corner shop or at
the Sharon Church. This is exactly what happened. But at
this moment, we simply wanted to identify the minders.
Some of these we will meet in the next chapter. In total, we
encountered and got to know extremely well not only the
two who were registered — but a further twenty-four who
were not. Later we were to learn that this was a modest
underestimate because once we created a friendly and positive drop-in centre',[3] three more minders came forward of
whom, despite all our research probes, we had no knowledge.
That, to our mind, reinforced our feeling that the law and the
parliamentary official and academic stances were entirely
wrong. Childminders should not basically be seen as people
to be policed, but as people to be supported. Only positive
services would bring the illegal minders forward, create new
standards of neighbourly care, and drive thoroughly unsuitable ones out of the child business and possibly into situations where they personally could be helped.

So Trafford in Manchester, though a strongly contrasting working community, emerged not as the opposite to Fartown in Huddersfield — but as its similar. We had taken great pains to choose working-class areas which were by no means in extreme circumstances. We had originally put aside, on these grounds, some areas we knew particularly well — parts of London, Birmingham and Liverpool. Within Huddersfield and Manchester we had carefully cut out districts which had become black ghettoes, demolition disaster areas, or planners' crimes. So far as possible we had worked from objective data and the best official statistics. We had listened to the views of the professionals, and in all innocence chose Huddersfield as a control area.

Our research techniques had to blend the classical with the innovative, for plotting a map of illegal childminding is as difficult as doing research into burglars. We had no precedents to go on. But the pointers were all one way. First, that a large number of mothers with children under five went out to work. Second, that in these urban working-class districts the number of such mothers out to work was necessarily larger perhaps double the overall percentage. Possibly the tendency also was to work longer hours. Third, official day-care provision through day nurseries was negligible.

Meanwhile all that other provision through nursery schools, reception classes, playgroups — which had so dominated the landscape of the pre-school debate for a third of a century — was, though admirable, both very small and largely irrelevant to the situation of a working mother. Fourth, industry seemed to evidence very little commitment to the needs of the children left behind, and the day-nursery waiting list had become a mass illusion: it was like queuing for a ticket for the first public rocket to Mars. Possible in theory, enshrouded in forms and particulars, but seldom likely to 'lift-off' during a child's pre-school lifetime.

But lastly — and maybe this could be potentially good news — there *was* a day-care service in operation. Out of difficulty, and often out of desperation, people in both Fartown and Trafford had created a backstreet childminding service. Little of it was known to the authorities. None of it received much help. But it was there.

At this moment, the signs were that in urban districts like this there were probably *at least* ten unregistered minders to every one registered one. We felt fairly confident that we could replicate such results in any other British city. And, more cautiously, that — allowing for different cultures and widely different styles of provision — that some similar general pattern would emerge in any advanced industrial society.

That degree of interim certainty had been won, with much personal difficulty, from hard, thinking, fieldwork. The knowledge could have come no other way. But before thinking further, it is necessary to meet at closer quarters some of the childminders that we found in Manchester and Huddersfield.

9 Portrait gallery

In painting, the most brilliant colours, spread at random
and without design, will give far less pleasure than the
simplest outline of a figure.   Aristotle, *Poetics*

How many CSEs do you need to be a childminder, Miss?
— fifteen-year-old girl, coming back to
school after her first visit to one of these
childminders as part of this action research

We have counted and computerized the scalps of tens of
thousands of childminders; the easiest task of all. We have
explored and recorded the dense neighbourhood detail — that
fine tissue of logic — of a substantial number. We have come
to know some personally very well indeed, and are in the
midst not merely of researching them but of then trying to
help them aid themselves. Let's go back to the field notebooks
and see if there is more to be illuminated by them.

Here are a score of extracts. Let's consider them first as a
portrait gallery, and then as the basis of a typology from
which action could be effectively sprung.

Pat Aldiss

Very early one morning I followed a young girl with a baby
in a pushchair along a maze of cobbled streets in Old Trafford. She dropped her baby off at a half-derelict house. The
hand-over was swift and almost wordless. It is in the original
Dawnwatch report.

Later that day I called at the house. Pat, the minder,
opened the door after a long wait. We went into the back

kitchen where there were four children — two babies in prams and two West Indian toddlers. There were two six-year-old girls in the front room. The back kitchen was in semi-darkness. The curtains drawn closely over the window. The carpet was dirty and threadbare. Along one wall was an old sofa. A sideboard and table with four upright chairs were the only other things in the room. There were no toys.

I asked about the children. 'None of them are mine. I've got one boy but he's grown up and left home now. I look after this lot for friends. I charge them a bit, but not much. About £2 a week.'

But what about the older children in the front room?

'Well Jackie, she's the pretty one. She's my godchild. She's living here with us. Actually she's just come out of a Council home. Her mum and dad split up and Doreen, that's her mum, couldn't cope. She was in the home for almost a year. Doreen asked if I could look after her for a while till she gets herself sorted out. She should be at school really because she's over six. But it's a bit difficult, not knowing how long she's going to be here. The other girl is just a friend she's got in for the day.'

Pat was very apologetic about the state of the house. 'I'm under the doctor with my nerves. Don't seem to be able to get down to anything. These pills he gave me give me a headache the whole time. We've had a death in the family you know. It was last April.' At this point she started crying quietly, but continued. 'Wyndham had been with us for years. He was like our lodger. Only there was a bit more to it than that. Would you like to see his picture?' She opened a heart-shaped locket on a chain around her neck and showed me a photo of a dark, middle-aged man. 'How does your husband feel about your wearing that?' I ask, half-jokingly.

'He doesn't know I've got it. And even if he did he wouldn't mind. He loved Wyndham as well. Wyndham and me were together for years before I met my husband. We could never have got married though. He had habits I couldn't put up with. Then I met my husband and we were all happy here until it happened. It was a heart attack. I couldn't believe it. I ran out into the road and screamed. They thought I'd gone mad.

'I started off looking after children when he'd gone. I used to go out to work before that but after he died my nerves went to pieces and I couldn't face going out. That boy over there — does he remind you of anyone? Can't you see the likeness? It's Wyndham's boy. I've never held it against his mother. I enjoy having him here. It's like a bit of Wyndham is left.'

Pat admits she finds it hard to cope with the children. She screams at them continually — even when they're doing something as innocent as flicking through the *TV Times*. She screams at her neighbours as well. That first time I was there a friend popped her head round the door and Pat yelled at her to go away. 'Can't you see I've got a visitor?'

Pat takes the first child in at seven in the morning. 'I don't mind. I have to be up at 6.30 to see Frank out.' The remainder arrive between 7.30 and 8.30. The last child leaves at 6.30 p.m. Every time I've called on Pat around lunch time she's been giving the children breakfast cereal. She puts three Weetabix and milk into an enormous plastic bowl for the two babies, and feeds them from one spoon. Jackie sometimes wanders into the kitchen to help herself to some bread and jam.

Pat doesn't look ahead. She sees minding only on a day-to-day — or at best — week-to-week basis. She wouldn't consider registering.

Amongst the minded children is Jeanette. She's a very tiny West Indian girl. Surprisingly for a West Indian child — they're usually impeccably turned out — she's very scruffy. Her bare feet cramped into shoes many sizes too small for her, thin shift dresses even on cold winter days, skimpy openwork cardigan covering her painfully thin arms. Her legs and arms are covered in large scabs.

Jeanette delivers herself to Pat. Her mother, who is unmarried, turns her and her two elder brothers out of the house at 7 a.m. when she leaves for work. The children spend the next couple of hours roaming around the derelict streets and rubble heaps of Salford, Jeanette tagging along until she's too cold or fed-up to stay. Then amazingly she finds her way to Pat's front door. Sometimes, if there's a pot of tea on the go, Pat will give her a drink. Otherwise she's just left in the back room where there's usually one or two other kids about.

The children's day is always chaotic. No order. No routine. Sometimes Pat will devote hours to them. Playing wild and dangerous games. Swinging them round the room by their ankles, encouraging them to jump from the sideboard onto the sofa. Lots of shouting and cuddling. Other times she goes for hours without opening the door to see what they're doing. Even forgets to feed them if she's off her food herself. They witness scenes of incredible viciousness between Pat and her neighbours. Scenes of screaming and fighting when someone says the wrong thing when Pat is having one of her 'bad days'.

There are no real toys in the house, but access to anything in the room, (which includes Pat's pills, matches and sharp knives). After they've been left alone for a few hours the room is always covered with cut-up bits of newspaper, and plates and cups brought out from the easily accessible sideboard.

If the children need to go to the toilet they squat outside in the earth of the back yard.

Although Jeanette is a chronically neglected child — both by her mother and minder — she's extremely resilient. I've seen her stealthily collect a plateful of food from Pat's kitchen — cornflakes, powdered soup mixed with cold water, jam and bread. And sit in a corner quickly consuming it before either another child or Pat discovers what she's up to. She's capable too of defending herself on her dawn rambles around the Salford streets. When confronted by bullying older children, or those aroused stray dogs that abound in the area, she fights and kicks her way out of trouble.

I was with Pat one day when a health visitor knocked at the door. She'd called to see one of the babies and a neighbour had told her it was with Pat. Pat was very nervous and jumpy whilst she was there. The first thing the health visitor asked was whether Pat was minding and who the children were. Very quickly Pat said she'd only got them there for that day, and no, she didn't do it regularly. 'You realize you'll

127

have to report to us if you do it on a regular basis, don't you?' said the health visitor. After she'd left Pat was furious that anyone had given her name to an obvious official! 'You just wait — I'll find out who that was and then there'll be trouble.

Maureen Williams

Mrs Williams's name was on the list of registered minders I received from Manchester Social Services.

She lives in a spacious and beautifully kept house in one of the better-off districts of the city.

She broke into my preamble about the Advisory Centre for Education (our previous work) by saying she knew all about it, and had subscribed to *Where* for the past four years.

She's registered for two children and has one pre-school child of her own. Her husband is an engineer.

We talked in her smartly fitted out kitchen. The week's lunchtime menus were pinned on a board over the washing machine, together with lots of the children's paintings.

'I feel I'm doing something really useful. I wouldn't consider going out to work anyway until Alan was at school. I see minding as a job like any other. And it's good to feel you're helping people out at the same time. Both these children's mothers are unmarried. As it happens, they're both teachers, which means I don't have them after 4 p.m. which is good. But I wouldn't object to keeping a child until, say, 5.30 p.m. if necessary. I charge £6 a week and give them a well-balanced lunch and sort of nursery tea.'

There were lots of good toys around, and a sandtray in the corner.

'I usually get the toys from Galts. It's cheaper in the long run. And you don't have to worry about the children swallowing nasty plastic bits. I've been minding for two years now. Before that I was involved in playgroups. I I prefer this. Anyway, I feel I've got the space and experience to provide the children I mind with a really good environment. Probably better than a playgroup. I've got a car of my own and we quite often go out for trips. Belle Vue and places like that. The garden is large so there's no problem in the summer. I just strip them off and put them in the paddling pool all day.

'I've got a fairly good routine going. In the morning they just play with the toys. Then lunch at 12.30. After that I put them down if they're sleepy. And then we read stories and sing. Occasionally I'll put 'Playschool' on if I feel like a bit of a rest. But normally we all do things together.'

I asked Mrs Williams how she felt about taking black children.

'There's not many around here. I expect if someone was sent and I thought it was the sort of child that would get on with the others I'd take it. But it never arises because I don't have vacancies. Two of my friends are waiting for me to take their children so they can go back to work. I'm booked up for the next four years!'

Mrs Susan Moseley

I knew there was someone at home because even through the door, the vacuum cleaner sounded like a pneumatic drill, but I had to knock and call for almost ten minutes before there was any answer. Outside the house looked much better cared for than its neighbours, on a rubbish-strewn council estate. Clean windows, neat flowerbeds in the well-fenced garden, fresh paint — even the stones bordering the path had been whitewashed.

At last the door was opened by a wispy-haired woman in her forties with a pale lopsided face and gaps in her teeth, rather attractively dressed in grey with a red belt and buttons. She just stood there looking at me twisting her face into odd contortions and vaguely waving her arms. I started to explain my purpose but it was impossible above the deafening noise of the Hoover, which she made no attempt to switch off.

At last I pointed to it and shouted please, couldn't she unplug it, and she began to laugh, moved the switch and turned back to me again with the same strange gestures and honking sounds, touching her ears and mouth. Only then did I realize that she was deaf.

The front door opened directly into the sitting room, conventionally furnished with a three-piece suite, sideboard with photographs, thick patterned turquoise carpet and a modern gas fire. Two girls and a boy were playing on the floor with a broken toy push chair and a dilapidated doll.

I found that Mrs Moseley could lip read if I spoke very slowly and simply, and gradually her speech became a little more intelligible to me. When we got stuck, she pushed me into a chair and darted next door to fetch her neighbour, Angela, to act as interpreter.

Susan Moseley has been a registered minder for two years, and before that, for seven years looked after children informally. Really she would prefer to go out to work. 'I tried and tried to get a job, but they won't have you with being deaf, so I thought OK I'll look after children. It's for the money mostly'.

She knows nothing about the three children she looks after, not even their names, though all have been with her for several months. Angela told me she had a list somewhere, and fishing it out from the back of a drawer was able to identify them as Marie, Paul and Sharon. Marie she thought was 'about three', the other two younger. None of them spoke while I was there. They pushed each other, made quiet grunting noises and pointed.

Mrs Moseley did not seem in the least worried by my unexplained visit. She sat on the arm of my chair and often touched me and laughed. Communication was very slow and difficult, but she remained patient and friendly.

She looks after these three children Monday to Friday 7.30 a.m. to 5.30 p.m. and gives them dinner and tea, for which she charges £1.50 including food and £1 without it. She does not ask more because it would just be deducted from her supplementary benefit. Even this tiny sum is not paid regularly — she often has to go and collect it on Saturday morning. Money is a terrible worry to her. 'I'm very careful. Pay everything as I go along'.

She never knows if Marie's mother will bring food or money. Meals are haphazard — lunch might be a few chips, some rice pudding, stew left over from the night before, or just a piece of bread and butter. She cooks at teatime when her own four children are home from school. The two eldest are children of her Jamaican husband, who left fourteen years ago, before the younger girl was born. John and Heather, aged eleven and ten were born of casual relationships with two different men.

The minded children are turned out in the back garden most of the day, except when it's raining. Mrs Moseley does not like toys in the house because they make a mess.

She does take them out about twice a week, shopping in town or to visit friends. Apart from that there seems to be very little interaction between her and the children. None of them approached her while we were talking, and she ignored them completely. I never saw her make any gesture of warmth towards a child. She claimed they could understand her, and she them, but if so, it must be at some very basic level, invisible to the onlooker. When they are 'naughty' she smacks their bottoms.

Was there any difficulty about her registration I asked? No none at all. She just had to buy a fireguard. That was very expensive. (There was no sign of any guard round the blazing range in the kitchen). She has been regularly visited since registration, about every three months.

Do the visitors (she has no idea who they are) give her any help? 'Do they hell! You've to do everything for yourself'. What she would most like is an automatic washing machine — she seems to be washing all day long. And large play equipment to keep the children happy in the garden, not nagging to come in all the while. A playgroup would be good to let her get on with the housework in peace. She doesn't think the children need any more toys — they've plenty already.

Mrs Moseley comes from a family of seven, two of them born deaf. 'Mother had too many children to have time to learn me to talk. I never spoke a word till I was fourteen.' She's very brainy', Angela interrupted, 'she sews all her own clothes. She can't read or write though because she never

131

went to school — only recognize her own name'.

Had she looked after many children? I asked. 'Oh, yes', Angela answered proudly for her, 'she's had *hundreds*'.

Joan Robson

The first three times I called Mrs Robson made excuses to send me away — the electricity had broken down, her husband would be coming home to dinner. Finally she burst out,

> 'I'm fed up of people coming to the door doing surveys on childminders. Why don't they just let me get on with it. Every week there's someone round. It's all since that Brian Jackson started talking about childminding . . . .'

After some persuasion she invited me out of the freezing wind into the small hall and through into the living room, light, well-carpeted, a guarded electric fire, black and white television, large cardboard box full of toys in the corner.

Joan Robson is a pleasant-faced, young-looking woman with cropped hair, in the last stages of pregnancy at the time of the interview. Once she started talking she enjoyed herself so much that she went on for nearly two hours, quite disrupting her daily schedule, and thanked me warmly when I left.

At present she minds three children, in addition to her own four-year-old Sarah, but is planning to give up in a few weeks as it is getting a bit much with the baby so near. Twice before she has minded children for a while and then stopped — once to have Sarah, once when they moved house. Will she mind again after the baby is born?

> 'Oh yes, I couldn't be without children. They're so entertaining. If every one disappeared tomorrow I'd have to find some more the next day. I love to play with them and teach them. I love to pick them up and comfort them when they cry. The house really needs fettling, but I'd rather be with the children. It's a joint effort. I don't take a child on without consulting Dick. For quite a long time he worked evenings so he was home during the day. He

was a tremendous help preparing meals. He'd play for
hours with them, so I could get on with the housework.
Now he comes home at lunchtime and once I've got dinner
put out he'll supervise while I get my breath back.'

Joan has no problems with the children she looks after at
present. Their parents are all white-collar workers with relatively short hours who pay regularly and treat her with consideration.

Martin, Primrose and Helen played contentedly throughout the long interview only becoming a bit restless when it
looked as if they might miss 'Playschool' on television. Joan
enjoys playing with children; she makes up different games,
lets them help with baking or spreads paper on the dining-
room table and organizes a painting session. She has a good
stock of toys passed down from her own children or left
behind by children she has minded, and when the weather is
good they can play in the safely fenced garden.

She thinks a great deal about the children and wonders if
she is doing the right thing for them.

'I often wish I could get it clear whether you should play
with children or teach them. Is it my job to teach them?
I've had to train Primrose out of nappies, and that's something I don't like doing. Then so many parents expect
them to read and write before school. That's fair enough if
you've got children the same age, but it's totally unfair to
spend a lot of time reading and writing with older ones and
leave the others. We do us educational stint with Sarah in
the evening. Other parents should do the same.'

Mrs Robson is registered for four children but allows
brothers and sisters to come after school and during holidays, so sometimes there will be as many as ten. Numbers
don't trouble her. If they are naughty,

'Usually a raised voice is enough or a quick slap on the leg
to let them know who's boss. Then I always sit them down
and explain. I think it's worthwhile to spend a bit of time
to explain why they're being punished.'

Only once has she had any serious difficulty when she looked after two boys for an unsupported mother.

'It wasn't till the last day I had them that I heard they'd both been having treatment for mental illness. You couldn't talk to them. They took a kitten and put it in a box of straw and set fire to it and poked it around till it died. I had occasion to crack one of them and he belted me back. I got into a right state with those boys. It gave me a nervous rash all over. It weren't worth it for the money'.

Wasn't there anyone in the social services department whose advice she could ask? 'Oh no, they only come and measure the rooms and see about a fireguard'.

Mrs Prem

Mrs Prem, a handsome middle-aged Indian lady always beautifully dressed in one of her great collection of saris, is the only registered Asian childminder in the whole of Huddersfield. She started looking after children at the suggestion of a West Indian health visitor, and for her it has been a great success, lifting her out of the deep depression induced by the move from Delhi to Huddersfield.

Both Mrs Prem and her husband come from prosperous families. Her father-in-law is a magistrate, her husband has a BA in Commerce (so says the plate on the front door). She herself was privately educated, trained as a teacher, and taught four years before her marriage.

The only thing that makes England bearable to her is the good schools. 'Other people only think of when they'll be sixteen, to go and work in a factory. I think of A levels. I wish for my children the most education.'

For a time she worked as a packing supervisor in a factory, but found it too exhausting. 'I can't manage my home as well. I feel tired when I come home and can't take interest in my children. Now I am meeting them cheerfully. I sit with them till ten o'clock, ask about school study and take interest.'

Back in India, Mr and Mrs Prem had 'a lovely large bungalow, three servants inside, a man coming in to wash floors and iron clothes'. Now they live with their four children in a dark little house huddled with rows of others in the packed terraces of Fartown. This area has been almost entirely taken over by the Asian community, but Mrs Prem fights to preserve her sense of difference from those about her.

'The other women here, they are used to work hard from morning to night in the fields. They can work in factory. I am not strong enough'. She will only accept children from 'good' families, by personal recommendation. 'Illiterate mothers from small villages expect you to do it for nothing. Some issue orders. 'Change the nappy three times'. I feel insulted'.

'Usually I have four little children, not under a year. Now there is Kuldeep and Kamal who are babies, just walking and Rivindar and Rama who are two and three. I love children very much. I enjoy looking after them. I speak to them in English so they learn. Sometimes they feel sad and I tell them poems and singing so they are happy again. I put on a tape for them to clap and dance. The little ones have sleep, then play with toys till children come from school. After four o'clock they watch TV with my children.'

Mrs Prem charges parents £3.50 a week for babies in nappies, £3 if they are toilet trained. This doesn't include food. The parents bring what they like; tinned milk, fruit, baby food, half a pound of butter or a few eggs. The children have snacks of fruit and milk at 11 a.m. and 3 p.m, when they wake from their rest. Mrs Prem does not believe in cooked meals for young children – 'too heavy'.

Every time I visited them the four little girls were sitting silently on the sofa with their legs tucked under them. Mrs Prem never takes them out – she very rarely goes out herself. Her husband and the children do all the shopping. There is of course no garden, the bathroom built on at the back takes up all the tiny walled yard.

They spend all day in the kitchen, a dark, narrow room, furnished in the most functional way, with a complete disregard for appearance. The rest of the house is ablaze with gold and brilliant colours, even the ceilings; but here the dingy wallpaper looks as if it had been left by the previous owners. Two formica tables, a black leatherette sofa, worn lino on the floor. When she has a visitor Mrs Prem brings out a spotted tablecloth, slips upstairs to change her sari, and produces an armful of plastic toys.

The toys are clearly quite unfamiliar to the children. They gaze at them with sad dark eyes, and have no idea what to do. Mrs Prem tries to coax them to play, but they don't know how.

She senses that English people think children should play with toys. This box of plastic objects, pink, green and blue, arrived at our suggestion from the civic centre at Christmas time — the only contact she has had so far since she was registered. But toys make a mess and they throw them at each other. She feels happier sitting with them in her arms, cuddling them, singing to them. They are 'very good children' she says, 'They love me and obey me. I don't shout but always speak to them very politely'.

Mrs Prem is always so polite and amiable, it is hard to tell what she is really thinking. Only when she talks about her sadness at leaving India — 'I used to fight every day with my husband and beg him to take me back' — is the genuineness of her feeling unmistakable.

Is her reluctance to go out due to the difficulty of managing four small children or is there some deeper reason? She agreed politely with all suggestions for giving help to childminders — toys, books, play equipment, even said she would like a course or discussion group. But when the opportunity arose, she retreated.

Perhaps she can only feel in control inside her own home: in the threatening world outside her husband and children are so much better equipped. The younger ones are Yorkshire tykes, with the voices, manners and interests of their schoolmates. Neelam has renamed herself Elizabeth, and no language except lovely Yorkshire English is heard in the house. ('Eeh mam, we 'ad smashing spuds at school today.') All her own children are doing very well at school. Mrs Prem knows this is because of the way she has brought them up. She feels perfectly confident that she is doing just as good a job for the children she minds.

Mrs Bennett

Mrs Bennett lives in a small, multi-racial street on the edge of Moss Side. I first visited her at about four o'clock on a sunny January afternoon. The children were returning from school and playing around the sweetshop on the corner. Asians, Chinese, West Indians and white. This one short street contained a Chinese chippy, Asian grocer and West Indian greengrocer.

Mrs Bennett is registered for four children, but frequently takes more.

'What can you do when there's a girl standing on your doorstep desperate. It does worry me if I've got one or two over my number. But I can't turn them away when they're in that state.'

She's had two African boys for two years — since they were six months or so, and an Asian girl for three years. These three children form the nucleus of her group. The others come and go more frequently.

'I wish you could depend on the mothers more. I've had children I've kissed goodbye of a Friday evening and never seen again. That hurts. O.K. so they've found someone nearer or cheaper, but they still might let you know. It's very difficult from the money point of view as well. You can never tell how much you're going to have from week to week.'

The house is in the traditional three-up, three-down style. But Mrs Bennett has deliberately made space for the children by having the dividing wall between the two living rooms knocked through. The house is usually over-warm and a bit smelly but generally quite clean.

About three years ago Mrs Bennett miscarried.

137

'That was my last chance. I suppose it was silly to try.
After all I've got two grown-up children and I'm a grandma
twice over. But we suddenly felt we'd like another.'

She gave up minding for a while around this time and took
a job in a private day nursery.

'I didn't stay long. Couldn't stick it. She was registered for
twenty children. Never had less than forty. I was in charge
of the babies. There were ten in one room. All you could
do was keep them clean and fed. There wasn't time for
anything else. Feeding time was hell. She'd give me a big
bowl of baby food and one spoon. I'd have to sit in the
middle with the babies all round me and spoon the stuff
into their mouths one at a time. They were never free from
colds or tummy upsets. They hadn't a chance. It was a
wonder the mothers put up with it. Except that by collecting time things looked different. She'd always make sure
she was in the baby room with me come 5 o' clock.'

Mrs Bennett can hardly remember a time when she wasn't
looking after children.

'My mother was a prostitute. We lived in Falmouth then,
and it was mostly sailors. There was me and my two
younger brothers. We never knew who our fathers were.
She used to make me go down and answer the door to the
men.
    'One day, when I was nine, she just up and left. Just
went without saying anything. I looked after myself and
those two boys for six months before anyone found out.
Then the Welfare came round and split us up. They sent
me to a Convent orphanage and the boys to Dr Barnados. I
hated every minute in that place. You wouldn't believe
how cruel they were. I was beaten every day. You see I'd
got used to being the boss. I couldn't take being told what
to do. By the time I was fourteen I must have calmed
down a bit because they let me have charge of the little
ones. I suppose that's where all this started. Looking back
on it it was a good training. I didn't get any qualifications

but there wasn't much I didn't know about bringing up kids. When I was seventeen I got a job as a nanny to a family in Sale. They were lovely. It was a beautiful house. I still hear from my little boy. He's a lawyer now but he still writes to me every Christmas. Then I got married and had kids of my own..

Mrs Bennett is very eager to talk about children. 'There's certain stages in their development. If I feel a child is backward in walking or potty training or talking then I'll spend more time on him.' She feels very strongly that she's not given enough support from Social Services. There's a lot more they could do. The lady that calls is nice enough, but I never feel she's really interested.'

'Yes I suppose I'm a bit strict. But getting a good whack never hurt me when I was a kid. You've got to teach chilren discipline. When I think back to what my mother let us get up to it makes me shudder. It's just as well she did walk out. Otherwise God knows how I'd have ended up.

The African twins, aged two-and-a-half are Chuka and Lani. Their day with Mrs Bennett is ordered to the extreme. Everything is done by the clock. Their mother seems happy with this regime — the children are always delivered on the dot of 9 in the morning and collected promptly at 5.30.

They're given a drink when they arrive and then playtime with the numerous picture books and soft toys that Mrs Bennett has collected. Quiet play always. Shouts and bangs are discouraged. 'That's why I don't have cars and trucks about. I believe there's no need for children to be noisy. They can have just as much fun playing quietly.'

She'd spent a lot of time with the boys on their talking. Correcting them on their pronunciation and teaching them new words from the picture books.

Dinner is on the dot of 12.30. All sitting round the table with much emphasis on manners. The boys appear to enjoy their time with Mrs Bennett. They're both solemn and watchful, but do play with the things about them. They're smacked firmly if they're naughty. (Dropping plates or turning the TV on out of time). Mrs Bennett hits them in front of their mother if they misbehave at collection time. Both seem to be quite happy about this.

Madge Warner

'I've looked after 168 children over the years. If you'd come a month earlier you'd have seen a dozen prams lined up outside the door.'

Madge, when I first met her, was about to remove to Wythenshawe. Her furniture was piled up in the middle of her living room. She was entertaining neighbours with tea boiled on the open coals in the hearth. 'They're rehousing us. About time too. This lot should have come down years ago.' The street was rat-infested and damp — many of the houses were only partly habitable, with two or more rooms permanently closed off because of rotten floor-boards.

Madge is about seventy. A very fat, white lady. She has been a childminder for twenty years. She is married to a West Indian man many years her junior. They have no children. 'I did start one when I was forty-seven, but I lost it. Oh! I'd have given my soul to have had a child by him.'

She minded the children of the neighbourhood up until she knew she was moving.

'I had three of them still with me last week. But I had to let them go on Friday. I couldn't cope with packing up and everything. It broke my heart. I wonder what's happened to them. I know where some have gone — I've recommended people myself — but I do worry about the others. There's some funny people round here.

You know no one ever took a child away from me. Only if they were moving. I've kept them when the mothers have given up work. I'd reduce the money of course. They've been my life. Women bring sick children to me. Women I don't even know, but they've heard about me and they'd prefer to come here than go to the clinic. Mind you, they're all right up there at the clinic. Some days I'd trail along there with six or seven I was looking after if

there was an epidemic or they needed their jabs. They've
always been good to me. And I'm not registered you know.
Never really saw the point of it all. I've never hidden the
fact that I mind. Well, you couldn't could you — with all
that lot playing around out front. I've had babies brought
to me that were that tiny and weak. By the time I've had
them for a few months you wouldn't recognize them.
They're that bonny. I've always taken a lot of trouble
about bringing them on. Always the best milk and rusks.
I shouldn't think I've made a penny profit out of it all.
Well, you can see that by looking around. This isn't
Buckingham Palace is it? But that's never worried me, Life
isn't up to much around here. If I can help by giving the
kids a bit of love and good food then that's me happy.'

I visited Madge in her new house in Wythenshawe. It's a
small council house in a quiet cul-de-sac. She was a changed
woman. Philip was still with her, but he seemed restless and
cheeky. She said she missed her friends, and the children.

'I know Bellot Street was a slum. But people knew me
there. I was never alone for five minutes. And then there
were the babies. I've not heard of anyone round here who
needs a minder.'

Her husband has started going out in the evenings and
staying away until the early hours.

'I said to him — "It's a bit late to start that sort of thing
my lad" — but it's all to do with his work. He's got a new
job here and got in with a different crowd.
    'Do you know of any babies around here? I only charge
£2 a week you know. There *must* be some children that
need looking after. If you did come across a little baby — I
don't mind if it's Indian or anything — I'd take it in.'

Bernadette Watkins

Talking about minding to a woman in a local grocer's, I was
interrupted by the Irishman behind the counter with the

141

information that I should try Bernadette down Leicester
Street. 'She's a real good woman. A Kerry woman. The only
person around here you'd feel safe leaving your child with.'

I found Bernadette's house easily. It was the only gaily
painted and well-maintained one in a street of otherwise
dilapidated housing. There was a poster in the window
advertising a Save-the-Children Fund jumble sale.

Bernadette invited me in happily. She's twenty-four, fresh-
faced and neatly dressed. She had three small children with
her. Her own two-year-old son, a three-year-old West Indian
boy and a three-month Nigerian baby. The front and back
rooms had been knocked into one. The whole house was
spotless and very elaborately furnished. She had lots of
small tables dotted around covered in glass ornaments.

Bernadette has been minding ever since she was pregnant
with her son. 'Sometimes I have dozens. But that's only
temporary. Everyone round here seems to leave their children with me when they have to go out.'

She charges £3 a week for the West Indian boy and £2.50 for
the baby. She said she would put the money up by £1 in each
case. 'After all the mothers' wages are going up all the time.'

There were one or two home-made toys on the floor.
Rattles made out of coffee tins and squeezy bottles. The
entire time I spent talking to her, Bernadette was telling the
West Indian boy to stop touching the ornaments. She said
the main reason she was minding was because she felt her son
needed the company. And to help the housekeeping out a
little. She said she'd tried taking her son to a playgroup, 'But
it was too noisy. My boy was frightened. Anyway I like doing
things my way. Didn't fancy being with those other mothers.
The hall wasn't very clean either.'

She wasn't registered.

'I shouldn't think I'll bother. I know you should really,
but I spoke to the health visitor and she said, "Mrs Watkins,
it's not people like you we're worried about. You could
eat off your floors, and you're very careful about your
fires." I know what she means. There're people round here
should have their own children taken off them, leave alone
have others to look after.'

Josie Corrigan

Josie's name was thrown up by the day-nursery waiting-list survey. A mother had used her for a short period before getting her child into the nursery. The first time I called she flatly denied minding. About the woman on the waiting list she said, 'She was a friend. I just did it to help her out.' She didn't ask me in, but was very friendly and enjoyed chatting. She told me she had four children of her own and was divorced. She's Irish.

A couple of weeks later I returned with some toys. This time she let me in.

The living room was carpetless and bare apart from a table, four upright chairs, a shabby, smelly sofa and a television set. The large gas fire was full on despite the warm June weather. On the floor in the corner was a four-year-old boy asleep. There was a baby sitting up in a pram and two very scruffy little white boys sitting on the sofa watching the TV. Josie felt some explanation was necessary. She was helping out another friend. No, she didn't take any money.

I tried to explain what I was doing. Eventually I convinced her I wasn't from social security. This was what was worrying her. She appeared to know nothing about the need to register in order to mind.

That first visit I stayed two hours whilst she talked and talked and talked.

'I had to divorce my husband. He used to hit me and the kids. Leslie has never been a normal child. When he was a baby and cried at night my husband used to pick him up and shake him. He went on and on. I used to try and stop him but he'd start on me then. He was always walking out on me. He brought a woman back here one night. Just walked upstairs with her into our bedroom. What sort of woman could do a thing like that? He earned good money labouring. And you know something? Even though he'd knock me and the kids about I sometimes think I'd have been better off keeping him. He always gave me my money. Whatever he'd been doing during the week, he'd hand me that money on a Friday. £20 every week. All I get now is what the social security give me — £16 a week. I have to pay my rent out of that and buy the food. I've had Irene off school for a week. She's got no shoes. They won't let her wear gym shoes. Wrote me a letter about it.'

I tried to get her talking about the children. It was difficult. She had no toys. Even the ones I left that day had disappeared by my next visit. I've never seen her feed the children anything other than toast. She'll talk a little about her own children. Leslie, her youngest, is a sick child. She worried that he sleeps all day. Even when the noise level is high with the TV on and children crying, he still remains immobile on the floor. Occasionally she gives him a shake. 'Look Leslie. There's a nice lady here brought you some sweets.' But he just squints at me and turns over. I ask her if she's taken him to the doctor, and she says yes, but he doesn't know what's wrong with him. Months later I discover the whole family suffer from continual thread worms. When — during a meeting at Sandra's house — she's shown the medicine she should take herself and give to the children, she says, 'It's too sweet. I can't stomach it.'

The children she minds come and go quickly. She's had seven or eight different children in the six months I've been visiting her. Usually it's a case of a child never turning up again after a week or so. Maybe because of the thread worms. She charges £1.50 or £2 per child. She has said to me on occasions that she'd 'like to do it properly. Have six or seven in.' But she's terrified that the social security people will find out.

One day when I called she was in a terrible state. A man with a briefcase had called that morning.

'He said he wasn't from social security but he asked me all sorts of questions. Said he'd heard I was seeing my husband and that I'd got a job. Do you think he knew about the children? I can't think how he could because I've told the mothers not to say they pay me anything if anyone asks. After he'd gone I rang up the social security and asked what it was all about. They said it wasn't anything to do with them and they didn't know anything about it.'

Later that day I went round to the Community Advice Centre and asked if they knew anything about the 'man with the briefcase'. 'Oh, he'd be a private detective. Social security are starting to use them around here.'

Josie has been to all the action meetings we are evolving from this open research. After the first one she said how much she had enjoyed it. 'This is the first time I've been out of the house of an evening since Christmas.'

She asked at one meeting what she should do if a child chokes. 'It happened to that baby the other day. He swallowed a buckle. I just ran out of the house and got Mary down the end of the road. By the time we got back he'd brought it up. Oh Christ, I *was* scared.'

I suggested to her that she might take Leslie and the children she minds to the playgroup nearby. I arranged for them to attend free of charge. She never went. Next time I called she said she'd been feeling ill all the week. 'Anyway I don't think the mother would like me taking them out. Supposing something happened to them?'

The impression Josie gives is one of complete desperation. She's minding children because it's the only way she can earn a little money without social security finding out. She has the extravagant habits of the very poor and depressed — the child sent out for half a pound of ham for a quick, unplanned supper. The grill left full on in the kitchen to heat the room. Although she's willing to join the group of active minders, she comes along primarily for the break it brings in her otherwise monotonous life, and to talk. Towards the end of the last meeting when we'd been discussing alternatives to hitting children she said, 'I'd never hit the ones I look after. But I took the belt to Leslie tonight just before I came out. His eye's swollen up really bad. I didn't mean to hit his face. But I get so mad at him sometimes. He just *lies there* on the floor.'

Sylvia Hawkins

It was eleven in the morning when I first called on Sylvia. She lives along one of the curving, cobbled streets in the middle of Old Trafford. At first no one answered my knock. Then

145

the waist-level letter flap opened and a child's voice asked me what I wanted. 'Mummy's in bed.' 'Well, if she's asleep I'll come back later.' 'No, she's not asleep — I'll go and get her.'

Sylvia opened the door in a flimsy nylon nightie. Her face smudgy with the night before's heavy make-up. She's pretty, blond and about twenty-two.

'I put a card in the window of the newsagents along Stamford Street. So far I've only had three people call and they've all been black. I'm sorry but I won't take black kids. For a start my husband wouldn't put up with it, and anyway I don't particularly fancy them myself.'

'I have my friend's two boys normally but they're not here today. She's off work. They're right little buggers. But they take more notice of me than their mother. They come to me some days black and blue where she's hit them. Worries me sometimes. But what can you do? I couldn't report her.'

Sylvia has an evening job. She's the hatcheck girl at Barnaby's — one of the largest nightclubs in the city. She works there from nine at night until two — sometimes three — in the morning. I asked her whether she didn't think it was a bit unrealistic for her to start minding children at 8 in the morning after such a late night.

'No. They're very good. My friend lets them in and they play around with my girl until I get up. I do get a bit tired sometimes. But it beats going out to work. I'd like to make a bit more money out of it though. I charge my friend £8 a week and I give them their dinner out of that so there's not much left over. If I could get a couple more it would be great. We're saving up so we can get out of this dump. It's really gone down around here. All these blacks.'

Lilly Owen

A damp, dark kitchen in a crumbling Victorian house in Old Trafford. A very old woman is slumped on a commode in the

146

centre of the room. There are four West Indian children ranging from three to five years silently lined up in front of the
fireguard. An Asian girl of about three is sitting quietly rock-
ing herself on the floor in a corner. Outside in the draughty
hall are two small black babies in prams. Lilly is making tea
in the scullery at the back of the house.

'Look at those bruises. The other arm's as bad. That's what
she did to me this morning before she took Glynis away.'

Glynis is Mrs Owen's granddaughter. She lives in the house
with her unmarried mother. There had been a fight between
Mrs Owen and her daughter about the West Indian man her
daughter had brought into the house to live with her. The
daughter had taken Glynis away and Mrs Owen had heard
nothing of her all day.

'God knows where she's taken her. They won't take her
into the nursery.'

That first visit Mrs Owen was too upset to talk about minding. Her estranged husband was dying in Crumpsall hospital
and she was clearly very upset about her grandchild. All that
could be established were the facts.

Lilly Owen is registered to mind seven children. She is in
her late fifties. The family has been minding for nearly forty
years. When her mother had a stroke thirteen years ago, Lilly
took over, and it was at this time that she became registered.
She charges between £2.50 and £3 per child.

By the time I next called, Glynis had been returned to the
care of her grandmother, and Mrs Owen was much calmer.

'Of course, before the war, things were much better. The
children were nicer, more obedient. Not so many of these
coloured ones then. This lot's no good at all. You have to
keep your eye on them the whole time.

'I don't believe in toys. I can't be expected to give them
things to play with. It's hard enough getting them to keep
still. That one over there — if you didn't watch him, he'd
be all over the place.

'When they're naughty I've got a good way of keeping
them quiet. See that nylon stocking? I tie them on the
chair with that. It doesn't hurt them. If they're really bad
— breaking things and screaming - things like that, I put

them down in the cellar for a while. I've got one here, he's
that bad he's never out of the cellar. If they're *really*
naughty — I paddle 'em.

'Feeding them is difficult. It all costs so much nowadays.
Some of them bring their own food but that's more bother
really. You have to remember who brought what.'

Mrs Owen has a part-time, afternoon job. I've never been
able to establish what this is as she'll never openly admit to
going out to work. But every afternoon she's picked up by
car at 2 and returns at 5.30. During this period an elderly
neighbour comes in to look after granny and the children.
The children are terrified of her. There's never much noise
in the house when Mrs Owen is there, but the minute the
neighbour walks through the door the children become completely still and silent. She openly lashes out at the children
when I'm in the room.

The children are never taken out. Unlike most of the other
minded children in the area, they're not even allowed into
the backyard.

Granny, although unable to·move, keeps strict discipline
in the room. For some strange reason she likes the children
to line up in front of the fireguard. It's almost as though she's
a sergeant major parading her troops —'Over there! Over
there!' she snaps if there's the slightest disturbance.

Mrs Owen has never hidden her dislike of the children she
minds. She complains continually about them in their presence. She also makes no attempt to hide her favouritism for
Glynis. Whenever I've taken fruit it's always Glynis that has
the orange peeled for her. The remainder are put firmly away
in the cupboard. The only child I've ever seen given a proper
meal is Glynis.

One of the children is Jimmy, aged three. He's West Indian,
one of four children. The others are all over school age.

His day with Mrs Owen starts at about 8.30 a.m. Although
he's quite capable of walking the few streets to her house,
he's brought by a silent and preoccupied elder brother,
bumping and tumbling in the old trolley Mrs Owen insists on
him having with him. She insists on the trolley because he
likes to move about. With the energy of a normal three-year-

old, he tries to explore and get something from the cramped environment of his daytime world, Mrs Owen's tiny back kitchen. Climbing behind the sofa, swinging on the cupboard doors. But this just isn't on. There are six other kids in that room, and there isn't space for a randomly moving child. Amazingly, most of the others don't behave like Jimmy. They do remain more or less in their allotted spaces — staring, rhythmically banging heels against chair rungs, sucking fingers, watching telly.

So Jimmy remains strapped into his pushchair most of the day. He's let out to go to the toilet and usually manages a slight detour around the room after using the pot outside the back door. But escape is short-lived. He's plonked back in and straps tightened once more.

Naturally, what frequently happens is that he tips himself out. Trying to reach a cup, or just getting himself in a position to see the TV in the corner. He chats a bit to the other kids, but talking isn't encouraged. They're quickly told to shut up once the noise reaches a certain level.

Sometimes Jimmy is collected quite early — 4.30 or 5.00 in the evening by an elder brother or sister. Other times he has to wait for his mum to come at 6.30 p.m. Because of the uncertainty of his collection time he's always dressed for home by 4 p.m. And on winter days that means thick coat, scarf and woolly hat. And there he sits. Sometimes for up to two-and-a-half hours in the turkish-bath atmosphere of Mrs Owen's overheated kitchen.

Jimmy won't have seen or held a toy in his hands all day. Winter or summer, no chance of moving about in the fresh air. No conversation, no exploration. Just the restricting straps of the pushchair.

I once asked Mrs Owen why she was a childminder.

'Don't know, really. Never thought about it.'

Janet Salmon

'I don't mind children - see, his mother's a relation of my husband's cousin. I only have him till his sister comes to fetch him after school. His sister comes at 3.30 — well four o'clock. See, if I didn't have him his mother couldn't go to work. I wouldn't look after no one else. I'm not one of them childminders'.

Janet, an enormous pasty-faced woman, always wears a short pastel-coloured crimplene dress, from which her immense mottled legs emerge like pillows, ending in incongruously fluffy slippers.

Ever since she gave up laundry work when her only child, Cynthia, was born, she has had a houseful of other people's children, but like many illegal minders she sees her job as temporary, almost accidental. Next week, next year something else will turn up. Her eyes are fixed on the time when Cynthia starts school and she can go back to work, anything to get out of the house. 'If you stop at home all the while you get fed up and then you feel miserable.'

Meanwhile she minds children. Janet knows she is breaking the law and is careful to cover herself. They are all in some way related to her and she looks after them for nothing. Parents and older brothers and sisters, less familiar with the law, told us she charged £2.50.a week, at that time the standard rate for unregistered minding.

Janet has no thought that if she applied for registration she would be turned down. Her reluctance is to label herself as a childminder. She doesn't see it as a job, just 'helping out'. On the rundown council estate where she lives many mothers go out to work and just leave the children locked in the house. That would be the likely alternative for the children she looks after.

It comes naturally to Janet, having children around the place. She herself was the middle one of thirteen brothers and sisters brought up in Bermondsey, and lived there until, in her mid-thirties, she met her Jamaican husband and came to Huddersfield with him. Janet thinks a lot of her husband, 'one of the best' she says. He is 'right fond of children' and always spends an hour or two talking and playing with them if they are still there when he gets home from work — driving a dustcart.

Janet herself never plays with the children. The most she can rouse herself to is an occasional walk round the grimy streets when the sun shines. The nearest playground is twenty minutes' walk away and that's too far. Mostly when she has done her housework she just sits in a chair with a cigarette or in summer leans on the garden wall while the children tumble round her.

The garden is a patch of rough grass scattered with sweet-papers, empty packets, torn pieces of newspaper. Steep uneven steps run down to a broken front gate. A single iron rail guards the six foot drop to the shop forecourt on the other side. Janet stands there chatting to passers by while the children run up and down the steps and swing on the rail. Each time they catch her attention she shouts at them to stop it, come in, get down, stand up — you'll catch your death sitting in that puddle. As soon as she takes her eye off them they go back to whatever they were doing.

The house was in a modernization programme, now abandoned or indefinitely postponed. Inside the walls are peeling and Janet keeps a roaring fire in an endless fight with the damp. She worries a lot about the children throwing bits of paper on the fire while she's not looking — that's the naughtiest thing a child can do in her view. She can't quite work up the energy to buy a fireguard and then it hardly seems worthwhile. It's not, she says, as if she was a regular childminder.

Janet will go on minding children for at least another two years, until Cynthia starts school. During that time another ten children may pass through her hands. They will learn nothing from her except to disregard adults. She screams at them continuously, almost always to stop doing whatever they are doing, or issues one word commands but is too lethargic and distractable to see that they are carried out.

Toys she sees only as targets for vandalism ('You can't keep nothing round here, the kids break everything up'), or a cause of arguments. Talking about help for childminders produced no response at all except for the suggestion of a playgroup for minded children with transport provided. 'Yes that would be good — so as the minder could get on with her housework'.

Elsie Howes

Elsie advertised in a shop along the main street. 'Lady willing to look after child during the day. Coloured children welcome.'

I found the house. An old, crumbling bay-windowed terrace. The front door was broken and permanently ajar. An old man answered my knock. I said I'd seen the advert and he eagerly took me through into the back kitchen. The smell of dogs and stale food hit me as I entered.

'Mother — this lady's come about the card' said Mr Howes. Mrs Howes jumped up. 'I knew it. I knew it. I prayed last night that God would send me a baby. I knew he'd answer my prayers.' I had to explain I didn't have a baby. She was disappointed but asked me to sit down and have a cup of tea.

Elsie is about seventy, but looks older. She has two grownup and married sons. They're both in the army overseas. She has two grandchildren. 'I've never seen them. I wish they'd bring them over.' Her husband is seventy-three.

'We both love children. Children and dogs. Life's not
worth living without them, is it? Of course we've only
lived here a few months. Our other house was much better.
We had lots more space. You should have come round then.
I sometimes used to have ten in. Everyone knew me there.
I never did it for the money. Just for love. I'll get some
here soon, I know. When people get to know me. Trouble
is I can't get about much now with my leg.'

I asked her how she coped with ten children. 'We just used to play. Play all the time. And go out for walks. We've always had lots of children around. We used to be foster parents you know.'

Mrs Howes stopped here and her husband took the story up.

'We had some trouble though. That were before my youngest boy went into the army. We had this little girl with us
then. We'd had her for about three months. She were a sly
little thing. Only ten. Well, she went away for the weekend.

I don't remember where. Perhaps it were back to the home. Anyway on the Monday this woman came back with her and starts asking questions about our boy. We couldn't understand what was up. Then she came out with it. She said our boy had been interfering with the girl. It was terrible. He'd never do a thing like that. If you could meet him you'd know. There was an awful fuss. They never sent us any more children after that.'

They both talked of 'doing the house up' so they could accommodate children. At the moment they could only use the downstairs rooms as the roof leaked badly. It was obvious the landlord would never consider doing anything to it as the whole street is under a compulsory purchase order.

As I left Elsie said 'Who does she remind you of, Dad? Janet. She's my eldest son's wife. I thought when you walked in that it was Janet come to show me my grandchildren.'

I returned to the Howes about six months later. The house was in the same shocking state. Once more Mr Howes opened the door. He didn't appear to remember me. I asked if Mrs Howes was in. He said she was asleep. Didn't get up until after dinner now. I asked about minding. 'Oh yes' he said, 'I'm looking after one little baby.' I asked to see it and he took me into the tiny back room. There was a very young black baby in a pram. Mr Howes said he made the feeds up himself and changed the nappies. 'But Mother likes to give it a bit of a cuddle when she gets up of an afternoon.'

The baby is two-month-old Julie. Her mother is seventeen, unmarried, living in a commune of young black people, squatting in one of the derelict houses. She drops her baby in at the Howes at 7 a.m. on her way to work at the Harp brewery at the end of the road.

At seven in the morning the Howes household is still centred around the bedroom — the damp and cold front room that serves also as store for ladders and bikes and endless cartons still unpacked from their previous home.

As Mrs Howes rarely gets up until after midday and Mr Howes is retired, there's no pressure on them to start the day. So Julie is taken from her mum's arms by Mr Howes still in his pyjamas and brought into bed to sleep between the two old people until she becomes restless for her next feed. Then Mr Howes gets up, gives her her bottle and puts her down in the old pram in the back kitchen. Then he potters around, lighting the coal fire, feeding the cats and dogs.

Julie is left in the pram until Mrs Howes gets up. Sometimes Mr Howes will change her. 'Can't say I'm keen on it. However many times I do it I don't ever seem to get those damn pins in right. And I'm *that* scared of pricking her. She's such a tiny little thing.'

After dinner Mr Howes leaves Julie with his wife whilst he goes out shopping for their supper.

'I'd like to take her with me. I'd think a breath of fresh air would do her good. But mother likes that bit of time with her alone — talking to her and giving her a cuddle. Anyway I reckon I'd get a few funny looks — pushing that little mite round the precinct. What with her being coloured and all.'

Usually Julie's mum comes for her at about 5.30. Sometimes, though, it's much later. Nine, ten at night if she's been off somewhere with her friends. When that happens things become difficult. Julie gets restless. Her mum only sends enough dried milk for the daytime feeds and she often wants more towards the end of the evening. And the Howes have had enough by then. All they want is to put their feet up, doze and watch the telly.

'We don't like to say much to her mum when she comes. Wouldn't like to upset her. She might take Julie away and then we'd be lost. It's not the money I worry about. It's nice to have the couple of quid, but we'd manage without. No, it's mother. It's like Julie's all that's keeping her going.'

Marlene Connor

Marlene Connor started minding just after her second child Sharon was born, partly to help out a friend, partly to bring in a bit of extra money. Her husband, a chef, has found it difficult to find work in Huddersfield at a suitably skilled level, and as he is 'quick tempered', several of his jobs have ended in quarrels with the boss. Marlene finds the child-minding money very handy when he is out of work.

She is proud of her status as a registered childminder. Unlike many of her neighbours she refused to take children until her registration went through, but she isn't too fussy about how many she looks after — up to six sometimes, though she is registered for only two in addition to her own. She says she could easily manage three more.

The Connors live in an unmodernized council house on an estate with a reputation for toughness. The houses, old and therefore cheap, tend to be allocated to poor families and those with multiple problems. Streets littered with paper, broken windows, overgrown gardens witness the familiar cycle of council neglect, vandalism, demoralization. When the crumbling terraces of the old town centre were bull-dozed to build a ring road, most of the displaced tenants were rehoused in Brackenhall. Like Marlene, her husband and nearly all their friends and acquaintances, a high proportion came originally from Ireland in search of work.

At present Marlene minds the two daughters of a West Indian nurse, Lisa and Erica. They were passed on to her by a childminder down the road who decided to go back to work when her own child reached school age. The little girls' mother, who is on her own, works two different shifts — 7.30 to 5 or 11.30 to 9 p.m. It is hard to imagine any other kind of day care accommodating her needs. Marlene looks after the girls for over ten hours a day, gives them three meals, and often takes them across the road and puts them to bed before their mother gets home from work half an hour later. For this she is paid £5 a week, including food. 'She can't afford more than that, with no husband'.

Before she could be registered, Marlene had to buy a nurs-ery fireguard and gates for the stairs and garden — she bor-rowed the money. Two years later, the tiny kitchen where the children play all day, is heated by a freestanding radiant oil heater (strictly forbidden), the fireguard has never come out of the shed where it was stored last summer, and the gar-den gate hangs on the hinge.

When she talks about her 'work', Marlene means cleaning the house, not looking after the children. Before her marriage (at just sixteen) she worked in a hotel and still follows the rituals she learnt there. To an outsider they seem to make little impression on the ingrained shabbiness of the house, but she keeps trying. Like the day her sister-in-law came in to give her a break and she went out and bought a tankful of tropical fish.

Despite her cheerful manner, Mrs Connor looks thin and worn, much older than her twenty-four years. She adores her husband, but when he has been drinking — usually during intervals between jobs — they have violent quarrels, which have more than once ended in a black eye for her. He 'taps' the children too if they bother him. 'But if he's in a bad mood when he comes home he'll just shout at them to be quiet and they do.'

Marlene treats all the children, her own two, the minded children and baby Joanne, with the same rough affection. Most of the day they play on the patched lino around her feet and between the table legs, with a few broken dirty toys while she gets on with the work. Her day begins with cleaning at 6.30 a.m. Then she fetches Erica and Lisa from across the road, gives the family breakfast, sees the oldest off to school. Washing and ironing next, until it's time to start making lunch. After dinner the little ones have a sleep, and once a week she tries to take them out 'for fresh air'. In winter the garden is usually too muddy, in summer, if the fence isn't broken then they can play outside.

From four o'clock onwards they watch television while Marlene prepares a meal for her husband. Teatime is 'all hell let loose', and by the time she has cleared up and taken the two little girls back across the road she feels ready for bed herself. But she tries to read a story to Julie and Sharon before they go to sleep.

All the children Mrs Connor looks after are, like herself, friendly and talkative. Her own two, grubby and unkempt beside the little West Indian girls, with their neat plaits and pink and white frilly dresses, are nevertheless unmistakably loved and cared for. She chats to them and cuddles them, and gives them plenty of good food.

Marlene's problem is lack of resources. There is not a penny of spare cash to turn the garden into a playspace, for machines to lighten her domestic load, to adapt the kitchen or create storage space, least of all to buy toys or books. She responded enthusiastically to suggestions for helping child-minders. Grants for books and toys? 'That would be lovely — they break them that fast'. A travelling toy library? 'Yes, oh yes!' Playgroup? 'Ideal — wouldn't mind about transport. If there was just somewhere we could take them so they wouldn't get bored'. Loan of equipment. 'Smashing. It's so expensive. My husband was going to make me a stairgate, only he never got around to it'.

Most of all she would like a regular visitor to give her time off for shopping or to travel across town to see her bedridden father-in-law. She was very keen to attend a course or dis-cussion group, 'there's a lot to learn about children'.

Robert Evans

I blush and stumble through my opening, 'I believe you're a registered childminder'. Sandy hair, small moustache, fashion-able beige trousers and matching roll-neck sweater. It must be the wrong address. But after a moment's hesitation Mr Evans invites me in.

'I expect you think there's something funny about a man doing this job', he says, expertly crinkle-cutting chips for the children's dinner. I have to admit that it's unusual — Mr Evans was the only registered male childminder we came across, though quite a few men look after other people's children in a casual way.

That isn't Mr Evans's approach at all. He took up child-minding when his wife left him with two small children. The choice was between that and a back-street greengrocery. 'Dark little flats smelling of cabbage and potatoes — I thought this is no place to bring up children.'

Hawthorn Avenue is a leafy cul-de-sac of large detached houses, 'a very posh place — everybody's rich except me. I felt a bit of an outcast to begin with'. Mr Evans tidied up the front garden, rode out the complaints, and now feels quite

settled in his neat little bungalow. On the whole he feels he
made the right decision, though he sometimes gets fed up
with other people's children all day and his own in the evening, 'bread plus bread isn't a very satisfying diet'.

For Mr Evans childminding is a business, and he approached
it in much the same way that he might have done his greengrocer's shop. He worked out the economics of it ('ludicrous'
he says), calculated how many children he would need to
keep himself and his own family on the fees and set about
equipping himself and the premises to accommodate them.
Everything is designed to run as smoothly as possible — the
modern kitchen with automatic washer, tumble drier, chip-
frier; playroom lined with shelves for toy storage — every toy
has an educational purpose he told me proudly; doors leading
to the patio with swing, slide and sandpit. Then he went on
a course for playgroup leaders at the technical college. It
took some courage, being the only man in sight, but he found
it a great help. Before he just used to deal with children by
instinct — now he thinks about it. For example he used to
have a lot of trouble with children biting each other. He
thought he should tell the bitten one to bite back. But discussing this at the class one day a playgroup leader turned to
him and said, 'Dogs bite, people don't'.

With the children Mr Evans plays the jolly uncle role,
sallying into the playroom at intervals to lead a singsong or a
rough and tumble. He leaves the job of continuous caring to
his assistant, Marjorie, who for a tiny wage looks after the
twelve children from 8.30 to 12.30 and 1.30 to 5.30. Unlike
most childminders, he insists on set hours and set charges —
£1.40 a day including an excellent lunch. There is no shortage of parents willing to pay these charges — high by Huddersfield standards, and though a fair sprinkling of them are doctors, teachers and white-collar workers, Mr Evans says that
many working-class parents are just as eager to pay for what
they see as a superior service. Among the children he has at
present, Cheryl's father is a milk roundsman, Jasmine's
mother works in a restaurant, Tony's family run a small
building firm and Martin's father is a fireman.

The children are tucking into fish fingers and chips now —
Marjorie has lunchtime off. Mr Evans is eager to talk, starved

of talk it seems. He is enthusiastic about all our ideas for helping minders, but unlike most of the women he is quite sure what really matters — childminders won't ever be any good until they get paid a proper rate for the job. 'It should be accepted that looking after other people's children is not financially viable. 15p an hour, that's all I make, and that's only if they all come and all pay.'

Mrs Jolly

'How many children have you got here today Mrs Jolly?' I asked once. 'I don't know love — I have to light a candle to see.'

School holidays. Every child in the neighbourhood seems to have gathered into the narrow living room — twenty-four I think, but I may have missed one or two.

For once it isn't raining so the rickety back door stands open and older children rush in and out, knocking over any little ones in their way. Mrs Jolly turns round and round in the middle of the room like a distracted hen. 'Who inside stay in and who outside stay out because we are in a mess here.' Children perch like birds on the sofa backs and armchairs, while Mrs Jolly's Norma, about fourteen, doggedly sweeps the rubbish into a pile. Suddenly Mrs Jolly remembers a baby upstairs. How long has it been there? Two hours, three? Norma slips silently from the room and returns with a nine-month-old black baby. She dumps him on the floor and changes his nappy, roughly and clumsily, all without saying a word. Mrs Jolly rushes outside as the noise crescendos — Winston has opened the rabbit hutch. No use trying to talk today.

Other days it's quiet. The children sit lined-up on the sofa, never stirring unless Mrs Jolly calls them to the table for a drink. Though she rarely speaks to them she's always ready to talk to a visitor.

Five minutes after I first knocked at the door I was 'watching' fifteen children while Mrs Jolly bathed a baby upstairs. 'I frightened to leave them alone because they touch fire' — two unguarded oil heaters, one of them piled round with drying clothes. Typical illegal childminder I thought. It was like stepping into one of those horrific newspaper reports that sparked off the 1948 Act.

But when Mrs Jolly reappeared she told me proudly that she has been registered for twelve years, and though she hasn't seen any health visitor this year or last, the fire officer is always coming.

I sit there half a day sometimes while Mrs Jolly tells me about her childhood in Jamaica, her auntie that brought her up, her disappointment that she couldn't be a nurse because her father died and she must work to help her mother and all her brothers and sisters. (Is it just a fantasy? Mrs Jolly never even went to school and can't read or write. She does her shopping by telephone so as not to be shamed by her inability to read the labels.)

'Always I want to serve. If I didn't take children it would be old people that couldn't look after themselves. I love children, all children. But what I really like best is babies. Every day I dream of finding a baby, a little baby that nobody wants.'

Mrs Jolly bustles about, burrowing for baby pants in a huge heap of clean washing, dishing out biscuits, wiping a nose, searching out the stepladder for a neighbour, throwing words over her shoulder all the time. When I unpack my bag of toys the children fall on them eagerly. Mrs Jolly pushes the older ones out of the way, 'You not a baby to play with toys'. They retreat obediently to the sofa, ignoring Mrs Jolly's casual slap. She can't let the chldren play — she keeps taking a toy from one child and giving it to another. Then she'll change her mind and snatch it back. Henry, a little black boy I've never heard make a sound, wants to play with the pull-along duck. Mrs Jolly keeps jerking him roughly back into the armchair. A tear runs down his cheek. 'Why can't he play?' I ask at last. 'He changed into his clothes. He know he not allowed on the floor after he changed or his mother when she come, she look me up and down.' Henry gives up and goes to sit by a beautifully dressed little Indian girl who has been curled up quite still all these hours sucking her thumb.

'What's her name, Sally?' Mrs Jolly passes on my question to her own three-year-old, noticeably livelier than the others.

At 3.45 p.m. the room begins to fill with returning school-children. One, dressed like a prep-school boy in cap, blazer, wrinkled grey socks, looks at me blankly when I offer him a Smartie. 'He mental that one – he just come off school ambulance'.

'Now then baby Jolly' she throws at Sally, 'time to mash tea'. The tiny creature balances along the sofa back on to the table to reach a tea bag from the high cupboard.

Other little ones are all buttoned up in coats and bonnets against the raw Huddersfield wind. The room is stifling. When will the parents come? Mrs Jolly is casual about times. People know she won't complain if they take the chance to earn a few pounds extra. Not that any of it comes her way. She charges £3 with food and £2 without. It's a problem, she says, when children bring food they can't eat, like baby Sharon who was pushed through the door this morning with a bag of potatoes.

The room is still full when I leave at seven o'clock. Mrs Jolly often keeps children all night. The line between minding and fostering blurs into invisibility. When Jonah's father was sent to prison Mrs Jolly just kept Jonah. Not only that, but took him to visit his dad in prison and sent one of her own older children to look after his council house so that he'd have somewhere to go when he came out.

Mrs Jolly is registered for ten (we checked). Sally is her only helper. Social workers are frightened to visit her – 'It would be like Pandora's box', one of them told me. 'And after all she really does love children'.

Death of a minded baby

Two eighteen-year-old girls, one from Jamaica, the other from Grenada, met in the maternity home, decided to keep their babies and set up house together living with the mother of one of the girls. The fathers of the babies have never been mentioned. There appears to have been no support from the authorities and therefore when the maternity grant ceased,

161

the girls had to find employment and a minder for the babies.

Mrs Jolly, already had her full quota of ten children but could not turn these girls away and took both babies daily from the age of six weeks.

'I have the babies for four weeks already and they fine, they doing well. I take them at 7.30 in the morning and put them upstairs in the cots until their next feed. On the Monday the baby's mother brought a dirty bottle — she say she haven't time to clean it but the baby been fed — she say nothing about the baby being sick all weekend and being very sick that morning. The baby poorly that day and when she came for it I tell her but she say the baby have a very bad cold that all.

'The next day she bring the baby with the other one and dirty bottles as before and she say nothing so I put them in the cots as they just been fed before they come but I see the baby not well. I go upstairs twice by 9.30 to see the baby but then I see it very bad. So I get my neighbour to come mind the children while I run for Dr James but I can't find the doctor — I forget his surgery has moved to Fartown Clinic — so I run back home. Now the baby very bad, so I ring the police.

'When they come I tell them I do nothing to the baby and the baby still warm — they give it the kiss of life, but it just die.

'When the mother come for it I tell her and the other girl not to bring the baby back but she have nowhere to take it so I still have the one and it not well either so I scared to take it upstairs. I leave it in the pram all day so I see it living.

'I do nothing to that baby, it just die. I have no trouble with any of the children before but I do it now for thirteen years, and you know number thirteen.'

Mrs Jolly could not get the baby's mother as she didn't know her surname or her place of employment — she knew her as Shirley and the other girl as Joy and had forgotten the names of the babies until she asked her own children to remind her. There has been no health visitor or social services contact.

An unqualified social worker had called once just prior to this event but Mrs Jolly had just received a telegram summoning her husband to Jamaica to bury his father and she was so distressed that the visit was postponed.

After the death no help or advice was offered to Mrs Jolly, indeed no information was given about an inquest or funeral. I called and took five children to a playgroup to give her a breathing space the next day after the tragedy but I left more children in her care than I took with me, as the other children could not come for a variety of reasons — one had a dreadful cough.

> 'I tell that baby's mother he have whooping cough three weeks ago but she say it soon get better. I keep asking her for medicine but she never bring none so today he coughing that bad I go to the chemist and buy with my own money.'

Two were asleep, one was sick, another's mother was due to collect him and the baby was too young. The children had shared a cold roast chicken for their midday meal.

Mrs Jolly found out from the other baby's mother that the dead child was to be buried the following Monday, no inquest would be needed as the hospital had signed the death certificate saying that the baby had been ill for some time prior to a lung collapse. So Mrs Jolly sat with her coat on waiting for someone to take her to the funeral. No one came.

These are leaves from field notebooks. They could be repeated a hundred times. All the minders here come from two small, densely researched districts in Manchester and Huddersfield. Poorer areas than these would reveal more minders, and more harassed and neglected ones. Prosperous areas would of course reveal fewer, and more confident ones. What we have here is, in our experience, a working-class norm.

But pausing in this portrait gallery helps one to think in fresh ways about childminders. Because the state licenses childminders, officials have really placed them into two 'types': registered and unregistered. It is then an easy mental step to assume that registered must mean good, whereas unregistered probably means unsatisfactory. But that is not what the portraits suggest. Would you want to leave your toddler with Susan Moseley, who is registered but illiterate, totally deaf and unaware of the children's names?

Registration clearly produces bizarre results because it is not based on any clear concept of child-care – only on checking out a number of disparate, external elements (fireguard, lavatory, X-ray and so on). We can see that at work in a number of these miniature studies. When the health visitor calls on Bernadette Watkins, she is impressed by the *cleanliness* of the home and brushes registration aside. She does not notice that houseproud Bernadette is continually nipping off the children's natural explorative behaviour, lest they damage her child-high collection of glass animals.

So we can place the minders in two 'types' – legal and illegal: the result of parliamentary decisions in 1948 and 1968, often magnified or sharpened up by local officials. But it is clear from the portraits that the consequence is that many of the minders who need most help, and many of the most deprived children are not known to the social services or are actively avoiding social workers. What does this suggest? Should we consider a national amnesty and remove the fear of prosecution, at least for a while in an attempt to contact illegal minders and their children? Should registration be more widely and attractively advertised? Should registration become a positive resource – bringing something of value to the minder (money, support, toys, links) – rather than a control device? But can we, looking at the portraits, risk giving up control altogether?

Let's try another way of 'typing' these portraits. We could divide minders into 'stable' ones who do the job for a long time and 'intermittent' ones who move in and out of it. This is not of course the same as good or bad. Lilly Owen and her mother could not be more 'stable' in this sense: they have been minding together for forty years – but none of us in the team would ever want our children to be left in such care. No, the point of looking at them in this way is that many people do drift in and out of minding. Janet Salmon, for instance, is clearly a childminder at the moment, but she doesn't see it that way. As far as she is concerned, she is just temporarily 'helping out' until she spots some more attractive work. It would be hard to put a figure to this division. It is clearly affected by the prosperity or poverty of a neighbourhood and by the ebb and flow of the employment situation for women. But our experience is that the ratio of 'stable' to 'intermittent' minders is generally 60:40. There is a stable core to build around, but a large and often disturbing group of temporary minders. If we are to transform childminding into a satisfactory child-care system then we have to go for an increase in the proportion of stable minders. It is, for example, of limited use offering training courses for all childminders if in a year's time 40 per cent are back in the factories and another unknown, untrained and possibly unsatisfactory 40 per cent have invisibly taken their place. What policies are required that would produce greater stability?

There is a further question here. Obviously 'stable' minders are a pre-condition of 'stable' children — 'stable' again in the sense of attending one minder for a reasonable period. But they don't guarantee that. Parents can be very casual about moving their child around. ('I've had children I kissed goodbye to of a Friday evening and never seen again. That hurts.') It may hurt the child too. We heard of one child who had been to thirty-six different minders. Should a new policy for childminding also place some onus on the parents which is likely to reduce such capricious behaviour?

We can next divide the portraits into two fresh 'types'. First, those who see childminding as an essentially passive activity. And the very word childminder is drenched in passive meaning: you mind the dog, you mind the shop when the real shopkeeper is out, you mind your own business. Then we can distinguish a 'type' who see it as an active role. When Marlene Connor talks about her 'work' — she means cleaning the kitchen. When a playgroup is suggested to Janet Salmon, she is very enthusiastic — it would allow her to forget about children and concentrate on her housework. And old Mrs Owen lining the children up before the fireguard has that undisturbed classical sense that 'minding' children means restricting and marshalling them, a situation we discovered in our original pilot studies. But again we have to watch our value-judgments. Life is awkward material to analyse. The passive minders include very many of the most loving minders of all: minders who cuddle and kiss and smile at the children in their charge. But, alas, love is not enough. What is so often needed is love expressed in practical ways.

Thinking of minders in terms of different typological grids is of course only a simple intellectual tool. It does not mean that we 'type' each minder, for clearly one person can belong to different (indeed opposing) types simultaneously, and few will ever perfectly exemplify one typology. It is simply an abstraction to think with: but within modest limits allows one to escape from the anecdotal, go beyond the individual, and probe better the condition of all childminders. You just have to build up different typologies, and see which — if any — yield fresh information.

Let's try another. We could divide these portraits into minders who are *retreating* from the public world, and those who are *advancing* towards it. This typology of our small portrait gallery already suggests first of all the likely effect on childminders and children of a *punitive* policy (fines, imprisonment, regulations, policing — and little support); and second, of a *passive* policy (you register or do not register the minders that the child market throws up instead of recruiting and training for an early childhood profession).

We could next think of childminders who positively sought the work, and those who would find it difficult to earn a living in the larger public theatre. Susan Moseley is totally deaf and wholly illiterate. When we first met her she seemed the most astonishingly unusual person to register as a childminder. But closer enquiry shows that this is not really so. She represents a distinct and not uncommon type. A passive policy logically leads to the passive 'type'. Since the state does not actively recruit or train childminders, it does not attract minders of the 'active' type such as Maureen Williams who with her playgroup experience and reading of current educational periodicals, clearly sees childminding as teaching activity. What happens — and must happen — is that one 'type' of minder will be someone who would find it difficult to cope with public work, or may even be in retreat from the world. So it is not surprising that minders will include a number of illiterate women who might feel frightened of shop or factory work, but more secure in their own home with children. Similarly it will, under our present conditions, attract people whose emotional hunger for children should make one pause. Seventy year old Elsie Howes is not really capable of looking after baby Julie but 'it's like Julie's all that's keeping her going'.

There are of course other 'types' of childminders than appear in the portrait gallery. For instance we found a man childminding, and this is something which might increase since we have a rising number of fathers, separated from their wives, who are bringing up their own children alone. It is a simple step to look after someone else's child too, and turn their situation into a profession. They could indeed be a good source of active minders, if strongly recruited. On the other hand, we have also noticed that in poorer districts there is a great deal of minding being carried out by older children, though this shows up in none of the official statements. Sometimes it is done by teenage children who should still be at school, but whose schools are neither anxious to have them back nor active in pursuing them. Sometimes it is a result of the shift system, and we have come across children — often very young — who are essentially childminding from 4 p.m. till midnight — but at this point the accepted borderline between childminding and 'babysitting' (of which I become increasingly dubious) is very shadowy.

Besides the basis for an elementary but illuminating typology the portrait gallery reminds us of two more aspects of childminding: first of all, minding as a form of income, and second, minding as a serious branch in the future of the educational profession.

Lily Owen charges £3 a week for a toddler and £2.50 a week for a baby. Josie Corrigan, who lives nearby, undercuts her, and charges £2 or £1.50. Sylvia Hawkins, the hatcheck girl, who lives close to both, does several hours of her minding in her sleep — but charges £8 for two children.

This, in our experience, would be a fairly typical cluster. In a prosperous middle-class district, where you might, for

example, find a former teacher minding, the charge could be
— at this same moment in time — as high as £16. But in working-class areas, though we found regional differences (a £7
average in Nottingham or Edinburgh compared to £3 in Bristol or Glasgow) it is clear that a very low price is put on the
work. £3 a week for eight hours minding on five days of the
week is 7½p per hour. The minders naturally would all like
a bit more — but their thoughts are of a further 50p or £1 a
week, not of a dramatic increase to professional levels. The
parents grudge every small increase, and may quite commonly shop around for a cheaper minder. This is especially true
of the Asian or West Indian parents with whom we work.
And it must be remembered that the £3 is *relatively* a large
proportion (commonly around one-sixth) of the mother's
take-home pay — pay often earned by long unpleasant hours
on routine production lines. They see the minder as having
much the easier job.

The minders, of course, may have another source of
income as well. In Brixton it was sometimes an early-morning
cleaning job (5.30 a.m. to 7.30 a.m.); in Manchester it was
more likely to be an evening job at pub or club. Some of the
unregistered minders may be drawing social security, and
very little of the money paid for minding in such areas will
be declared for tax.

This has led some social workers, who see the whole activity as undesirable, to claim that minders are making money
out of children — and to apply pressure to reduce it. Our
experience is quite different. Whenever we have correlated
the fee charged and the quality of care given (as measured on
our checklist score), the result — with odd exceptions such as
Sylvia — has been that the more you pay, the better service
your child gets. But by and large this simply reflects the
social class or educational background of both minder and
parents.

Minders in traditional working-class areas, where charges
are low; and in immigrant areas, where they can be lowest of
all, are often worried lest some official discovers their earnings
and then, in some undefined way, harasses, taxes or prose-
cutes them. This is one of the barriers to their coming forward for registration. But if we looked at minding through

business eyes, it is often clear that the financial gain is tiny and that sometimes (when one allows for the heating, light, washing, TV consumption and food required) it represents a net *loss*.

It is worth probing the charges in these ways, rather than simply recording them, because any major improvement must involve the minder being paid more *for the specific task of caring for and educating the child.* The present free market is clearly most damaging to those children most at risk, though it works well enough in middle-class areas. Which, then, is the direction forward? Can the minders, for instance, be unionized? Should local authorities subsidize minders by paying a retainer? Or should they lay down guidelines as to what current charges might be?

This question of charges, as we see in these portraits, is always going to be enmeshed in how the minders perceive their role. Most of the minders here sense their first job as housework — cooking, cleaning, shopping.[1] They may do this because this is what their husband pays them for. Remember Josie's regret at losing her '£20 a week man'. It is also fair to say that many of them feel most secure when pursuing or relaxing from the familiar housework routine. Either way space is not being made for the child — the child is simply, in its most passive sense, being minded.

After this, the next level of attention is overtly loving the child — cuddles, kisses, sweets. But as I remarked earlier, this is hardly enough. You see this most clearly in the crucial area of language development. Susan is deaf and registered, and perhaps unusual. But it is very common to find minders and children, especially in migrant areas, who cannot converse because they speak quite different languages. And very common indeed in other areas to observe minders who simply do not listen to the children nor actually converse with them (as opposed to giving orders). Now control of this whole area seems much more important than many of the regulations on the statute book. In what directions could we improve it? Should we actually be trying to relieve minders of housework? For instance by allowing them home helps, or by using mobile services (for clearly the child-feeding situation can be very unsatisfactory) or by linking them to bulk-buying schemes? Should registration involve attention to language? Many minders need language help themselves. Home tutoring may not only aid them, but the children could be brought into it too. And should not linguistic mismatches be actively discouraged?

At another level, we can see that some minders actively play with the children, use toys, take them out and share experiences. They are so clearly on the verge of playing a key educational role that it seems startling that they are so neglected. What do they need? Is it courses, links with other minders, travelling toy libraries, relationships with playgroups and schools? And can we reasonably expect social workers to provide the educational support and direction? Or must we draw in others?

This is to look optimistically towards a better future. But before concluding, it is as well to reflect on these portraits from the angle which gave us our present 'social worker as policeman' view of childminders. Pat Aldiss has dangerous pills, matches, sharp knives lying around. There is no guard round the blazing fire in Susan Moseley's kitchen. Josie Corrigan and her children have threadworms, and don't take the medicine ('It's too sweet') and Lesley's eye is swollen where she hit him with a belt for literally doing nothing. Marlene Connor, who is registered, keeps the children in the kitchen all day with a freestanding radiant oil heater. And Mrs Jolly with a dying baby in the house does not know its name, nor where its mother works, nor how to get a doctor. The baby dies. There is no post mortem, no enquiry. Mrs Jolly carries on minding in the same way as before.

These portraits we suspect, can be replicated again and again in working-class districts. They show that we must protect the health, safety and lives of minded children. This is what the law is designed to do. Yet clearly it is a huge failure. These children are as much at risk as ever. And the basic reason is that we have not recognized childminding for the major profession it could be in early childhood. We have neither seen it, nor valued it, nor supported it. It is time to make the case afresh.

10 Childminding: a classic case in the cycle of deprivation

Why is it that, in spite of long periods of full employment and relative prosperity and the improvement in community services since the second world war, deprivation and problems of maladjustment so conspicuously persist?

Sir Keith Joseph, positing the existence of uncharted 'cycles of deprivation', 1972

He his fabric of the Heavens
Hath left to their disputes, perhaps to move
His laughter at their quaint opinions wide
Hereafter, when they come to model Heaven
And calculate the stars, how they will wield
The mighty frame, how build, unbuild, contrive
To save appearances, how gird the sphere
With centric and eccentric scribbled o'er
Cycle and epicycle.

John Milton,
Paradise Lost, Book One

We began with a bleak December Dawnwatch in the back streets of seven British cities. Back in the warm leathery quiet of the University Library at Cambridge we found that the Oxford English Dictionary was blank where childminding might be. It is time to pull the strands together.

Despite its absence from the modern debate on early education, childminding must have a long history. There is a superb chapter — 'Minders and Reminders' — in Charles Dickens's *Our Mutual Friend* in which the wealthy Mr and Mrs Boffin, together with their secretary set about seeking an orphan to adopt. But

171

either an eligible orphan was of the wrong sex (which almost always happened), or was too old, or too young, or too sickly, or too dirty, or too much accustomed to the streets, or too likely to run away; or it was found imposs- ible to complete the philanthropic transaction without buying the orphan.

At last they hear of one, cared for by a Mrs Betty Higden, and set off in their phaeton:

The abode of Mrs Betty Higden was not easy to find, lying in such complicated back settlements of muddy Brentford that they left their equipage at the sign of the Three Mag- pies and went in search of it on foot.

When discovered, Mrs Higden lives in

a small home with a large mangle in it'. The room was clean and neat. It had a brick floor, and a window of dia- mond panes, and a flounce hanging below the chimney- piece, and strings nailed from bottom to top outside the window on which scarlet-beans were to grow in the coming season.

Betty Higden is nursing the orphan sought for adoption. But there are other children in the house.

'These are not his brother and sister?' said Mrs Boffin. 'Oh, dear, no, ma'am. Those are Minders.' 'Minders?' The secretary repeated. 'Left to be Minded, sir. I keep a Minding-school. I can take only three, on account of the mangle. But I love children, and fourpence a week is four- pence. Come here Toddles and Poddles.'

The word 'Dickensian' has often been applied to the condi- tions of backstreet babyminding today. But always wrongly. Dickens was, of course, a great social investigator. To the prosperous Mrs Boffin and her knowledgeable and efficient secretary, the apparently simple and generous act of adopting a deprived working-class child turns out to be beset with a thousand difficult questions. And to discover childminding in a poor district at first hand (having left the posh phaeton safely at the *Three Magpies*) is a matter of astonishment.

Nevertheless, Dickens (despite the false image) offers a warm view of a necessary activity. And Betty Higden — even if fourpence a week is fourpence a week — sees herself as a humble educator: 'I keep a Minding-school'.[1]

Perhaps we need to find a fresh sum of the strengths of that modest service. But of course there were terrible distortions and handicaps too. In 1908 the Board of Education Consultative Committees[2] reported that a poor working mother must either 'leave her children unattended' or 'send them to be taken care of by a neighbour or professional minder'. And their view of childminding at that time was bleak:

> The 'professional' minder is nearly always unsatisfactory. The Committee are informed that it is common practice in some districts for ignorant women to earn a living by minding neighbours' children. The minder takes an average of 8d a day. There is no inspection or control. They are often dirty and unsatisfactory, often conducted by women of the grossest ignorance.

The rate of pay had doubled. The official Committee takes in its knowledge, unlike Dickens, secondhand. And it is very free with the label of ignorance. Yet conditions must have been grim and stultifying for many generations of children trapped in this near-invisible situation.

What is surprising is that a century later — with present-day children growing up in the modern approximation of these conditions, good and bad — childminding is not, as I said, a major matter of debate in early childhood education in this or any other industrial society.

It has cropped up in the newspapers when a child has died, and people (like Simon Yudkin after the 1939-45 war[3]) have tried to draw attention to it. But we do not even know the scale on which it exists today. Perhaps it is time to try the first speculative calculation as to the number of children involved. Possibly we shall never be certain of the exact num-

173

ber, but it could alter our thinking if we could reasonably demonstrate the points between which the actual number may lie.

A number game

Childminding numbers first appeared in official records in 1949. This was the year which followed the first Act requiring them to register — taking up the simple point made half a century (or ten generations of under fives) earlier by that Board of Education, 'there is no inspection or control'.

Table 10.1 shows that, from 1949 to 1968, city officials discovered more and more childminders and registered them. I think the first point to pause over in this investigation is that this does not mean that there were only 271 childminders in 1949, and that these increased twenty-five-fold. It only means that these were the ones who had come forward, passed registration and been logged. No doubt some of them (like Lily Owen in 'Portrait Gallery') had been childminding for forty years or more. Nevertheless, the mists rise — more and more of the landscape is seen.

In 1969, the second Act affecting childminders came into being, and at once the formal figures (largely reflecting both the publicity and the new spurt of official energy) reflect that. Look at 1968 compared with the next two years in Table 10.1.

The number of childminders went up fourfold, the number of permitted children almost doubled. Did they really not exist before? I doubt it. Like so many official statistics this records the energy, perception and limits of inspecting officials — not the actuality of the territory that we have met in previous chapters.

The next year was 1971. Official records showed a nil return. Did this mean that all registered childminders had abandoned their profession, or perhaps gone illegal? I consulted the ministry. 'There were no figures for 1971. This was because of a change of the dates to which the information related.'[4] Once again we are back to the *Oxford English Dictionary*. No entry, no existence.

Table 10.1 Government returns on childminding 1949-72

	No. of registered childminders	No. of children permitted
1949	271	1,703
1950	415	2,638
1951	468	3,506
1952	560	4,178
1953	638	4,737
1954	715	5,570
1955	777	6,090
1956	881	6,964
1957	949	7,536
1958	1,138	8,981
1959	1,313	10,192
1960	1,531	11,881
1961	1,780	13,999
1962	2,202	17,600
1963	2,597	20,800
1964	2,994	24,000
1965	3,393	27,200
1966	3,887	32,336
1967	5,037	42,696
1968	5,802	47,208
1969	18,168	70,531
1970	25,595	84,861
1971	—	—
1972	29,191	90,036
1973	30,333	91,878

Then came 1972, and this produced a fresh crop of figures, because of amendments to the 1968 Health Services and Public Health Act.

So the effect of the law here has been to uncover not 1,703 permitted children as in 1949, but 91,878 in 1973. And this refers to England and Wales only. Separate data for Scotland and Northern Ireland is not easy to come by,[5] but by this date there were 1,351 permitted children in Scotland and 131 registered minders in Northern Ireland caring for perhaps 377 permitted children.

But there is one more sum to be done on these official figures. Suppose each year we simply divide the number of childminders into the numbers of children. This has not previously been done, but it yields surprising results. First of all we have the initial head-count of minders after the 1948 Act. It shows that the first wave of childminders looked after just over six children each, and that this rose gradually to — a perhaps more realistic average — of rather more than eight children by the time the 1968 Act is passed.[6] And then, overnight, the average drops to three children each. What happened? Did all those mothers stop working? Did all the children go home? Did all those childminders suddenly decide that eight was too much on average but three toddlers was right, manageable and economic. More likely the earlier figures told a truth. The new regulations meant that local officials protected themselves (the 1968 debate and Act enshrines the idea of a two- to three-child household) and overnight produced lower levels of official numbers permitted. It is very doubtful if this had any effect on the actual number of children minded. We demonstrate the arithmetic only to suggest that, once again, we have good evidence that the official data underestimates the number of children affected. For example, a small survey commissioned by the Department of Health and Social Security from Berry Mayall and Pat Petrie showed that their sample of thirty-nine registered minders on the day of interview were looking after an average of 5·7 children each: well above their quota. If something like this were true of all registered childminders, that would give us 171,000 children in their daily care. This may or may not be too high, but it is again an upward pointer, and one — derived from a government survey — which adds further doubt to the official figures.

We may then reasonably say that childminders — at a minimum — are permitted to look after around 100,000 children. But there are several more illuminating stages in this hidden arithmetic. From being an apparently trivial 0·05 per cent of the under-five population in 1949, it is by 1973 just under 3 per cent on official figures. The real proportion now seems to be quite different.

For example, consider first the regional nature of the figures. How is it that England and Wales have 91,000 children with minders and Scotland (a much poorer area) has only 1,300? And Northern Ireland a mere 377 children with registered minders?

So far we have evidence pointing to a baseline figure of 100,000 children. There could be two reasons for the rise from 1,703 in 1949 to that figure. One could be the rising number of women going out to work. Between 1951 and 1971 the number of married women going out to work rose by 2.5 million or 76 per cent.[7] Unfortunately — but interestingly in line with one of the main trails in this research — no figures were gathered before 1971 on the employment of working mothers. Again a curious detail in the invisible world of the poor. But by 1971, there were 588,600 working mothers with children under five and a further 48,000 classed as 'economically active' but not actually out at work on census day.[8] So clearly we could say that the increased numbers of childminders come from the increased demand made by increasing numbers of women going out to work. But we could also say that the predecessors of many of these 100,000 children with minders were certainly there in previous years — but were unknown to the authorities. Rising numbers are in part the result of rising discoveries of minders by social service departments or rising awareness amongst minders of the requirement to register.

So we could next try to calculate the number of illegal childminders so as to get a realistic overall sum. At first sight this looks impossible, and no one has published any number at all. But even if we can't get the answer right, we can make calculations to give us bearings on its approximate range. Here are the four main markers which emerged as this research unfolded.

In one of our pilot probes[9] we especially looked at the situation of the West Indian mother in Britain. We estimated that by 1971 there were approximately 120,000 West Indian children under five in England and Wales. This was an under-five population (in 1966 when we were still opening up this field) of 21 per cent compared with a host population figure of 8 per cent. Two out of three West Indian women were out at work. Later evidence showed that even higher numbers of West Indian mothers with children under five might be out at work in the poorer parts of industrial cities (Leicester 85 per cent Manchester 71 per cent) — which is exactly what had been seen in Dawnwatch.

With this we related medical papers published by Professor Eric Stroud, paediatrician at Kings College Hospital, London, and Dr G. Stewart Prince, a consultant in child psychiatry at the same hospital, who had noticed that twenty-one out of twenty-three successive West Indian children referred to him (often for apparent deafness or speech defects) were withdrawn, aloof, apathetic, unused to play, and fearful of necessary exploratory behaviour. Looking at their backgrounds, he recorded that the majority (63 per cent) had been left with unregistered minders whilst their mothers went out to work.[10] As we have followed the childminding trail, other similar reports, very small but careful, have come in from the medical field, all confirming this high use of unregistered childminders by the West Indian population in Britain.[11]

Because the data is clear cut here, we can actually combine it across disciplinary boundaries and make a reasonable estimate. Our initial calculation was that probably 60,000 children with West Indian mothers spend the day with an unregistered childminder. Possibly that number is declining. Partly because of the downward trend in the birth rate here, partly because a small but increasing number of West Indian minders (largely minding only West Indian children) are appearing on the local registers in the more advanced local authorities. Nevertheless, we may well still be left with some 50,000 children here put out to unregistered minders.

A second marker came from the series of *Action Registers* we published as part of the strategy of 'open research'.[12] The idea was to report findings on childminding as they were discovered, and invite officials and voluntary bodies to say what they were doing about them.

The data thrown up by these ancillary surveys illustrated the remarkable variation in the number of childminders from one place to another. The whole of Scotland had roughly the same number of registered minders as the county of Kent. The whole of Northern Ireland had less than the small area around Huddersfield. The city of Liverpool reported twenty-six minders whilst smaller Leicester noted 1,300.[13] At one stage Glasgow recorded two registered minders whilst thinly populated Cambridgeshire had 477 and Oxfordshire 525. Just before the reorganization of local government in England, we looked at two adjacent towns in East Anglia: Lowestoft and Great Yarmouth. Only the River Yare divides them, and for a working mother in either, there was only one real employer: the huge fish freezer works. You could see mothers from either turning up for the day's work. Yet the town on this bank had large numbers of registered minders, whilst the town on the other bank had hardly any at all.

What is the explanation? Of course there must be regional and local variations in the employment of women. There are differences too in the local survival of the extended family: grandmothers looking after the kids. But by far the most obvious variable was the attitude of local officials. If they were indifferent to, unaware of, or disapproving of child-minders then the chances were that very few would be registered. If they were concerned about childminding, publicizing the requirement of registration, and setting up supportive services, then the odds were on much larger numbers registering.

Putting it all together, we can say that if all local authorities were as positive as the best ones are about childminding then registered numbers would double — might increase by up to another 100,000.

We then tried a third marker. We asked local authority officials what *they* thought was the extent of illegal minding. A long shot but worth a try. Sixty-seven authorities expressed concern about illegal minding, but refused to make local estimates. This was really what we expected. The pressure on officials is towards extreme caution, and never more so than when asked to estimate the extent of an illegal activity for which they carry formal responsibility.

Nevertheless in November 1976, sixteen local authorities — carried largely by the public drift of this open research — were prepared to put in numbers of what they thought their

179

own situation was. The pioneer areas were:

Solihull	Waltham Forest
Tameside	Wandsworth
Wirral	Barnet
Calderdale	Camden
Cornwall	Hackney
Hereford and Worcester	Hillingdon
Lincolnshire	Harrow
Southwark	Hounslow

A weak sample because it was small, because it contained so many rural areas (Cornwall, Hereford and Worcester, Lincolnshire) and because the big cities (except for parts of some London Boroughs) were absent. So even if they knew the extent, and even if they were prepared to stick their necks out, they could only come out on the lower-than-reality side. Their average estimate was that compared to their number of registered minders, they expected to find another 86 per cent unregistered minders in their streets and villages. If, for a moment, we let that figure stand across England and Wales, it could imply a further 85,000 children with unknown and unregistered minders.

If we look back over the hard and often surprising trail of the earlier chapters, the miniatures tell their own story. We learned to know two inner-city wards thoroughly. And knew where every child under five was. In these poorer working-class areas it was rarely with gran or auntie — for all that had been broken down. Nor was it with nursery nurse or nursery teacher — for such provision was tiny or invisible. It was with a childminder, and usually an unregistered one. In one section of the Huddersfield ward there were twenty-one minders, all unregistered. In Old Trafford, there were twenty-six minders — and twenty-four were unregistered. The cornflake kids and the day-nursery eternal waiting lists all led back to unregistered minders.

Two other small pieces of research prompted by this project tend to confirm this. From Dawnwatch onwards we had seen childminding as being very much a question of small children in busy cities. It was not until early 1976 that we had the opportunity to look at one of Britain's new towns. This was Telford, a vast new city, planned out of the industrial dereliction of the pioneer towns that made the modern age, including Ironbridge itself, and then the miles and miles of wet cow pastures that spread away from what Shropshire people call neither a hill nor a mount but The Wrekin. Telford strove towards a new population of a quarter of a million by 1990. It had to attract young couples seeking new opportunities. Inevitably it was to be a city of children. Yet of children whose parents (all this would apply equally in New Zealand or in any other society substantially built on migrants) must both seek work to achieve their common desires. Day nurseries were lacking, and when present were not educational and very inflexible. Where did all the children go? The old question found again the old answer. Three per cent of children between three and five were in full- or part-time nursery education, but 28 per cent were with registered childminders. Local officials estimated that illegal childminders would double this number — and then there was the question of children under three. It was clear that the great and possibly crucial weakness in this future-looking city of children was overlooking the early years of its fresh generations of small children with working parents.[14]

Nor originally had we thought of childminding in the countryside. This only came home to me when, after giving a seminar on the research so far at the National Children's Bureau, a rural social worker who had travelled from Suffolk to join in invited me to look at the kind of large modern farm that now dominated the county.

'There have to be women to help with the seasonal spring, summer and autumn trade. So they just bring their children along early in the morning, and make a metal pen out of the moveable cattle fences, give them a few toys and that's that. If it rains, it's easy to switch it all to one of the sheds. Is that childminding?'

And indeed we had forgotten that the farm is a factory. One group who responded to the 'open' style of this research was the Research Unit of the Social Services Department of

Cornwall — another rural county.[15] They conducted a simple, systematic but illuminating calculation. In their selected area there were 1,500 children under five with mothers out at work. Only twenty-four of these were in day-nursery places. Not many more were with registered minders (only thirty in Camborne and Redruth). Social workers reported that many of the minders themselves worked evening shifts after a day minding, and that the extended family — aunty, gran and uncle — as substitute parents simply did not exist on the scale that television or social planners imagined. Where then were all the other children? Again, all the contacts, indications, experience and logic suggested that in a rural area like this, there must be considerable numbers of unregistered child-minders. And as an appendix to these calculations, we must remember that many of the childminders presented in the previous chapters do not only look after pre-school children but sometimes for long hours the after-school child too. Minded child blurs into latchkey child.

If areas like these are at all typical then after the family the major day-care service for the poor is not only child-minding, but illegal childminding. National numbers are impossible to state with certainty, but it is just possible to make a reasonable estimate.

We can say, at the moment of writing, that there are between 820,000 and 1,250,000 children under five in England and Wales alone who have a mother out at work. Maybe a quarter to a fifth of these live in the poorest districts. We simply cannot account for the day care of the majority of these 250,000 — 310,000 children except by substantial numbers of unregistered minders. And this is exactly what our eyes, ears and trampings of the streets have told us ever since Dawnwatch. It would be surprising if the figure we were talking about on this measurement — unregistered child-minding in the poorest districts — was less than 100,000.

So we are left with a sum. Up to 100,000 children registered with minders. Perhaps 50,000 West Indian children out with minders, mostly unregistered: a declining figure. A calculation that if all authorities were as positive as the best, then we should expect another 100,000 children to emerge who are today with illegal minders. A frank request answered by sixteen local authorities suggesting a further 86,000 children in unknown care, and with the probability that this is on the low side. And lastly, a speculative enlargement of our own micro-research, which would again lead to 100,000 children with unregistered minders.

Further evidence lies in the penumbra of childminders awaiting registration. Their scale depends entirely on the positive attitude of a local authority. A good example of an authority in 1975 which tried to be helpful to childminders was Wandsworth. It had 308 on its books, and a further 221 awaiting registration — in other words 70 per cent more minders were formally known and willing, leaving aside the unknowns and the unwillings.

Many of these numbers must overlap, sometimes considerably so. But using them to take bearings we could probably say that 200,000 children today are with childminders and that 100,000 of these children are unknown to any caring authority other than the parent and the minder. Possibly the real figure is around 330,000 but it is not easy to see how that can be firmly established, and the conservative minimum here is large enough.

The main feature is that childminders (registered and unregistered) offer full day care to far, far more children than any other agency except the family itself. Nursery schools, playgroups or infant classes do not by their very hours cater for the child of a working parent (though sometimes attendance at them can be combined with spending the rest of the day with a minder). State day nurseries serve around 25,000 children (1974) and there is — not surprisingly in all this — a mushrooming of private kindergartens or factory crèches at least in times of full employment. But in terms of scale alone, we now discover childminders to be (outside the family) the biggest part of the pre-school jigsaw; and for the poorest, often the only part that matters.

Babies and toddlers

Apart from their numbers, another characteristic of childminders now emerges. They may look after six-week-old babies or top up with nine-year-olds waiting after school until mum's shift finishes. The child who died upstairs at Mrs Jolly's was six weeks old, and almost any teatime at Mrs Owen's you can see up to ten school-age children joining the toddlers for two or three hours.

As the research progressed, we became aware of how especially important childminders are for the care of babies and children under two. The reason of course is that no one else will readily take a child as young as this. Most pre-school services are really for toilet-trained children between the ages of three and five. It is also not every mother who leaves a child as young as this. Often in this research we have seen it to be the poorest who are forced back most speedily to work. No one knows how many very young children are involved. The earlier medical studies of childminding arose because the hospitals were following up recent births or helping patients with babies. The survey by the Office of Population Censuses and Surveys,[16] partly prompted by the earlier published findings of our research looked at a sample of children which included 898 under the age of twenty-four months. Of the small proportion who said their child was in day care, half were with registered minders. All the signs tend to confirm our observation, that childminders have a specially influential role with very small children — and that most of those children tend to be the small sons and daughters of the poorest.

A child's day

A third feature to emerge and be analysed is that child-minders may look after a child for very long hours and — for good or bad — have more prolonged contact with it than its own parents and certainly far more than any future school-teacher. Naturally some children are only with a minder for relatively short periods. The Office of Population Censuses and Surveys report just mentioned finds that 20 per cent of the children under five on its sample had a mother who worked less than 30 hours a week, whereas a further 6 per cent had one who worked 30 hours or more. Clearly in global terms this is very much a minority. But there are two errors very commonly made in interpreting these figures. First of all — and this has been the drift of our previous analyses — there are two groups of mothers of small children who tend to work very long hours. There is a small number of professional women (in medicine, in the media, and so on). There is a much larger number of poor or unsupported mothers. For example, our survey of Fartown — a working-class district — revealed that 36·5 per cent of mothers with children under five were out at work, and that half of these were on fulltime day shift, and almost 12 per cent on night shift. We also saw how the longest hours were worked by black mothers. The average for Asian mothers was 9·4 hours a day, and night shifts (though only four days a week) could be much longer — 10 to 12 hours. The *shortest* working day we found for an Asian mother in Fartown was 8·5 hours. Thus it may well be that the child of the poorest parents, growing up under many stresses, is precisely the one who is left for the longest hours in the care of a childminder.

The second error is to think that the hours that mum works are the same as the hours that the child is left. Not so. Go back to Dawnwatch. Some of the mothers on the streets there (many of whom we came to know closely) had to clock on at the factory by 7.15 a.m. or 7.30 a.m. They dared not and could not be late. Four minutes late loses fifteen minutes' pay. And a possible reduction of your chances when it came either to redundancies or overtime. That is why we so often saw hurrying mothers dragging small children through dark streets. To get to work for some of them meant first a bus journey to the city centre, and then sometimes a second bus trip to the works. Allow up to an hour for that, especially with the bus stop waits. Before then they had to deliver a sleepy child to his minder. With our then innocent eye we noticed how often on these early morning child-exchanges few or no words were spoken. Everyone was tired, hurried.

You may be lucky, and your childminder is only two streets along. But as those Dawnwatch trails suggested, many people have to look much further away. Allow five to ten minutes for this. Beforehand you have to wake a small child who does not want to be wakened, dress a small child who does not want to be dressed, try to feed a small child who does not want to be fed, and put on an overcoat, shoes and gloves on a small child who does not want to tramp the dark bleak early morning streets. Think of all this in a child's time-table, and it can be — as we saw so often — that a mother clocking on at 7.15 a.m. meant a reluctant child being woken up at 5.15 a.m.

And when evening comes, the same pattern unwinds itself in reverse. Except that it is not uncommon for a mother who has had a hard monotonous day in a factory to take a break before picking up her child, call for a coffee, a shop, a few minutes at the club. In the end it means collecting an exhaus-ted child, the bedtime struggle, and the toddler straight to bed at 7 or 8 o'clock.

Of course, this may be towards one extreme. I can only say that it is an extreme which we found common amongst the poorest. But the same logic works when mother works part-time or is not under quite the same pressure as the Dawnwatch mums. Getting a child ready, going to a minder, setting off to work, taking a break on the journey back, or fitting in some essential task (like buying supper) all mean that the child's day and the mother's hours of employment are quite separate statistics.

There are many points to develop from this. Not least whether a mother should be in this position at all. But per-haps the most immediate one here is to note the huge disad-vantage at which such a child can be. The true price of the mother's labour can be the educational future of her child. Against that stands the sometimes frail hope that the long hours with a childminder could be transmuted into a strong influence for good.

Footing the bill

There is no reason why services for the poorest should be services which are the cheapest. It can also be true that some of the richest services are those which the community itself provides at very little cost.

Our research throws up this dilemma. Let us begin by con-sidering the cost of traditional day care, and who bears it. As we now see, a parent — without an extended family ready at hand and able to look after the child as part of the complex transactions of kinship, has three possible choices. First is a state day nursery. Second is an all-day company crèche. Third is a childminder, registered or unregistered. These are the triple anchors. Some of these arrangements may be combined with some time in a playgroup or a nursery school or an infant class or a self-help mother and toddler group or with a relative. But without one of the three originals it is impossible to leave the child, and earn.

Consider the cost of each. A day nursery has three main costs — the cost of the buildings, the cost of training and paying the staff, and the cost of running the place.

In 1975 the cost of building one day-nursery school place for a child was £3,000 and rising fast. To plan for a hundred children meant on average an initial £300,000 at those prices. The strength, of course, is that the buldings exist, and can be used for many children.[17]

Second, the staff have to be professionally trained. This is normally a two-year course at a direct cost of around £2,000. To avoid too much complexity we must discount the capital and running costs of the buildings in which this must take place — or we get lost in a hall of ever-reflecting financial mirrors.

At the same moment the annual running cost for each single child was £700. Or £70,000 for a hundred children. Of course, compared to the cost of educating university students this is very small beer. The older a child is, the more successful a child is, the more the citizenry spend on him. It is an absurd logic. But it belongs to another argument. Here we need only note day-nursery costs as our attained bench mark in this forgotten but decisive educational field.

Such is the cost of state day care. Next consider private enterprise. Many mills, factories and huge international corporations realize that to attract young mothers into their workforce then they must move in — where the state is absent — and build an all-day crèche for the child. If we look at other industrially ambitious societies as culturally diverse as China, Israel and the Soviet Union, we can see that the state itself has favoured and begotten considerable day care on industrial (or intensive agrarian) sites.

Great Britain is very much lost in the middle ground. Small state provision, and yet small encouragement towards free enterprise to create an attractive alternative. The best inform- ation we have on the scale and cost of private industrial provision is an overall survey of twenty-eight such ventures (out of the then total of eighty-one).[18] On the whole it seems that industry tends to use spare parts of the plant for a crèche, to be willing to subsidize such a service and not be too sure about the real costs, and lastly to accept a lower staff-to-child ratio than we usually meet in a day nursery. Consequently the cost of an industrial nursery is much lower. By using company building, company equipment, company workforce, it looked as if the initial capital cost of providing for a hundred children could be cut to around £100,000. There is still the same cost of drawing on qualified teachers from the state area (our earlier figure of £2,000 direct train- ing costs again). Running costs again tend to be lower. Some as far down as £150 a place, others nearer £600 a place each year. The reason may partly be the willingness of companies to subsidize the service (several in the sample put in an extra £8,000 a year to support between 25 and 72 chldren). Or their readiness to tolerate these lower ratios of adult to child. For example, one employer who insisted on reaching the equivalent ratio to a state day nursery found that it cost him £800 per year for each child.

So we can see that private enterprise, by imaginative use of existing resources, can provide a similar service at a lower cost, though with a real risk of a drop in quality.

Now compare the childminder. The capital cost is nil. She uses her own house. Perhaps she has to buy a new stairgate, fireguard, or fit in a lamp. This may be a big dip in her purse, but in this financial comparison it is trivial.

Second, she has had no training for the job. This is entirely wrong, but the very best training and back-up service that we have yet seen amounts to no more than £7 per child per year.

Third, there are running costs. Support and services for the childminder. The government has suggested that these may vary from £2.50 a year in an area which offers little back-up service to £20-£34 a year in an authority which does

Table 10.2 Comparing the costs of three main forms of day care for small children

	Setting up for 100 children	Staff training per single teacher	Annual running cost per single child
State day nursery	£300,000[a]	£2,000 per person[b]	£700
Company day nursery	£100,000[c]	£2,000 per person[b]	£200—£800[d]
Childminder	Nil[e]	0—50p[f]	£48[g]

(This table excludes direct charges to the parent and leaves out private day nurseries for which comparable figures are not available — but likely to lie near the range for company day nurseries)

a excluding loan charges.
b excluding cost of training college and tutors.
c excluding company provision of plant, equipment, conversion costs.
d assuming lower staff ratio or company subsidy.
e excluding occasional need for stairgate, new power point, fireguard.
f most authorities offer nothing. Birmingham is taken as an example of a 50p authority backing childminder in service training.
g can rise to £20—34 in the most positive areas. Normal situation though is £2.50.

all it can to aid childminders (courses, toy libraries, loans of equipment). According to the last survey of local authority support only 5 per cent did offer anything like strong support.[19] At that time an average of £4 annual running costs per child could only be queried as on the generous side. Table 10.2 shows how the figures stand. If we compare those figures – even if we disagree about details – the first conclusion is glaringly obvious. Childminding is cheap. It directly costs society very little indeed.

But there is a private cost – the one paid by the parent.

Four forms of day care

Table 10.3 Average costs to a parent earning £20 a week (1975) with one small child

State day nursery	£4.50
Company day nursery	£3 – £4.50
Private day nursery	£5 – £10
Childminder	£3 – £6

Obviously these costs will rise – have risen – year by year. But they will tend to march in step. The personal charges are roughly of the same order, except that our research suggests that the poorer you are, then the more likely you are *not* to get a state nursery place and *not* to get a company-subsidized chance. Both are so small in scale. You are going to end up by paying a childminder – and our experience is that the poorer pay least and get the weakest service for their child, and that the better-off (like ourselves) pay a little more and get excellent service.

The question of quality trembles precariously in a narrow financial band. A personal pound or two tossed in here, or saved up there reflects major differences of quality for one child. Ten thousand pounds of public money per child added to conventional day care insures against the worst (excluding the institutional) but does not guarantee the best.

Clearly the financial equations and priorities are not only

wobbly but wrong. But whatever the details, a strength of childminding is that to improve this service very considerably costs relatively little public money. It may also mean the parent meeting a higher personal charge — unless this is the point at which any available state support should be switched.

Serving the poorest

We kept records of the occupation of parents who left their child with a minder. And while it is difficult to obtain strictly comparable data drawing on groups from this place and that, the overall pattern was both very clear and in line with common sense.

Some childminders (usually very good ones) took the children of professional parents. These were registered minders who lived in fairly prosperous districts. Maureen Williams ('I'm booked up for the next four years') in 'Portrait gallery' is such a one. She buys excellent toys ('cheaper in the long run'), takes the children out in her own car, gives them the run of a paddling pool in summer ('I just strip them off'), uses children's television very selectively, and has a clear plan for every day. Indeed she is quite confident that the quality of the service she offers is superior to that of a playgroup, if only because she can concentrate full-time on three small children.

We constantly unlocked this cameo behind the wrought-iron gates in leafy suburban avenues — Edgerton in Huddersfield, Didsbury in Manchester, Henleaze in Bristol. As rising costs put even the au pair girl beyond the reach of all but the most affluent families, childminders are increasingly used by middle-class mothers.[20] This must be good. Services reserved for the poor are invariably inferior. It is no accident, for example, that the English primary school became the envy of the world at just that time when middle-class parents began to abandon their exclusive dependence on private education. The childminders who serve professional families are often professionals themselves — teachers or nursery nurses keeping their hand in while they bring up their own toddlers. Though, formally part of the same system, they are a different species from most of the minders we met in 'Portrait gallery', and as we noted there, usually operating on quite a different scale of charges. Registered childminders in prosperous streets are only a minor part of the jigsaw (unregistered childminders are as rare as the Great Northern Diver in such spots). The total number of women going out to work as doctors, architects, civil servants, social workers is far less than that of women (living in quite different streets) who are tied to semi-skilled or unskilled jobs.

There is also of course a large workforce of skilled women, not attaining the professions but certainly not on those production lines with the mothers of the 'cornflake kids'. Often they, too, turn to a childminder. But our observation is that this is a group which —when it works — works part-time, and is able to give such a high priority to the young child that if work conflicts with the toddler's happiness, then work is abandoned. Such mothers make highly intelligent use of nursery schools, playgroups, mother and toddler sessions. And indeed usually take the lead in many of these: the very encouraging rise of the pre-school playgroup movement is largely their achievement, and that of imaginative and educated mothers who do not need to go out to work but have time and energy to spare. Childminders do appear in this world, but often part-time, or combined with other forms of provision (including mum down the road) or frankly as emergency stop-gaps.

Overwhelmingly, childminders serve the poorer groups in society. The families who look to them are first of all ones in which the man earns a low wage, and when the woman of necessity works too, take-home pay still remains relatively modest. All this reflects a poor educational background, and a lack of those skills which the prevailing market will buy. Close to this you also find families who do indeed have formal employment skills, but who are desperately trying to achieve a higher standard of living or a new social status. This probably locates the main group of clients. But there are two subgroups, which are in many ways part of the main and yet special to themselves. One is in migrant families — from the West Indies, West Africa, the Indian subcontinent — fighting to establish a beach-head in the host society, and prepared or compelled to transmute family patterns of child caring to do so. These families — picked out by the colour of their skin — were clearly there in the origins of this research. We see them on the streets of Dawnwatch, meet their children in our pilot probes in Birmingham or Liverpool. They were part of the spectrum of the inner city, but struggled against extra hazards — discrimination and the often utter cultural indifference to how best to rear a small child. But larger, more intractable, and rapidly overlapping were children in one-parent families.

Add all this up, and it now becomes clear that one element of childminding — for good or ill — is that it is a service on the whole forged for the poor by the poorer. If it is done badly then the chances must be that the child inherits the problems of the parents. If it is done well, the odds must be in favour of helping to break — if it exists — any recurring cycle of deprivation. Analysis now shows that the probability is that instead of the normal social middle game in which one strives awkwardly and doubtfully to improve the common lot, just a little, childminding presents much more the win-or-lose challenge of a one-armed bandit. And unless one really thinks and works at it, the long-term odds must always be against it.

Five finger exercise

Take all five points together. If only as an elementary exercise. Childminders care for more children all day than all other comparable forms of provision totalled up. Then childminders care for much younger children than any one else outside the family — they supremely illustrate the ancient and modern wisdom that the essential educational influence usually makes its mark in those critical learning years between babyhood and school. Any school teacher might envy their daily length and potential intensity of contact at such a hopeful moment. We see that costs are relatively low, and borne by the parent. Only a slight pull of the social levers might multiply (or, alas, begin) support — with a good chance of qualitative change.

We have moved a long way from dingy back rooms and dank morning streets. As the landscape has cleared, the unknown childminder — now or in futurity — becomes a more and more central figure in education.

The *potential* influence of a childminder — either negative or positive — clearly raises the question of whether very poor early care (of the kind we originally saw in Birmingham) produces irreversible limitations to growth. Of course that isn't so. There are several — if too sparse — reports on small children reared in even worse conditions than the most severe examples that are touched on in this study. Wayne Dennis in *Children of the Creche* reports small children in the Lebanon left in bleak, deadening crèches who by the age of twelve had an average IQ of 54. On the other hand when some of the children were adopted and brought up in a more sympathetic and stimulating ambience, they recorded IQ scores of 85. And those pulled out of these conditions at two (a nodal age in childminding) showed IQ scores of 96. There are other examples of children removed from destructive environments amongst very impoverished societies in Africa, or Central and South America. And one could consider, as an extreme, the situation in modern society of 'wolf children' small boys and girls brought up in atmospheres of total rejection and incredible lack of responsibility (like being locked in the hen coop or attic for their first years).

Yes, a lot is still — almost miraculously — salvageable. But one could easily be misled by the optimistic and frequently quoted strain in this kind of evidence.[21] Two human calculations must be remembered. First, though children are often surprisingly resilient, and catch up much lost ground, they hardly ever reach the normal level of achievement and fulfilment. And second, there is quite as much evidence to show the enlargement of growth that can be achieved by early, intense and systematic attention. Whether or not we accept the notion of IQs, childminders *could* lift them far above expected levels. If one pauses to think the question out, there is little doubt of the decisive potential of bad or good childminders — whether or not the succeeding world treats the child ill, agreeably or with excellence.

Childminders as necessary agents in any industrial society

Before considering what might be done to unlock the potential of the childminding system, it is worth standing back and considering how this is not only a challenge in the backstreets of Huddersfield – but an inevitable dilemma in any industrial society – in cultural worlds as otherwise different as Japan, the United States, Rumania or New Zealand.

In an industrial society women will be drawn into the workforce in such increasing numbers as that economy can stand. The ancestors of some of the 'cornflake kids' were pale mothers dragging coal trucks for twelve hours a day, three thousand feet under ground. Perhaps their future sisters will have more rewarding jobs. But whenever an industrial economy expands there will be this pull – a pull of mothers into work and away from a young child, and there is also a push: women searching for relief from child and home, women seeking a materially higher standard of living, women expressing a *need* to work or asserting in practice a *right* to work.

At the same time the requirements of the child left behind may only be met reluctantly and partially by society. There will always be those who feel it is wrong for a mother to leave her young. Others who believe that the family should and could cope with such an aberration. Nor is the working mother of a small child usually in a strong political position to claim resources for day care. As for the child, he has neither voice nor vote.

It is always difficult to draw and compare data from differing societies. As an outsider one cannot be sure that the information is complete. Information from embassies, or statements by governments often presents a shop-window view – as you see if you read overseas accounts of social provision in your own country. And then there are considerable cultural traditions. The French – ever realistic – have a history of accepting working mothers as a fact; next door in Holland, the Dutch most certainly have not. British policy towards them is criss-crossed with guilt – should they be helped or driven back to the domestic hearth? Czechoslovakia and Hungary have broken new ground by modestly paying the mother of a child under three to stay at home – and paradoxically discover and accept that more and more mothers (especially the better educated ones) choose to work. Australia and New Zealand take a pioneer view of a family setting up house and largely turn a blind eye to the dilemmas of day care, though in my experience it is a most serious problem in cities like Melbourne and Auckland. Japan sees day care as very much a paternal responsibility of industry. The United States veers from a free-market solution — selling day-nursery franchises to people anxious to make quick profits — to colossal welfare programmes (Title IV-A of the Social Security Act apparently provided for 300,000 'child care years'). The Soviet Union, aiming to nurture a collective ethic, aims as far as it can to separate child from mother during large parts of early life, as in different, though often oddly similar ways, do Israel or China.

It is also technically very difficult to compare pre-school provision across boundaries. In Britain, children start school at five (and if there is room, they may begin earlier). But in Sweden or the Soviet Union school begins at seven. And in France, West Germany and most European countries it is six. So the very definition of 'pre-school' is different. The plethora of pre-school provision can be very confusing. In Italy or Holland it is dominated by churches. In Britain a nursery-school place may only imply three hours attendance a day; in Belgium the school may be open from 8.30 a.m. until after 4 o'clock. The names and formats of different types of provision (from One o'Clock Clubs to Écoles Maternelles) are endlessly baffling. Even our old friend the childminder is hard to pin down under her varying names: day care mother in New York; 'upbringer' in Leningrad; 'day mama' in Oslo; gardienne in Brussels. The boundaries between childminder, foster parent, or nursery-school para-professional continually blur.

Yet even allowing for all these dilemmas. I think we can establish three universal points. The first is that in every industrial society more and more women (including mothers of small children) both work and seek to work. In Britain, between the censuses of 1961 and 1971 the number of mothers going out to work with children under five rose by over 60 per cent. In the United States one in every seven women with a pre-school child was out at work in 1954. By 1960 it had risen to one in five, and by 1970 it was nearly one in three. It is not easy to obtain figures for every society, but the same trend is recorded in Sweden (startlingly), Italy (modestly), Austria (probably), Australia, Switzerland, Holland, Belgium, New Zealand, Canada, France. Of course the figures sometimes reach plateaux (I only know of two: the Irish Republic and West Germany) and they may be throttled back by economic recession. But even when the wind blows chill, it is no longer as mechanical as it was to eject women from the workforce. They are increasingly reluctant to see themselves as expendable, second-class labour, and most of these societies now have equal employment rights and safeguards in law. All the evidence, too, is that had they the opportunity (a reasonable job and adequate day care for their child) then many more women would move in to work, and many part-timers would seek full-time employment.

The fact that so many women work part-time can be used in this dialogue to argue that full day care is not desired all that much. I think this is to misunderstand. That women in large numbers work part-time, whereas men seldom do, directly records the problems women face in seeking employment. The Office of Population Censuses and Surveys in *Low Cost Day Provision for the Under Fives* (DHSS and DES, 1976) reveals on inspection that one in five mothers with a baby under one year desired day care, and that nine in ten mothers with a child of four wanted it. This was precisely our experience.

The second universal is that pre-school provision does not match present need nor future aspiration. All industrial societies record quite high rates of part-time provision for children aged between three and six. For five-year-olds, Britain scores 100 per cent, as do France, West Germany and Belgium, with Holland at 94 per cent. Other similar nations may not always equal those figures, but they cluster very closely. With four-year-olds, the figures are still high (if we accept this part-time element, which is usually not, as we have seen, relevant to a working mother). Belgium maintains a figure in the nineties, France one in the eighties, West Germany begins to droop and lies in the thirties. At the age of

197

three, Belgium has dropped to the eighties, France to the fifties – and Britain is down to 4 per cent, whilst Sweden is at 2 per cent.

Here lies another threshold. Under three there is little day-care provision in any society. The onus is on mother staying at home and then of the extended family coping with her absence. The Soviet Union offers some nursery provision to 10 per cent of children under two, Britain to 6 per cent (mostly childminders) and thereafter in all societies the figures fade away. Right across the board, pre-school provision has come to mean part-time education for children between three and six, an extension of the school system downwards.

The third universal is that the first two do not add up. There is a present and rising demand for day care for young children. There is small provision to meet it. What provision there is tends to be for the older children (and then usually part-time) and not so planned or so flexible as to meet the requests of a working mother. It is into this gap that child-minders wander.

Take the United States: 'over 91 per cent of all day care services take place in private homes'.[22] Yet at that date only 140,000 places are licensed with childminders. Meanwhile, 4,200,000 mothers with children under six were in the work-force.[23] Are all the rest with husband or grannie round the corner? It sounds too like the trail we have followed in Britain: a trail which led one right athwart conventional wisdom. An estimate based on direct interviews by the National Council of Jewish Women places the daily number of children with minders not at 140,000 but at 2,000,000.[24]

One sees much the same laws at work in a tiny country like Belgium. With the older age-groups (three to five) there is, as we have seen, comparatively generous provision – over 90 per cent attend some kind of nursery school, but for children under the age of three there are only 12,000 childminders. Even here, with one of the best examples we can put forward, the gap between service and demands rapidly widens for the very young child of a full-time working mother.[25]

Childminding is not some pocket of Victoriana preserved in old inner-city streets of Britain. It is a universal and necessary consequence of the way we live now.

11 On refusing to write a conclusion

> I knew a wise man that had it for a by-word, when he
> saw men hasten to a conclusion, 'Stay a little, that we
> may make an end the sooner.　　　　　Francis Bacon,
> *Of Dispatch*

So now we have a new question. And to raise childminding is
to ask a question rooted in working-class experience, when
the great international debate on pre-school education has
been implicitly and perhaps inevitably bred by middle-class
needs and perceptions. It has been dominated in state terms
by kindergarten provision for older children, with all the
buildings, and professions that requires; or in voluntary ways
by part-time playgroups. That particular source of change
lies in the child-rearing patterns and desires of the more prosperous — they are the social capital on which it draws. To
start a playgroup, for example, you normally move from a
background of education, free time, opportunity, the support
of people like yourself, a child-centred perception of early
schooling, the social and residential position and skills to
claim the needed resources (persuading the vicar to let you
have the church hall).

Not so with a childminder. As we have seen, childminders
are isolated, do not usually have strong formal educational
backgrounds, have no free time or extra resources, live in
districts which don't bristle with opportunities or encouragement, are unused to making their own claim, and may indeed
tend to have an authoritarian rather than child-centred sense
of early schooling — always supposing they accept (which
most in our surveys do not) that they are part of an education system as well as being part of a community mothering

network.

We have a question and we have a map. As the question is hard but crude, so the map is promising but sketchy. We must hope that further research refines both. And at this point it would be tempting to conclude our study with a series of recommendations.

Certainly it would have made for an easier life. But we decided to go one step further and, rather than simply print conclusions, to test them out in a series of pilot schemes. There were two reasons for this: first, an interest in 'open research', and second, one in 'action research'. The case for open research is noted in Chapter 1. We were determined from 'Dawnwatch' onwards to make our findings as widely known as possible, so as to stimulate action on childminding. Of course there are dangers in such open research too, but by and large it removes the *voyeur* element from research and helps attract resources to the communities under study. It also whets the appetite of the researcher to ask: what happens to conclusions in action?

And so one moves easily to action research. This means — where possible — setting up one of the conclusions in action and seeing how it works. That is what, with many colleagues, we then tried to do. Some succeeded, some failed, and many changed before your eyes once you applied evaluated action instead of pure research. To move one's own research thinking to its conclusions, however tentative, then to set up those conclusions in being — and then to evaluate *those*, is enormously to extend your research thinking even on so modest a question as this. All this is commonplace to agricultural scientists. You observe, assess, record, conclude on the phenomena in their habitats. You then create habitats suggested by your conclusions, and evaluate again. But alas, in social research we have often dropped off the bus long before that stop is reached.

That at least was the theory. But what was the action going to be like?

Part II

Seedtime

12 Research into action

A thought which does not result in an action is nothing much, and an action which does not proceed from a thought is nothing at all.   Georges Bernanos in
France before the World of Tomorrow, 1955

Other people talk about how to expand the destiny of mankind. I just want to talk about how to fix a motor-cycle.   Robert M. Pirsig, *Zen and the Art of Motorcycle Maintenance*, 1974

Black in Brixton

It was spring in Grantchester, and the apple blossom just about to burst the bud: all tight pink tips and not that petalled shower of white which would soon rain around us. We took honey and tea in the gardens behind the Red Lion. The honey, I noticed disapprovingly, came in plastic packets from Philadelphia. There was that pacific, springtime beauty about Cambridge which marvellously helps you analyse your work and ideas, and treacherously seduces you into believing that your plans can so easily be carried out.

A strange place to talk about childminding. But open research had brought a letter from the National Elfrida Rathbone Society. They were interested in putting one of the conclusions into action, and had raised funds to do so.[1] We knew little about the society except that it was concerned with (to use an ugly word) disadvantaged children. Under the apple trees we talked to Anne Evans, the society's emissary, about possibilities for action. Anne said the society would like to run the first training course for childminders. The ones most in need. Illegal West Indian ones — our original point of concern. Perhaps only ten, but done intensively. Show, hopefully, what startling changes could be made if one tried. Brixton was the place; one of the poorest and most tense migrant areas of London. The neglect and violence of the big-city ghetto seemed a long, long way away that day. Julia McGawley agreed to move from the Manchester research to observe and write up the experiment. Six months later we were to come down from Huddersfield, visit the minders again and record the lasting result. It was a brave experiment: no doubt of it. Cambridge lured us all, and it was tempting to retire to the University Library, write up the conclusions of our survey and from its long windows watch in turn crocus, daffodil, tulips and cherry blossom as the final pages fell into place on a note of untested optimism. But Brixton? it was hard to say yes, yet impossible to turn down this unlooked-for opportunity.

Well, we had something else to go on besides what we have reported so far. Sonia in Huddersfield and Julia in Manchester had asked childminders what *they* wanted. At the time none of the minders received anything except formal registration and expected little. Open questions ('what help would you like?') led nowhere. So we presented them with ten possibilities and asked them to choose. Most of the suggestions were novel to them.

We began by asking 43 minders on our Huddersfield sample. And then 26 on our Manchester sample. During the course of this we were approached by the Community Relations Commission who, concerned by the situation of the black community in our early research reports, adapted this part of our questionnaire and tried it on a sample 127 white minders, 20 Asian and 30 black in Leicester, Slough, Manchester and Lambeth.

In all three surveys clearly defined tools — safety and play equipment, cut-price food, the travelling toy library — were most welcomed. Whereas those which released the minder from the stove, sink, washing line and cooker in order to work full time with the children were most resisted. We encountered much outright opposition to links with playgroups. Partly this was a challenge to their own competence. Partly a cultural dislike of messy, play-based early education. But even more so, it was a new idea meeting initial resistance. It was the less tangible but most fundamental elements of raising the quality and educative nature of day care that clearly were likely to be most difficult. But we had at least the first sketch map of what childminders at this stage saw as their needs.

Into action in Brixton

It was at this level of knowledge that we observed the first course for illegal minders. Julia played a full part in running it with the society, but carefully set aside time to describe what happened as she saw it, as the organisers saw it, and as the childminders saw it.

A plan was drawn up to provide a course in basic child development for ten to twelve unregistered West Indian childminders. The course was to run for five weeks, from 10 a.m. until 3 p.m., four days a week. The minders were paid £12 a week for attending the course, with a 15p per day charge made for lunch. A playgroup for the minders' children was provided, together with a minibus service for collecting and taking them home. At the end of the course, the minders, who had attended throughout were given a certificate.

Finding the minders

A local community relations officer was asked to contact unregistered West Indian minders in the area and interest them in the idea of attending the course. This was difficult. The minders had to be found. This had to be done informally and delicately, and very much through the community network. Second, they had to be persuaded that it was in their interest, and in the interest of the children they minded that they attend the course.

It had been decided early on in the planning of the project that the minders should be offered payment for attending the course. This was a sensible and realistic decision. There can be little doubt that, initially at least, this incentive played a large part in recruiting the minders.

Ten minders, three of them registered, were contacted in this way. Of these seven subsequently attended the course.

When it became obvious that there would be spare places on the course, the social services department suggested the names of three of their registered minders who they felt would best benefit from a course of this nature. Between them the ten looked after nineteen children.

Before the course started, we visited the minders in their homes and went through a fairly detailed interview schedule with them. This was to obtain information on how they saw their role prior to attending the course. The course was held in a hut at the back of the Brixton Centre in Ferndale Road. This was as near perfect an arrangement as was possible. The hut contained a large, secure room ideal for the playgroup, with two smaller rooms attached.

The programme was as unstructured as possible. Everyone involved felt that a formal timetable and work structure would be daunting for the minders. A fair amount of emphasis was put on outside visits to playgroups, schools, etc. Two films were to be shown and visits planned by child development specialists, social services representatives, a fire prevention officer, etc.

Once the initial snags, the strangeness and uncertainties had been overcome, there was no doubt that the course was an immense success. The strongest feeling all of us took away was that the minders had enjoyed it. It had been a unique break in an otherwise isolated day-time world. The certificate ceremony on the final day was beautiful. As each minder received her certificate she gave her own little individual speech of thanks. There was a moving moment when Diane sang a song she'd composed especially for the occasion.

'Farewell to the course
And farewell to all our dear friends. . . .'

Lunch was magnificent — saltfish and goat's meat curry. The dancing went on and on. Everyone was reluctant to leave. But was there more to the course than enjoyment? As Rose said, as she was about to climb into the minibus for the last time:

'It was just too short. If only it was going on for a year. I've learned so much about children. I wish I could leave the housework and spend the rest of my life understanding children.'

Six months later

Six months after the course we revisited the ten childminders. Our desire to evaluate the course in the dimension of time was strongly based on our readings of sociologists who had monitored the much more massive social intervention programmes in America — such as Headstart. We guessed that the most immediate result of our open research would be that an increasing number of local authorities and voluntary bodies would see courses for childminders as the 'solution'. This is exactly what happened. Almost every course for childminders that has stemmed from our ongoing work has been felt as a great success — by the media by the course organizers, by their directors of social services, by the tutors, and by the childminders on the course. Indeed to join in with this early innovative work has often been an immediate springboard for professional promotion for all concerned.

But can radical change be that easy? Courses for childminders *are* an excellent and necessary step. But remembering the American experience, not in childminding, but in other attempts to improve pre-school learning, we had some doubts about a policy likely to be carried out by social workers, poorly informed about the previous and very considerable educational and sociological knowledge that has been so bitterly won.

The simplest way of thinking out this doubt was to take the National Elfrida Rathbone Society's adventurous and well-endowed course, and by interview, observation, and scale assessment try to see whether the children in the care of those ten course members were better off or not, and why.

First of all, with each minder we conducted an interview

207

either before or (with last-minute joiners) at the very beginning of the course. This recorded something at least of their
attitudes to their profession, and gave the facts on how long
they had been minding, what children they had, what provision they offered. We had also used our Childminders Checklist as a small, but hopefully objective, scale test. This list,
being the first of its kind, is naturally vulnerable and open to
improvement through experience. But it has the virtues of
relative objectivity, and of comparability, not only between
one childminder and another — but between the same childminder past and present. The checklist gives the minder a
score on two counts — the physical conditions she offers the
child (Is the room safe? Is there space to play?) and the
quality of care she presents (Does she talk to the child? Is the
child washed or taken out?). Wherever possible the checklist
is filled in with the minder present so that it is an open and
possibly educational dialogue, and not just a private research
screening.

This draws us our base line. Then we have the immediate
account of the course which gives us the experience that
everyone concerned had, took away and reported. Now, six
months later, we repeat the interview, repeat the checklist
assessment, and then get far away from it all to record and
compare the differences as coolly as we can. If we can analyse those differences, however disappointing they may be,
then we can plan courses which — in time — may bring
fundamental changes in child care, and so in a child's chances
of an equal and full life.

Brixton

So it was back to tramping the kaleidoscopic backstreets of
Brixton to find again the course members.[2] A full account of
the follow-up visits to all ten childminders can be found in
our report to the Elfrida Rathbone Society, *Changing Childminders.*[3] Here we return to just two of them: Rose and
Sylvia.

Rose

Rose is 33 and comes from Dominica. She is badly lame in one leg, and pays a great deal of attention to her appearance. She is very beautiful and relaxes eagerly into talk of boyfriends and the eternal problem of how to meet more men. On the drier hangs a pair of knickers with the slogan 'I'm giving way' printed in scarlet across the front. She has two children at primary school and is unmarried.

Rose has been minding for five years. She is registered and glad to be so – 'I feel safer'. Before the course she minded four children for whom she charged either £3.50 or £4. She provides all food. She would like to put up the rates but doesn't know how to – and doesn't think the parents would agree.

> 'I like a lively child. Not like Denise there – she just sit and wet herself. I don't like children who mess in their pants – some just stand there and do it. I don't like them to scratch at each other, or pull the bedclothes off. But I don't smack them much. I don't hit people's kids, unless if their mother tells me I must give them a good slap on bottom. Then I do.'

Rose is serenely indifferent to the children around her. They sleep, squabble, cry. It is as if she doesn't notice or hear them. She lives on social security and doesn't declare her earnings from childminding (which indeed probably represent a net loss).

Rose thought the course was marvellous. Her certificate is framed in the front room next to her favourite painting of a long, naked white lady with golden hair. 'I see that picture for £1.90 in Brixton Market and I fall in love with that picture. She's a real person that, on TV – my friend tell me.'

Her only criticism was that there were too many black people. 'I'm a black, but when too many black, nothing goes right – black people criticize too much.'

After the course, she kept visiting three of the other minders for some months, but this was never easy since they were widely scattered, and eventually faded out. She had also joined the literacy class at Brixton College and very much enjoyed it. When the College decided to charge 15p for looking after children in the crèche, she stopped. For her this would have meant the impossible charge of 60p for every lesson she attended.

Rose is the only minder who tried to put some of the ideas of the course into action. First of all she gave the children scissors — she'd been surprised to see very small children using scissors in the playgroups they visited and in the course crèche. Unfortunately she only had huge wallpaper scissors, and nothing to cut up. Within minutes Bruno, who is four, snipped off two-year-old Marie's pigtail. When Marie's mother arrived, she went crazy and, after screaming at Rose, rang the police. The police came, tried to pour oil on troubled water, and rang the social services. The social services came (their only visit to Rose after the course) and advised her to keep scissors away from children. She never saw Marie again.

Next she tried giving the children paint. She only had ordinary house painting brushes and some half empty tins of domestic paint. The children simply splattered her kitchen walls, and that ended that. Lastly, she tried water play. She put the children in the bathroom, put in the plug, turned on the tap and left them. An hour later she noticed the water dripping through the ceiling: the children were wildly happy, the bathroom was awash. That ended her programme of experiment.

Six months later the minded children were confined to one boxroom where they listlessly slept on the bunk bed. There were no toys, no window they could see through. Outside it was a sunny afternoon, and Rose's children were in and out of the front door. The minded toddlers remained shut up and silent. I picked up and cuddled the baby.

Rose's scoring before and after the course was identical.

Sylvia

Sylvia is very good at making soft toys. Her front room is full of piggies, teddies, and Disneyland animals. She is unregistered and has been minding for five years. She has never had a white child. 'Maybe if I was a real Nanny, I would have one'. She hates Africans. 'Don't like, don't like — Africans *always* give trouble.' She herself is thirty-nine and born in Jamaica.

She minds two children. One, Martin, she took at three weeks. He is now four and has not yet spoken.'

'Martin, he's a dull boy. Not bright child, want more tender care, more looking after him. Mustn't be rough with Martin. Can't leave him alone — he goes silly. He don't talk or play about — more like a silly child.'

Sylvia casts a sleepy spell around her. She talks very slowly and lethargically, moves little and sleeps a lot during the day. The children she minds tend to sit still and doze all day. Even conducting the interview had a hypnotic, sedative effect on me. I began to nod.

Just as Martin is — at the very least — plainly autistic, so possibly Sylvia has some undiagnosed chemical condition inducing this extreme lethargy. Sylvia enjoyed the course, but slept through most of the morning sessions. Her husband works as a motor mechanic in New Jersey, and comes home once a year. Sylvia only comes to life when she speaks of his visits, and that, of course, could be her root problem.

The highlight of the course for her (as for so many) was the visit to a school for handicapped children ('I was so frightened by them dumb children, and the children with no arms — we hardly know so many children like that around'). Her only complaint was that the children were allowed to come into the discussion room for cuddles: 'If we learn something we don't want no children there.' Otherwise for her the course has slipped into oblivion. No one has visited her since.

Six months later Martin still does not talk. In twelve months he will be starting school. There was no difference between Sylvia's scores before and after the course. This was the story, with variations, at every course member we revisited.

It may seem a little unfair to take this pioneering course for such brutal evaluation. But if courses for childminders are ever to succeed we need to know what are the principles that make for success. The Brixton course was planned far more

211

carefully than almost all local authority courses to date, and probably most in the future. It had an array of tutors and visiting specialists which hardly any authority can realistically hope to repeat. It had the minders attending full-time, for four days a week, for five weeks in succession — an intensity of teaching not easy to replicate. It had the financial resources to pay the minders a salary for learning. And at the end of the course it was clearly felt by most people to have been a considerable success.

Yet assessing the minders on our checklist scale as they were before the course and then six months later, we get this result, abstracted from the basic data profiles.

Table 12.1 Assessment results from the Brixton course

| | Physical conditions | | Quality of care | |
	Before course	After course	Before course	After course
Janet	7	7	6	6
Patti	5	5	6	6
Beryl	3	3	5½	5½
Dianne	6	6	5	5
Rose	3½	3½	1½	1½
Sylvia	4	4	2	2
Violet	4	4	½	½
May	6	6	3	3
Grace	3	3	5	5
Ella	7	7	9	9

Absolutely no change. Neither over a period of time, nor in one minder's service compared with another's. Whatever effects the course had were *short-term* — after that everything rapidly reverted to nature.

Is this stationary score a function of the checklist itself? Undoubtedly as the very first checklist in this field, it is a blunt instrument and not without self-fulfilling elements. Since then we have improved considerably on it. But allowing for this, if one searches back to the single points and half points that make up the 'before' and 'after' scores then two things are evident. First, we are scoring *physical* conditions (is there a garden or playspace, is the room safe or dangerous?). Nothing has changed those prevailing conditions. Second, we are scoring *cultural attitudes towards child-rearing* (does the minder reason or talk with children, are toys and books available and used?). And this, of course, is the tenaciously resistant cocoon defending parent, child and minder from the different and brief dynamic of the course.

Naturally, as the interviews show, the course did have some effects. It was a lively, interesting and happy experience at the time both for the minders and the children in the crèche. It heightened several of the minders' awareness of themselves as black people in a white world. It inspired Patti to ask for registration and to start literacy classes. It encouraged Janet to see if her children could play as she had seen others do in the nursery schools. For many it created new friendships, and an interest in improving their reading and writing. It helped some see how hopelessly uneconomic childminding was.

All these were real enough effects, but almost all had died out after six months for reasons of cost, distance, discouragement, lack of positive support. What principles can we then draw from this miniature analysis to help us create courses which *do* have a lasting effect and *do* interrupt the cycle of disadvantage? I would suggest there are three cardinal ones.

First, physical conditions
It is a very hard task to change people's values, attitudes or perspectives on children. It is far simpler to reduce danger and increase the possibilities for growth by changing the physical conditions under which children are minded. It is no use simply deploring bad working-class housing like the social worker who visited Patti and told her that her house was not fit to live in. No good presenting lectures on stairgates and paraffin heaters. No good expecting people who have minded children safely for years suddenly to instal or meet the cost of improvements which could help the child. It's a hopeless route to unreality and no change.

But there is no reason why a local authority, using existing

213

powers, should not fit those extra lights, lend that fireguard, fix up a stairgate or even knock down an internal wall. All these cost money, but they are small costs. And they are the only way of changing conditions. This kind of positive follow-up to the course would have created the primary level of change.

If, too, there had been an aggressive attempt to link the minder with parks, with playgroups, with nursery schools, then a whole new level of change is possible. Almost every minder here could have been so linked up if the transport problem had been met. Again a cost; again a very small cost. And we see how attention to the physical environment easily blurs into changes in the quality of care offered.

I put this *physical* question first because it is the simplest, and yet can have profound consequences. It is no good despairing at physical conditions. Whether we like it or not, these are the conditions under which huge numbers of children will live. Absurd, too, simply to talk about it, or expect a poor and doubtful minder to transform her flat overnight into a home far surpassing much richer ones. The answer clearly is to intervene, and offer to provide the desirable features — from stairgate to a minibus link with the nearest playgroup, nursery or park.

Second, educational principles
This careful and intensive course clearly faltered on educational grounds. Why? First it tried to do a lot in a little time, and apparently got nowhere. It used the 'crash course' approach. This works if (i) the student is highly motivated and (ii) the skill to be mastered is clearly seen by teacher and taught. Hence a 'crash course' approach succeeds well in, for example, learning Russian in a language laboratory for a business trip or learning to drive for a licence test. But with childminders the motivation is weak and dispersed and the skill sought is cloudy and undefined.

One rock on which the course foundered (and many, many others may) was the tenacious belief by the minders that though they may know very little about anything else under the moon and sun, the only thing they *did* know about was children. I think they were quite wrong, but the psychological and cultural problems to be solved before this kind of mutual learning and teaching is possible are profoundly difficult.

The only educational strategy that might work here is the 'drip, drip' approach. Two hours every Tuesday for a year would have got somewhere. And one has to accept, I think, that this very difficult learning situation requires that kind of generous space to make any effect.

The second rule that was broken was the attempt to use informal, eliciting, heuristic methods with a student body that had always seen learning in authoritarian terms. This is why the minders asked for *instruction* on cooking or illness. And this is likely to be the pattern of most courses. The tutors will believe in discussion and self-realization; the childminders will believe in fact, formal skills, instruction and authority. Ultimately, of course, the teachers are right: qualitative changes in child care are not to be imposed on, but developed out of, the minder. However, few minders will see it like that. And none did here.

It seems to me one has initially to go for authoritarian teaching in clear-cut areas (medical, diet, safety) whilst developing mutual learning groups alongside. In this case no vital trace remains in their memory or in their practice of the many seminars (often led by distinguished specialists) that they attended.

Third, the course presented a cultural collision

It was essentially asking the minders to reverse in five weeks everything they felt, perceived or believed about young children. There are many ways of arguing this point. You can say that their culture (which enfolds their attitude to children) is valid, and to be respected. Or you can say that better ways of rearing children are known, and so a change-carrying cultural dialogue is needed. On this course the minders were West Indian, but the same consideration always applies since the childminder, whatever his or her colour, is usually working-class; always part of a submerged, dominated and different culture.

If there was to be dialogue, then that at the very least means the minder has to be listened to, talked *with* not *at*, that the teacher has to be a learner too. That did not happen, nor is it usually likely to happen. But for the maximum improvement in the quality of child care, it must. Has the social worker with her LSE diploma nothing to learn from the poorly literate backstreet childminder? Surely it can't be so; growth is a varied and mutual activity.

If the minder is essentially being asked to make a huge cultural leap (as she normally is) then that will not ever succeed without two kinds of support. First, self-support. It was not a tutor but a minder who composed the song that celebrated the 'togetherness' of the course. Again and again the minders tried to keep in touch with each other after the course. But the huge distances of a big city, the lack of private transport, and the everyday fact of toddlers and babies to be cared for, were too much. If a change in cultural attitudes was desirable (as I think it often is) then the crucial step is to help a group of minders support and reinforce each other. The necessary consequence of a successful course for childminders must be some kind of autonomous childminders' group.

The second factor is of course the most obvious of all, and hardly needs arguing. If a minder is essentially being asked to rethink her accepted cultural perspectives (remembering always that her husband, parents and neighbours are not very likely to do any such thing) then she must have positive and consistent support.

That is exactly what these minders lacked. Had they been regularly visited, in a helpful way, had they felt the presence of support systems (like a travelling toy library or links with a playgroup), had they been provided with the tackle to do their job then the final scoreline of this course could have been utterly transformed.

A setback. It was not so straightforward as it had seemed under the apple blossom in Cambridge. But it had reminded me how illuminating it was to carry over into action research, test out and monitor, the recommendations that were emerging from our work. Time to try some more.[4]

13 A tale of four cities

cities of men
And manners, climates, councils, governments.
Alfred Tennyson, 'Ulysses'

Huddersfield

It was raining horizontally in Huddersfield that Tuesday morning. We were down by the neglected canal near Aspley basin, and looking at one of the very black and splendidly confident mills along Frith Street. Now abandoned, many windows broken, it had passed into the hands of the Polytechnic, who used it as a base for their carpenters. It was huge, but the small group of workmen had staked it all out in the way that people always spread to meet the space available. Piles of old chopped wood lay everywhere. Would it ever be used? Here and there tiny transistor radios were perched on beams like modern birds buzzing out streams of pop music. In the largest room (where the tea was brewed up) was a huge picture of a naked woman. She really was very beautiful. But over her private parts someone had pinned a small cardboard flap. It said, 'Do Not Raise this Flap'. Everybody did. Underneath was a blank square of white paper with the message, 'Curious, Aren't You?'

Could this be the first childminders' centre? The Polytechnic were willing. But were the carpenters? I doubted it. But possibly there were other places. Working with the educational priority team in Liverpool we'd come away with a keen sense that even the most overlooked parts of our old inner cities had an abundance of what you can only call Victorian cultural capital. However grim the streets now were, the terraced houses were overtopped by vast monumental schools, churches, factories, municipal offices, chapels and meeting houses. The Victorians had believed in the city. And they had bequeathed a great array of underused or forgotten buildings. Like this mill.

Surely one of them could become a childminders' centre. There was not only the poetry of justice in the notion (for the mills created the childminder, and the modern neglect of the working-class city sectors enlarged their numbers), but after the Brixton experiment it made good sense. Little would be achieved by hit-and-run raids, and indeed damage could be done. We needed a permanent centre radiating support and services.

Out into the cold, prickly rain again and along Frith Street into St Thomas Road. Last week had been a great disappointment. The education department had come up with a splendid building. A Victorian working men's institute, which had then served a little as a youth club and place for a playgroup. It was now empty. We'd planned to move in sharply on Monday morning. And then on the Friday the roof of the nearby Mount Pleasant nursery school was declared unsafe. The children had to be placed somewhere. On Monday morning too. The education department had no choice but to claim back the building at the thirteenth hour.

There were four of us out in the wet street: Barrie, who had recently run our splendid 'Education Shop' scheme in Butlin's holiday camps, and now all eager to see a children's centre set up, full of balloons, toys, stickers, play-ins; Hazel, who had come late into teaching from industry, and had all the extra drive and wider horizons that that so often gives; and Stuart, deputy director at the Polytechnic, who now remembered the bus sheds.

The bus sheds, I asked? This was going too far even for my theory of cultural detritus. Well yes, he explained, it could *just* be all right. Sheltering in the sheds I saw at once what he meant. The new Metropolitan transport system had inherited the old Huddersfield trolley-bus sheds. Alongside the great bays, full of the fresh cream-and-green diesels, were offices. But modern systems, machines and manning meant that far less staff were now needed, and half the office quarters were

used by the polytechnic as a spill-over place during examina-
tions and other crises.

Out of the wet, and with a chance to root the idea in
action, our excitement transformed those long lines of diesels
queuing to enter into streams of multi-coloured playbuses
bursting out towards all the childminders in Yorkshire.

Reality was, of course, much harder. First of all there was
the need to equip the centre. The first 'toys' we obtained
came from the local woollen mills. The huge bales of cloth
often arrive wound round brilliantly coloured plastic bobbins
— which in turn end up in the works wastebins. But they
make ideal playthings for toddlers, and those first bobbins
are even today in action as skittles, imaginary telescopes,
objects to roll, blow through, pile up, pattern. So an early
task was to establish a fully equipped playroom, and as big a
toy library as we could build. And we were determined not
to buy them, but draw them out of the community. We visited the local hospital for mental illness where many of the
patients had sessions weaving basketwork as part of their
therapy. They had splendidly equipped workrooms, and we
asked if they could make toys for real children. They could
come and deliver them at the centre if they liked and see how
they were used. If they weren't allowed out, we offered to
bring photographs of the children. We approached old people's
homes in the same way, suggesting not only practical toy
making, but asking them to look in too, and be grandma or
grandad for an hour. We tackled the schools where older
brothers and sisters of many of the children that concerned
us were taking lessons in woodwork, metalwork, or craft.
Again we asked if they could sometimes not only make toys
but design them — that not only might give us a bonus, but
help them think about the nature of play.

By broadcasting our needs around we always found families whose children had grown up and left behind them boxes
of toys. So we had a toy library which we could use as a tool.
It supported our central playgroups; parts of it could be
crated and then regularly exchanged if we wanted to set up
local groups of childminders; parts could be put in our minibus and used as a travelling toy library round minders' homes;
and it was always helpful when knocking on strange doors to

219

have a bag of toys. But building a toy library like this had other strengths. We were making transactions across the community that were to yield rich and often unsuspected harvests all round.

The centre too had to become a familiar and enticing place. We arranged for a large exhibition of children's paintings from local schools on the theme of living in a multi-racial society, to cover the walls. The delicate beauty of some of the Indian children's art, the great rhapsodic swirls of colour from West Indian children, the intricacy of Chinese work, the uproarious self-portraits or pictures of 'my class' transformed the walls. They also brought coachloads of school parties, perhaps a thousand children and their teachers in a fortnight. All this meant more familiarity, more contacts, more ideas for co-operation. We kept a visitor's book at the entrance.

And then we arranged a grand opening. The mayor in his gold chain, a gigantic release by children of a multi-coloured pile of balloons, lots of pictures of the children and minders on television and in the local papers. And then a continuous round of tea-and-pie lunch discussions for social workers and teachers, highly popular jumble sales, wine-and-cheese parties for childminders. It was astonishing to see the effect this had on some childminders. It was there in the sparkle of their eyes, their new hairstyle, their dress. I suspect for some — indeed I know — this was the first wine-and-cheese party they had ever attended. They loved being free of the children, being somebody, being recognized. It turned out that the West Indian bus drivers in the sheds alongside us had a Steel Band, so Hazel arranged with the inspector for people to swap over each other's buses in unbelievably complex ways ('if you take the number 71 to Moldgreen and then Johnnie can . . .'). In that way the whole band could be free for an hour during the day, and make the centre dance to the exciting sound of their carefully converted oil drums. Everyone enjoyed it, but the West Indian minders especially were pleased and proud. We consulted the Chinese at the nearby takeaway, and discovered that Joseph Lee there ran a Kung Fu class, and was only too pleased to bring his boys along and ceremonially demonstrate their range of martial arts to rapt childminders, parents and social workers. One evening when events like this seemed to be happening at once all over the building (as frequently happens) I thought back to 'Dawn-watch' in Huddersfield, and reflected how hard it had been and yet how easy. Hard in terms of energy, application. But once the conditions for friendly meeting were created, every-thing flowed naturally. Looking round the room I was surrounded by endlessly chattering groups in which I could pick out not only childminders whom we had originally visited, but with them were policemen, councillors, officials, social workers, health visitors, school teachers, even the income tax man; all of whom they would once have feared.

This element of festival became part of the style of the centre and in some way of which I am not wholly sure, a deep strand in its organic growth. Perhaps it brought a bit of fun back into education, social work, childminding. Perhaps it nurtured those informal chats over wine, jumble, mushy peas, which often breed better results than any formal courses. Or perhaps it just raised morale. Certainly raising the morale, altering the self-image, of childminders was a first task. On the door of the room where they homed in to mash tea and talk amongst themselves we pinned up the label: Supermums. (The only criticism came from a male childminder who wanted recognition for Superdads too.)

However, it was then we tried to project the resource of the centre, the concern for childminders outwards, both formally and informally. Amongst other examples (folk evenings in pubs, stalls on the market, badges and T-shirts with 'Children's Centre' on them) we[1] set up Play-Ins in the middle of Huddersfield. Between the central market and the public library, overlooked by the glorious Town Hall and the Victorian offices of the *Huddersfield Examiner*, and strung around by the low-level chain shops that leave their mark all over Britain, stands a large patch of grass and paving. The developers had oddly called it the Piazza. At least that initial P was not bad: Piazza Play In sounded attractive. There is in most towns some place as suitable as this. We chose Saturday morning when most childminders were free, and mums were trailing reluctant children round the big shops.

The sun shone, and on the Piazza we laid out sand trays,

221

school easels and pots of paint, climbing frames, a Wendy House, pedal cars, books, stalls selling whatever we had to sell, bold notices everywhere inviting people to come and talk — and a small troupe of actors who performed a children's playlet every hour (in between they sat in the *Albert* recovering from the warmth of their reception). There never was any need for our so carefully drawn notices. Children were swarming over the tackle as soon as it came off the van. Mothers were asking what it was all about, and childminders and the project team were explaining. There were balloons and hot discussions, everywhere, and lovely cameos all around. I recall looking for my three-year-old daughter Ellen, and glimpsing her solemnly standing at an easel painting an all blue picture, with the paint running gently downwards and dripping on the grass. And on the other side of the easel was a tramp whom one often saw picking round the market bins. He was as absorbed as Ellen, transported by the sheer strangeness of playing with brush, paper and brilliant paint. Sitting down, intently observing them were three elderly and turbaned Sikhs whose own childhood must have been spent in the days of Kipling's Raj and endless skirmishes on the North West Frontier. Curiously, the right setting and the right tools brought the community into new relationships with itself — out of which action could be distilled.

Very formal events oddly had the same strengths. We made a point of using the town hall — a Venetian palazzo dreamed up by Victorian Huddersfield. Of course there were endless little difficulties but it was a revelation to many that they could actually use their own town hall; and when for example we arranged for the small Chinese community (who had now become enmeshed in it all, for no one understood the situation of the working mother or the invisible minority more than they did) to transfer their martial arts display on to this splendid platform of the choral society, the effect was electric. Again it was the extension of relationships, the new sense of spotlight, of pride.

Looking round for underused resources in the community, Hazel noticed that the technical college had a student crèche, but very few children in it. Courses at the college were either free or met by a nominal charge (which we could raise from a sale). Why not ask for a childminder's course, enrol a dozen and simultaneously give the children accompanying sessions in the crèche? There was some technical difficulty. Apparently they had to combine physical education with their 'main subject' in order to use the crèche. That was a tougher, much more doubtful proposal to put to the minders, but somehow the fun element that now flowed strongly carried it through. Yes, they'd have a go.

The result was startling. They were delighted to be freed from the children for a few hours each week, and we were absorbed building up the crèche into an educationally structural playgroup. The minders took little interest in the course which was dominantly about child development and at first in too academic concepts and terms. But they adored physical education. This turned out to mean 'music and movement', taking off that extra inch, discovering bodily grace. Some tried (as we could never have imagined in the early stages of the survey) riding, trampolines, squash, even cricket. Of course it was all done in a great giggle, but the effects on the children were noticeable. Minders were more relaxed, more positive with them.

It was with this broad technique that the courses were evolved. Within a year, and at a time when only 1 per cent of registered childminders had received any form of training and support, 100 per cent of registered childminders in Huddersfield had attended at least one course, and so had many unregistered minders.

The courses worked best in small groups of six to eight minders who over the weeks became self-sustaining groups, gradually taking over the planning of their own curriculum. Gradually we moved over to having a visiting expert join each group every second or third session, and leaving the other sessions for discussion. It was interesting what 'visiting expert' came to mean. We drew on the voluntary energies of whoever might help — infant-school teachers to discuss preparing children for school, doctors to raise the question of baby-battering, health visitors to talk about minor ailments and signs of matters more serious. But the most effective could be the most unexpected: the lady from the electricity showroom who showed ways of buying and cooking cheap 'one pot'

meals for children; the trade union official who signed them
all on for his union — NUPE — at the end of the meeting, and
got them thinking about pressing their own claims; the
income tax official about whom they were very doubtful lest
he insisted that they hadn't always declared their full income.
He explained — as he might have done to any businessman —
that if they realistically took their necessary expenses into
account — then they were probably running at a net loss, and
could sometimes even have a claim for tax back. And one of
the most stimulating sessions of all was with an Indian palmist.

In the discussion sessions, everyone was now much more
alert, curious, confident and ready to talk about the children in their care, and ways to enhance its quality. Nancy
told us about Jocelyn, a twenty-year-old parent whose little
girl Mandy she took every day. Jocelyn had tried to suffocate
Mandy, and was now on tranquillizers. Mandy could be fear-
somely difficult: who could Nancy tell — except her tranquil-
lized mother? But from the group she drew support, fellow-
feeling, new knowledge. Soon she was able to say,

> 'I've got to play with her and not just shut her up in a
> room. She's so much better if I do. Her screaming and
> crying used to get me down and then I just went wild, I
> didn't know what I was doing.'

Later still, as confidence expanded and relationships grew,
Jocelyn might herself drop in and chat.

Such groups to my observation (colleagues sometimes disa-
greed) were always better if someone in the team remained a
regular part of them. There was so much knowledge to be put
in the coffee arena. But within a few months they were
undoubtedly able to run themselves — providing the place,
the facilities and the transport were there.

One of the main facilities was the parallel playgroup for
the minded children. We offered to assist in running 'education for parenthood' classes in six local secondary schools.
This meant taking timetabled lessons for children of fourteen,
fifteen and sixteen in schools. We would really have liked to
have started with the twelve-year-olds or earlier and built up
over several years. The practical sessions, which were part of

the school course, were in the playroom at the children's centre. We dovetailed this to match the childminders' discussion sessions, and so with this rearrangement everyone was learning and teaching simultaneously: toddler, teenager, childminder, visiting social worker.

Another crucial facility was transport. The minibus for taking minders and children to the centre, the park, the seaside was basic. So later was the double-decker Playbus (which we converted in the sheds: so our original dream on that wet Tuesday morning became more solid than we expected).

With transport it was much easier to set up local groups of childminders, whom we could service from the travelling toy library. It was once more a matter of smoking out underused buildings: church halls, schools, institutes. We never again found a half-empty bus shed, but some of the most valuable work was done by getting childminders and their children into schools or adult education centres. There could be resistance or thoughtlessness. When we moved into one adult education centre. Judi Thorpe came back to tell us,

'they told all the minders to go to Room 2123 — which was three miles and two floors away from the playroom: and make sure we were out in thirty minutes, so they could slot the cookery class in.'

But gradually, as they thought or argued it out, people accepted or convinced themselves that childminders had an equal claim on community education facilities.

Mary Crossley had the idea of getting the childminders and the children to meet in local health clinics. Some of these medical centres had plenty of space in which children could play and minders meet, whilst health visitors weighed babies at one end, and doctor saw parents in the side rooms. It was a fruitful conjunction, driving everyone more closely and usefully together. It reminded me, in miniature, of the vast, unnecessary and wasteful gulf we permit between medicine and education.

We had then a centre which served every childminder in the city, and every child for whom they cared. But around the centre grew many other activities, not central to this report. English classes for Asian mothers; one-to-one tuition for adult illiterates; classes in English and in written Chinese for that community (I joined the class for four-year-olds writing Mandarin — and was soon trailing far behind); meetings for prisoner's wives; Saturday-morning sessions for Caribbean children; meetings for pre-school playgroups or single-parent family associations; holiday schemes for children who needed that little bit extra. Naturally, it also drew many visitors, for example, thirty students taking a master's degree at Melbourne University flew over to use this as their practical term. We also had visits from the Chinese national basketball team from Peking, building bridges with the Hong Kong Chinese, and the Italian delegation to International Women's Year looking for ways forward from Maria Montessori.

All this was very welcome. It cannot be expanded here. But it illustrates the key position of childminders in a working-class community. Working with them opens up questions of baby battering (of which some have experience); of the needs of children from minority groups; of the pressures on children in homes where father is absent; or of being an Asian childminder with little English. In Huddersfield, at least, childminders were of the warp and woof of the community. The threads that led from them were organic to the whole.

In the week I write, a normal week, the centre works with 54 registered childminders and 10 unregistered ones, together with 397 children of whom 104 are in school parenthood classes, and the rest are under-fives. The direct cost to the local authority is negligible. For example, in the Brixton experiment it cost over £1000 to train 10 childminders. Three recent courses for 22 minders in Huddersfield directly cost £59.25. Of course there are hidden costs. There must be building, transport and above all staff to act as catalysts. In Huddersfield we raised the money from outside agencies.[2] But that was to launch the experiment. If it is desirable to run something like the Huddersfield Children's Centre in other cities, I see no reason why the invisible cost could not be met out of existing municipal budgets, just by using the money differently, so as to unlock community pride, expertise and solid resources.

Manchester

Turning round the corner from that tiny jam factory lost amongst the terraced houses — rows and rows of windowsills and doorsteps painted red or cream — you suddenly ran into the tide of scarlet-and-white supporters rolling along to a floodlit match at Manchester United's packed ground at Old Trafford. Odd to emerge, at the research stage, from the isolated world of childminding, and step only twenty yards away into this great gregarious Mancunian sea. Manchester is an ambivalent, undecided city. It has great pride, ceremony, presence, yet is utterly different from Huddersfield. The community was fractured, dissipated, full of separated and lonely existence. Perhaps that, in some elusive way, is why our alienated survey area yet also had the biggest, peacock-like and most aggressive football crowd in Europe. Certainly it was going to be much more difficult here to transform research into action, since there were not the rich community strands to pick and weave that we had found in a smaller Yorkshire woollen town.

First of all, we had to find a person to whom Julia could hand over, whilst she completed the Manchester survey and moved to the Brixton course. That person was Sue Owen, who was then the adviser on under-fives in the social services department. She also organized the Manchester Playbus which had recently met a disastrous end. The Playbus (quite a gem) was being driven to some forgotten streets near the football stadium. It was a beautiful double-decker bus, full of sandtrays, story corners, cushions, toys. It even had a small lavatory for the children on the upper deck. Unfortunately some public health official insisted on inspecting the lavatory whilst the bus was in motion, lest — in his view — it should be classed as a travelling health hazard. The whole notion was bureaucratic tomfoolery, but all the same he stuck to interpretation of old small-print bye-laws which had never imagined the existence of a Playbus. More than that, he determined to test the works properly, and locked himself in the lavatory just as Old Trafford came in sight. More unfortunately still — and especially for him — the driver didn't notice the height of the cables running to the Ground across

227

a side street never before penetrated by a bus. There was a great flash, and a crash, and a cocoon of cables encased the bus. Sue and the driver were perfectly all right. But the public health official was marooned in the upstairs kiddies toilet, desperately banging on the window and yelling 'let me out!'

So Sue left the Playbus and began to work to create a trial service for childminders, different from the Huddersfield experiment. The research itself had meant that some childminders now wanted to meet in each others' houses (menfolk were willingly exiled to the pub and meetings broke up rapidly as they returned at 10.30 p.m.), and Julia — feeling a touch of researcher's guilt — had gone to a lot of trouble to encourage this. Sue joined the group of nine childminders, of whom eight were unregistered (several appear in 'Portrait gallery'). And for the first few months little outside progress was made. It was simply lots of talk, and not very much talk about children. More dominant were man problems, rents, council house waiting lists. One poorly literate childminder needed weeks and weeks of support to disentangle her from unfair but multiplying hire-purchase agreements. There really wasn't all that much time to concentrate on child care until some of the other pressures had been aired, talked out, shared and sometimes slightly relieved.

But we had to find a daytime base, and rather than choosing something in the style of children's centre that was burgeoning in Huddersfield, we decided to move much more gently, and go for a drop-in centre, where mother or minder and their children could call in anytime, and expect tea, talk and toys. We looked first at church halls, and soon found one. We collected the toys, brewed the tea, spread the word around. Everything was set fair: but we were in for three months of disappointment. The West Indian church elders felt that 'something should be done about poor children'. What they had done was to set up a uniformed children's brigade, with much marching, salutes, obedience, cornets and hymns. This took me right back to the origins of this research, where we can discern a cultural conflict over the role of the growing child. Do you start from authority, accepted knowledge and impose that on the child? Or do you emphasize a change in the environment, a range of tools and stimuli —

and seek to elicit growth?

When the minders and children came, the church never accepted the noise, play, paint, smoking, tea-making, music. No matter how well we cleaned up afterwards, there was always a tension towards containment. Worse still, the minders often did not come at all, and there could be long hours of waiting and a feeling of defeat. But gradually the numbers did increase and slowly we realized that we had hit on a formula that, in the ways that mattered to us, was better than, say, the fixed hours of a playgroup. Minders, mothers, children drifted in and out as the rhythms of their life dictated. This fluid situation had to be planned for and used, quite differently from a structured one, but for the minders and children we were working with, increasingly it felt right.

Of course the first base had to be abandoned. But Manchester, like any Victorian city, is (should you press hard enough) full of underused buildings owned by the education department, housing department, social services department, the university, the churches, or old voluntary bodies. So rather than go for one major centre, this time we set up a string of four drop-in centres, in Longsight, Moss Side, Levenshulme and Old Trafford, together with other evening groups in Stretford and Moss Side, and the travelling toy library serving all these, and Chorlton as well.

Needless to say, this needed resources. And what we did was to accept students from Manchester Polytechnic on one-term practical attachments as part of their training courses in social work, education or any other course with a community service element. The toy library was garnered largely by the original childminders, together with some purchasing cash from the Save the Children Fund. The vital minibus came from Bird's Custard and we much enjoyed the urban poetry of the Custard bus ferrying toys to the cornflake kids.

Perhaps the first noticeable effect was change in some of the children. Children whom we had come to dread because of their screaming, shouting, destruction almost miraculously over the months became absorbed in play. The delight we felt over a small girl who had never smiled, played, joined in on the day that at last she did. Till then we had privately been bandying words like 'autistic' as if the child suffered from some near incurable condition. She simply needed a couple of months of warmth and change.

Not that all went so well. We sometimes showed short films including a very absorbing one on battered babies. The minders were now very ready to discuss children at length, and baby battering was something of which many had had some personal experience. But in practice it can be a prickly thicket to force your way through. One day a small girl cut her head open at an unregistered minder's. The minder had nothing to clean the wound with, and we were already very worried about the child's health. She had had so many cuts and bruises, not deliberately inflicted, we felt, but certainly unattended to; they seldom healed normally. Sue asked the minder if she could take the child, in the Custard bus, to the clinic to have the head wound treated. At the clinic the doctor looked after the wound but also felt the child had scabies and gave us suitable creams. The doctor recorded this on his card, which then in some minor office mix-up went to another clinic and a strange health visitor. She immediately notified the social services department that this was a suspected case of child battering at an illegal childminder's. The social services descended on the place, couldn't get the evidence, and left threatening fines and imprisonment for unregistered minding. In no time we were engulfed by an angry boarding party of childminders, parents and friends which looked very ready for violence on its own account. It was all talked out. I have no doubt of the child neglect here, linked to negligible health education and no supporting service. But the crude threat of fines did no good at all (that too had to be talked out with the social services department), nor was there any follow-up help from the health visitor who flatly refused to call on the minder 'in case I find the standards unacceptable'. I felt sure, despite the great flare-up, that our modest supporting services around the drop-in centres were a wiser course in a community as impoverished as this could sometimes be. For an awkward hour or two, we were touching the seeds of disaster. Uncoordinated and self-protecting medical, eduational and social services looked a poor bet for that small girl.

Gradually the centres grew stronger, bonding together

small groups of minders and mothers. Much happened that would have been inconceivable a year before — an amazing trip to Manchester Airport with fifteen toddlers in push-chairs, or a group of minders at one of the evening groups joining a union *en bloc*. We approached the question of children being given too little or too unbalanced food by encouraging communal lunches at the centres. We also tackled the other dilemma of children being left alone whilst minders shopped by starting a home play scheme. If minders wanted a regular hour or so off, we would arrange for someone to arrive with the toy library and play, talk, storytell with the children in the minder's own home. Sometimes this led to surprises. One unregistered childminder was being threatened with prosecution for looking after eight children, a figure we accepted when we interviewed her at the research stage. Only when she started drawing on the home play scheme did we discover for ourselves that she regularly took in seventeen children. Nevertheless, rather than lecturing the minders on nutrition, play or the dangers of leaving children alone, it proved better to provide positive services such as the lunches or home play schemes, at the same time as handling these questions in discussion.

But the basic difficulty was the law, and the law as administered by a local authority in a negative spirit. Most of the minders we began with were not registered and as the centres drew in more and more, it looked as if our research had probably underestimated their numbers. Some people were quite unaware that they were minders at all ('no', said one, 'there aren't any minders round here. I know that 'cos I look after my friend's little girl: she couldn't find anyone to take her.') Some had tried to register only to be frustrated: 'I thought they'd forgotten about me and then say I'd got a certificate and then I didn't see anyone else for three years.' Others were defiant about registration: 'I've been doing it for seventeen years and they've known about me and they've not done a thing, so I'm damned if I'm going to register now.'

One of the local authorities we dealt with was particularly negative to minders. We arranged to take their community liaison officer to visit some, and see for himself what might helpfully be done. We actually got him as far as the doorstep

231

of an unregistered minder, and then he refused to budge. We could hardly believe it when he said 'If I go in there, I'm conniving at a criminal act', and he returned to his tower-block office. This was by no means the last time that we met a 'don't want to know' response from social workers. So by default the centres became locally recognized as exchange points. Mothers looking for minders looked in, as did minders looking for fresh children: and we were able, to a modest extent, to match minder and child, and gently to discourage unsuitable minders.

Yet every week was full of threats of prosecution. We tried endless delegations, press publicity, prepared defences. We tried putting forward one of the unregistered minders offering the best quality of care as a 'test case' for registration. It took much persuasion on our part, but when the day came the social worker was so rude to her that she immediately withdrew her request and retired back into unregistered minding. It took two years of this battling before the council passed a formal resolution to say they did not intend to prosecute when cases of illegal minding came to their notice. That a council had to minute such a matter tells a lot, but though at the time we often saw our difficulties in terms of individuals, it was clear what was primarily needed was a change in the law.

And so the scheme continued, each month with some unexpected highlight. A general election gave us a chance to set up a childminder's coffee corner and crèche in the old school where polling took place : a neat example of taking the news and the service to where people are. One of the minders whom we had originally seen on 'Dawnwatch' joined us, under a government job-creation scheme, and was now able to help organize other minders. And on a typical week which we measured, we visit some thirty-eight minders and their children with the toy library, and forty-nine minders with their children call in at the centres. No costs fall on the local authority.[3]

Bradford

Bradford was our city for tools. Besides thinking our way forward in action on the local scene, it became clearer and
clearer that childminders would benefit if we could build up
a pile of nationally available tools for the job.

We began with toys, and retired to think it out over team
meetings at two lovely inns where we would not be disturbed:
The Peacock in Derbyshire and the Cavalier Club in Halifax.
Pooling experience from the research and from the action
projects, we hammered out a toy kit that, ideally, every
minder might receive on registration. By now, between us, we
knew many hundreds of childminders, and thousands of children in their homes. Some minders had no toys at all; some
received toys from our travelling libraries, and promptly put
them out of children's reach; some welcomed what we
brought; some had plenty of toys of their own — but very
much of one kind: either mechanical Hong Kong toys, or
promotion toys (Wombles, Daleks) linked with some current
television series. A minority, usually in middle-class districts,
and with much stronger educational and professional backgrounds, offered the children a more challenging range.

We designed a basic set. Toys that stimulated response to
colours, shape, size. Toys that excited visual or tactile pleasure. Toys that prompted fantasy. Toys that made for private
play, and toys that encouraged group play. It was important
to get an elaborated conceptual grid first, and then check it
out — even if the end seemed only a pile of jigsaws, posting
boxes, bricks, dressing-up clothes. A full range of deliberately
selected toys, available free on registration, could implicitly
create that invisible curriculum of play that was clearly lacking in what Dickens had long ago called a 'minding school'.
Having designed it we then approached a major manufacturer
— James Galt of Cheshire — who agreed to produce such toy
kits in attractive bins for local authorities to buy. Press publicity certainly produced orders from all over the country and
that was as far as we could go at the moment. A new tool was
on the market for authorities prepared to take it up.

But one should also record negative experiments. I was
very keen on developing the idea of the kitchen as a class-

233

room, and on the possibilities of a parallel junk kit. Earlier we had published a series of articles[4] on how the home — even without toys — threw up all the raw material you needed for a child to enjoy and learn. I tried a very simple idea, which could cut out all the cost of a national toy kit. I put a bag in the kitchen and popped into it all the useable household rubbish which would otherwise end up in the dustbin: milk bottle tops, tubes from lavatory rolls, cornflake boxes, envelopes with stamps on, polystyrene boxes with their AD 2000 shapes. And then showed in what varied ways these could be combined and presented to a child. Toys for free, all around all of us. But life is hard on ideas, and this one proved to be excellent for discussion groups or for childminders with a secure educational background, a more prosperous home, and perhaps only one or two children to mind. But it was running too far and too fast for the minders who needed most help. They had neither the time nor the conviction for this approach. Unexpectedly, the mass-produced toys — carefully selected — scored every time.

Next step was to design a model starter kit. The idea was that on registration, every childminder should receive an attractive folder which contained her insurance cover, contract forms to agree with parents, key telephone number when she needed help, information on her right to free milk for the children, guidance on diet and safety, a register in which photos of the children could be pasted together with all the basic information about the child — health, address, doctor, parents, place of work. And so on. I hadn't forgotten how the registered minder whose baby died in 'Portrait gallery' knew neither its name, its mother's name, nor where she was employed.

It was now time to open in Bradford the first National Conference on Childminding, and to make it an annual affair.[5] We welcomed the chance to pitch our tent in the provinces. Too much of the evidence and debate on pre-school was narrowly London-centred, and often read like news from a strange and much wealthier land. Bradford was far more typical of Britain. The annual conferences there gave us the chance to put all our research and action, however imperfect, into the arena. The conferences brought together childminders, academics, civil servants, social workers and teachers from all over the country who could, in the workshops, share their experience and initiatives. This annual forum gave an immense impetus to creative concern about childminding.

But more was to come as we published from Bradford a series of *Action Registers*. The notion was to make publicly available a record of what every local authority or major voluntary body was doing in the childminding field. We were able to report modest action in a small number of London boroughs, but only one authority outside London actually doing anything. There were others beginning to stir — Sunderland 'planned to review childminding'; Dudley was 'interested in the provision of advice'; Norwich aimed 'to hold quarterly meetings with minders', and so on. The number of children directly affected by these services was a few hundred. Six months later, when we published the second *Action Register*, it had risen to 5,000. By then forty pilot schemes were going in the London boroughs, ten local authorities elsewhere were in action and so were twelve voluntary organisations. This was very encouraging, even though in total this activity only covered between 1 and 2 per cent of registered minders.

A year later, with the issue of *Action Register Three* the patterns changed again. Day-nursery provision was still miserable. If a mother went out to work full-time in Barnsley a child only had half a chance in a hundred of quality-controlled day care. Places like Sunderland (0·86 per cent) or Gateshead (1 per cent) were not much better. But concern and interest in childminding was clearly rising. The number of local authorities now taking a positive attitude had now moved to sixty-four, and the number actually in action with their schemes was thirty-four. Clearly the spreading of information, however raw, the meeting of people, however simple, and the spread of tools, models, ideas were having a considerable ripple effect. The question now was how to build in an even more powerful multiplying force. And for that we turned to Nottingham.

Nottingham

Nottingham has a BBC local radio station. We asked them if we could use it to declare an Amnesty for Childminders. What's that, they enquired? Of course it was symbolic of what was needed nationally in changing the law, the status and the image of childminding.

We asked if for forty-eight hours we could run phone-ins, news items, features over the station — all on childminding. We would ask unregistered minders to ring in and tell us about their situation. And we would ask all minders, unregistered or registered, to phone in for advice, reassurance, information. If they didn't want to ring up live over the air, they could contact us on a private line — both numbers given out regularly from the microphone, and in all cases we promised not to divulge their name or address to officials unless they agreed. We also said we would try to set up visits to all who would welcome that.

The effect was electric. The radio station became dramatic as never before. Phone calls flooded in from minders and from parents. Puzzlement by some who didn't know they had to be registered (on a later occasion one of these turned out to be the childminding wife of a councillor who served on the social services committee); desperate cries for help from mothers who simply had to find someone to help care for their child. Even one from a parent in Denmark who accidentally picked up the Amnesty on his car radio.

Some cases were rather sad, like the neighbours who rang us — they hadn't known who else to contact — about the blind eighty-year-old lady who was babyminding. It was very dangerous and we had to end it, but we managed to get for her the social-work and home-help services of which she was unaware, and yet needed and welcomed.

In forty-eight hours we contacted more unregistered minders than a conventional social services department met in ten years. We were using a free, multiplying service — BBC radio — and radiating knowledge, help and support. There were lessons to be learned from this.

But first, we tried to build back a service into the community which had responded. With help from the government's

236

unemployment programme, we took on two jobless people with no professional experience in this field at all. But by now so much was common sense, or familiar tracks, using new tools that even with no specialist background they soon had a vivid and encouraging effect on fifty childminders and their children. Their initial reports repeated the story of Birmingham, Liverpool, Huddersfield, Manchester, Brixton.

By now, having essayed it in so many places we were confident that, if you knew how to look, most towns would reveal the same picture. The question was how to use the Nottingham amnesty experiment for a more national effect. And we did this by approaching the BBC and arguing for a national television course for childminders.

Needless to say it took a vast amount of work to make the idea first credible, then acceptable, and lastly practicable. But finally in January 1977, the BBC launched a thrice-weekly television series for childminders, called *Other people's Children*.[6] With it came a 'how-to-be-a-better-childminder' book, based on the pilot courses at the Huddersfield Centre and largely written by Sonia. Moreover it went quite free to every registered childminder in the country. The print order was based on the official figure for childminders. Such was the demand that within a fortnight the order had to be doubled. Someone, somewhere had got their sums wrong, but that we had realized long since. So now we had a major television series, a free book, the chance for social workers to call on every registered minder bringing this news and gift instead of inspection and threat, the growth of viewing groups and a projection of the presence of supported childminders as good and necessary neighbours in the world in which we live.[7]

This thinking in action hugely enlarged our sense of what conclusions should be drawn from the research, and gave us the confidence of basing them not only on looking and assessing, but on doing — which can be quite a different kettle of fish. It was time to draw up a childminder's charter.

Part III

Agenda for Whitehall and Westminster

14 A charter for childminders

Variations in what children learn at school depend
largely on variations in what they bring to school, not
on variations in what schools offer them.

Christopher Jencks, *Inequality*

We began with an alarum, moved through survey and investigation into monitored or exploratory action. Perhaps now it
is time for blueprint. Of what should a charter for childminders consist?

First of all, the background must be a new sensitivity and
an asserted priority for children under five. They live the
moment in life when later failures, costly in human and
material terms, can be prevented. They are our delegation to
the future. Yet Britain, a fairly typical middle-of-the-road
industrial nation spends half its education budget on that
one-tenth of our children who survive into higher education.
The care and education of children under five is nourished on
crumbs. Worse still, it is fragmented, disorganized, illogical.

Before a childminders' charter can bite, we need to unify
services for small children. The difference between 'caring' as
represented by our tiny number of day nurseries, and 'education' as demonstrated in our too-few nursery schools is a
shibboleth of yesteryear. Both are minority services, both
report to different local authority departments, are con-
trolled by different ministries, and have grotesquely different
hours of work, holidays and salaries for their professionals.
But there are also the new professionals, childminders and
playgroup leaders, who care, as we discover, for far more children. There may often be different tasks and rhythms here,
but all need to be welded into one unified profession. And so

241

do their services. Day nurseries need not only expansion (remember those hopeless waiting lists in Fartown and Trafford), but they need educational vivacity. Nursery schools, on the other hand, must extend their caring capacity by opening early, closing late, not observing the academic rites of terms and vacations — and so serving the children of working parents. And childminders and playgroup leaders must be seen as equal members — para-professionals, if you like — of a wholly articulated system which organically links the community and its needs with the professionals and institutions it funds. This great and most necessary reform can only come from government: for it is within government that the essence of this fragmentation is locked. It must mean, at the very least, a minister for the under-fives, responsible for initiating, co-ordinating, and accounting for a whole pre-school service. To tackle childminding without such root change is not enough. Much can be done by small immediate steps as the action research suggests. But without a clearer vision of an early education system, questions like child-minding will always remain difficult symptoms.

And next we must recognize that childminding, urgent though it must be on any pre-school agenda, is not the prime form of day care *except in the poorest and weakest groups*, which I feel is one of the most startling discoveries of this research. Nevertheless if we leave that aside for a moment, it is reasonable to ask whether it is necessary for all these parents to work while their children are young? Are there not basic ways of supporting the family which could — if only to a degree — ease the pressures on children that we have recorded in city after city?

A parent's wage

The obvious device would be to pay the mother, or single father, of a small child to stay at home. This could be done by making large child-benefit payments during the first three years. Whether this should be made dependent on the parent's not working is arguable. We certainly strongly support this new incentive: a wage to be a mother.[1] But, by itself, it is unlikely to reduce childminding dramatically. The only evidence comes from some East European countries which have tried modest versions of the idea. It has had only a minor effect; parents still choose to go out to work. I would guess that there are two main reasons. The economic one is that no state is likely to pay a mother as much to stay at home as she could earn going out to work. The human reason is that many of the parents we saw on our survey actively wanted to work. They wanted to get out of the home, they wanted long spells away from their children, they wanted companionship and outside interest, they wanted to exercise skills other than those of parenthood, and if they were women (though this feeling was only faint amongst the poorest) they wanted that right to leave the child and work that men customarily enjoy. And our observation was that they were not always less-good parents because of this. They might have been depressed, harassed mothers had they stayed at home, and it could be that the quality of the smaller span of time they gave to the child was better than the quantity of a less-attentive relationship had they stayed at home. I say 'might' and 'could' because though all this was sometimes true and often latent, it was more frequently absent, and one felt how much we had neglected teaching, raising, transmitting the arts of parenthood.

Baby benefit

A more modest but immediately effective idea would be to pay a number of substantial six monthly bonuses to parents of children under three. But increasingly as this research developed, I felt that we actually paid child benefits in the wrong place — at the post office. The baby benefit I suggest here should be physically paid at a health clinic. It should depend on the physical production of the child; and I suspect that would end or reveal many elusive cases of child neglect and child abuse. And it should come only after a full consultation — medical, social, educational — about the child. The little action probe in Huddersfield where the minders, children, parents and social workers met at the health centre suggests what a rich way forward this could be. I can think of little which would yield a higher bonus to society than this combined, positive and regular attention, in the right setting and linked to an attractive baby benefit.

Amnesty

This should be the backdrop to a charter for childminders. And that charter must begin by changing the law which as we have seen, creates such a negative image and atmosphere around the childminder. Possibly the sensible deed would be to declare a national amnesty on the lines of our little Nottingham one, and start all over again. The numbers of illegal childminders are very large, largest of all in the poorest communities, difficult to locate, and almost certainly we will never know the real number. They are the creatures of distant, ignorant and self-regarding legislation. It is legislation largely for the working class since, as we saw early in this thinking, major middle-class systems of day care, such as the *au pair* girl, are unthinkingly excluded (even though there must be many forms of unnecessary deprivation and neglect amongst children from more prosperous homes).

Day care parent

The new law could usefully begin by never using the word childminder. It has accumulated too many bad overtones. It is wrong at its heart. It suggests passivity — you 'mind' the dog, or the shop, or your own business. In the Huddersfield action thinking we had to break the old image violently by calling them Supermums (and the odd male minder, a Superdad). The new title should imply a professional, caring role. I think day care parent should oust childminder from the official vocabulary.

Insurance

Next, the law should first give benefits rather than restriction. One simple one would be for every day care parent to be automatically insured by the local authority on registration.

Towards the concluding stages of our survey, a childminder in Lancashire was sued because a child in her care had been badly scalded, and damages of £8,000 were awarded. The whole court scene was an Alice-in-Wonderland event spawned by the Poor law. The childminder (like many on our previous pages) only survived because she took in children. There was never any prospect of her paying £8,000. The award was a fiction which harassed her, but did not benefit the child. Naturally one doesn't want accidents to happen to a child, but nevertheless, given such numbers, they will. The childminder should have the same protection as the schoolteacher. Registration should bring automatic insurance cover. At 1977 prices this would only cost £2 per minder, but provide immeasurably better protection against the worst for child, parent and minder.

The milk muddle

Free milk (one third of a pint per day for each child) is the only entitlement that childminders now enjoy. Very few know about it, less take it up. The right is clouded in language which beats off all but the bravest. It was very much because of the publicity received by this 'open research' that in 1975 the government remembered to include childminders in the list of those who could claim free milk. The official rubric runs:

'Children under school age who are attending an approved day nursery or playgroup or are minded by an approved childminder are entitled to receive free of charge one third of a pint of milk, or National Dried Milk (NDM) made up to one third of a pint, each day they attend. The arrangements by which the children receive their free entitlement are that the day nursery, playgroup or childminder applies for approval by the Department on Form WF/DN 15 and, following approval, receives reimbursement for the cost of the milk supplied to the children in their care, as a result of submitting quarterly claim forms.'

Even if a childminder survived this preamble, and was accustomed to quarterly back claims, the form itself requires the reading age of a Cambridge undergraduate (or a senior man from the ministry). It is all hopelessly remote from the reality of the backstreet minder. As one said:

'Oh yes. I know all about free milk, but I don't get it. The form was too comical, sorry, I mean complicated. I filled it in and then they wrote back and said why did I include Bank Holidays? Well, I'd never thought of that. I mean, I hadn't put them in specially, but perhaps I hadn't crossed them out or something. I don't know. Anyway, Bank Holidays mean nothing to me. Most of my mums work in the betting shop, and that's a busy day for them. So they wrote, and I wrote, and in the end I gave up. It cost me too much to argue with them.'

All that is needed to cut through this gobbledigook is for a new law to make free milk an automatic right and service once registered. Let the bureaucracy sort out its returns itself behind closed doors; there is no need for the childminder to be involved at all.

Benefits of registration

But the main clause of the Act should set the need to register in terms of the benefits it brings rather than the penalties it avoids. Anyone wishing to mind should be issued with a preliminary certificate. It is best for the authority to know everyone who is minding and have access to their houses. Only then can one begin to improve the quality of care, or in some cases, dissuade them from minding at all.

The local authority should then be obliged to provide a day-care course, and full registration should mean that a minder has completed such a course, and will regularly attend refresher courses. Such a registration certificate would then become the minimum guarantee to a parent which is now absent. It should help end the scandalous situation where social workers may privately mark a minder's file as 'unsatisfactory' yet not pass on this knowledge to parents.[2] Minders should receive a formal certificate which they could display, if they chose, as on the Brixton course.

Registration must give the minder further recognition and rights. Recognition as an integral part of pre-school provision, and the right to practical support; a multi-purpose childrens' centre, visits from childminding advisers, the toy library, group meetings, relationships with schools, nurseries, play-groups, membership of a bulk purchase circle. The minder should receive a handbook (like the one written to back up the BBC television series), a toy kit (like the one designed in association with Galt), and a starter kit (on the broad lines of that designed in the action research). All these could perfectly well be centrally funded and designed through the ministry and (since we lack an Early Childhood Institute) through the Health Education Council.

Extending the library principle

We have for a century accepted the notion of a free, municipal book library service. Over the last twenty years we have added gramophone record services. If we look at most record libraries we see at once that, though they are subsidized by everyone, they are likely to be of most value to that 10 per cent of the population who are attracted by classical music. I have no quarrel with this. But perhaps we should think of extending the library principle further, and directing it to critical points of need. The voluntary toy library service clearly has ready clientèle. In our survey and subsequent practice it was very popular with minders (especially if it includes not only indoor toys but large outdoor ones — climbing frames, inflatable pools). The time is now ripe for this to become part of normal provision, and it could start as a service to minders (it has, of course, many other uses —

handicapped children, children in hospital and so on).

I think we also need to establish in social services departments a safety library: fireguards, extinguishers, escape chutes. This would end the nonsense of the Fire Officer inspecting childminders' houses (as we saw in Brixton), recommending £300 worth of safety equipment, and leaving behind a minder who could never afford that outlay, and who would in consequence simply mind illegally.

Going public

If positive legislation lay behind day care, then every effort should be made to end the days of touting for trade in children through tatty cards in corner shops. If a minder is registered it should be displayed on her house or in her window. Instead of the out-of-date, neglected, and often secret lists that are currently kept (remember how it took three years for an established research unit to obtain the list in Chapter 4? What chance had a parent got?), properly maintained lists of registered minders should be available in social services departments, health clinics and public libraries. Parents should be encouraged to see several in a preliminary way and choose the one they feel best suits their child.

There is another sense, too, in which childminding might go public. It was very striking to see what goodwill, fresh relationships and new knowledge were created by the 'Play-In' in Huddersfield or the Phone-In amnesty in Nottingham. There is no reason why local authorities should not use these existing opportunities and facilities in the community to radiate their interest in caring better for young children.

The rate for the job

Childminders are poorly paid for an important job. Many by business standards, run at a net loss. Almost all have great difficulty in deciding what to charge, and when to change the rate. Part of the difficulty can be met by including a clear contract between minder and parent in the starter kit. But gradually childminding has to be weaned away from the anarchic market economics in which it is now trapped. A second step would be for local authorities to remove some of the onus from the minder and recommend rates of pay. This needs to be done sensitively since a parent's income and responsibilities, and a minder's qualification and experience, may both vary a lot. Some parents may be leaving more than one child in day care, or combining childminding with other provision. But it is perfectly possible, and would be a modest step towards a better order.

Childminding — a salaried service?

An ideal to move towards would be for childminders, or at least the core of the childminding system, to be paid — as we pay nursery nurses or teachers — by the local authority. Part or all of the cost could be recouped from parents, though hopefully the time may come when day care becomes an extension of a free education service. /

All that may be a very long way away, at least in Britain, but it is helpful to look at what evidence we have at this stage. There has been an experiment in salaried day care in New York, and one in Angel Town, Brixton. Unfortunately neither have published an evaluation — an example of how very important it is to build a research element into the action. But a third scheme, in Lambeth, is the subject of a quite excellent study.[3] This project took place not very far away from the earlier experiment we reported in Brixton. But whereas that Brixton study had tried to work with ten minders who were already looking after children, the Lambeth scheme deliberately recruited ten women, not minding, but whom they hoped could be turned into good minders — with the special role of caring for young children on the local authority's 'priority' list.

The trainees took a six-week course, and were paid a basic rate of £20 a week. Once in service they were guaranteed their salary by the authority. The authors of the evaluation can throw new light on the costs of this approach. The cost of the scheme in 1975-6 was £18,000 (it included the salary of an extra deputy matron to link nursery and minders). This looks very high. But pause. The evaluation finds that at least three important objectives were achieved: the day nursery is used to create and support an improved child-minding service; very young children enjoy personal care under the supervision of trained staff; and, given these conditions, parents who all originally preferred the day nursery, are delighted with their childminders.[4]

The scheme attracted women who said they would not have considered ordinary childminding. With training and continuous support they provided, say the authors, 'a good standard of normal family care'. They showed 'unexpected enthusiasm and conscientiousness', not only in direct care of children, but in keeping the records and daily diaries required by the project. Yet these minders were drawn from an inner-city area very similar to Brixton and none had any professional experience of child care.

Over the thirteen-month evaluation period the minders looked after thirty-four children from the priority day care waiting list, thirty of them with a lone parent. Half were found after placement to have a serious health problem or be backward in some way. The scheme reached children urgently in need of good-quality day care with otherwise little chance of getting it — children of the kind who fill the waiting lists in every poor urban area.[5]

The report calculates that to attach salaried minders, providing thirty places, to every day nursery in Lambeth would cost £316,000 a year and, following the Groveway pattern, could offer day care to 360 more children within two years. The same number of day-nursery places would, at current rates, cost £484,000 and take ten years, even if (most improbably) the capital resources were available. So salaried childminding at its most costly, as here, can provide 50 per cent more places eight years earlier than the day nursery, taking the lowest estimate of costs.[6]

Could the advantages of attachment to a day nursery be extended to childminders without necessarily paying them a salary? Unsalaried minders, the authors suggest, could not be expected to accept the responsibilities, controls and supervision which produced such good results in Lambeth. That conclusion looks too pessimistic in the light of our Huddersfield experience — there is more than one way of getting good results. And also intermediate possibilities.

It clearly makes sense anyway to pay some good childminders a retainer if they are prepared to take children in need. This already happens in fostering, and has been noted earlier — the line between fostering and childminding can be a very blurred one. The only caution one would make here is that it would be a mistake to see the choosing of salaried minders as an alternative to supporting the minders that the community already nurtures. Both approaches have considerable strengths; but the organic community network, whatever its flaws, is primary. One must remember that even if many minders in the community are transient — moving into or out of minding as their circumstances change — this is, even then, a subtle and effective way of implicitly transmitting education for parenthood.

Confused roles

Looking back over this research, we see how childminders are more than childminders. They may also be parents themselves, wives, housewives. To improve the quality of care that they offer the child may demand that they reduce the quality of their household work, or make a considerably more economical use of their energies. Many of the minders that we have met simply added children to their existing routine. Others were caught in the conflict. The best, from a childcare point of view, distinctly lowered their standards of household management. We need more evaluated experiments to see how this duality of roles can be helped. Two lines of advance could be children's meals and housework. We provide midday meals in schools, and it would be thought laughable that the teacher should not only teach but cook the lunch. With old people we have developed a Meals-on-Wheels service, taking hot, nutritious food to them in their own homes. Throughout this research there have been many nagging doubts about the adequacy of the diet of some children with minders. In Manchester we tried a midday meal for the children at the drop-in centre. Perhaps what we now need is an experiment in taking school meals to registered minders' houses. How does it benefit the children nutritionally? Does it increase educational alertness? What are the difficulties? Which children have a claim to such provision? What are the costs?

Equally, this research suggests the need for a small, evaluated experiment in reducing the adverse pressure of continuing housework. We have an established Home Help system for new mothers, the old, sick or handicapped. Where we have a childminder with a substantial number of children, and one who seems capable of serving them well, we could try introducing a Home Help, so that the minder concentrated on the children. Of course there would be resistance to this. In our analysis of what childminders themselves want, this did not figure highly. They felt it a threat to their secure position in the household. But that need not be the end of the story: an experiment should be tried.

Self-help for childminders

The man from the trade union who came to the children's centre in Huddersfield, soon found himself with new members — the first childminders in the north to join a union. In Manchester one of the evening groups, led by a minder who first appeared on Dawnwatch decided themselves to join the union. The first annual Bradford Conference enclosed another first: a workshop on childminders and unions.[7] These are still springtime days, but clearly more and more childminders should be making their own case, voicing their own perception of the situation. Membership of a trade union should become a natural matter. So too should be membership of the National Childminding Association, bringing together local groups in a forum where not only pay and conditions, but educational responsibility, quality and potential are discussed amongst equals.[8]

Scatter-shot policy

Reflecting on this changing texture of ideas, research, action, blueprint it is noticeable how unfocused is government aid towards altering patterns of deprivation in early childhood. Initial funding came from trusts and foundations, but after that it was a scatter-shot policy. The Huddersfield centre drew modestly on Urban Aid, and it was one of the small successes of pursuing 'open research' that 'childminding' appeared for the first time as a heading on this government subsidy to local authorities. But the development of the Manchester and Nottingham work depended on the government's programme to take the edge off unemployment, and the Lambeth scheme for salaried childminders was sponsored by the Department of the Environment. These multiple sources of support have some advantages, especially at the pioneer stage, when the case is not established or widely accepted. But later it becomes wasteful. We have argued elsewhere in this account against the fissiparity of state services for children, and will argue more. For the moment though, it is clear that central policies for the inner city need to see and support childminders as an essential service.

Open college

Perhaps the most potent multiplying effect from this research and action was the major BBC television series for childminders, with its free supporting handbook, network of over 700 viewing groups, and huge 'eavesdropping' audience. A series such as this is usually repeated for a year or two. Dropping back from action into straight research, we will try to record its effect on childminders. But education is a crazy world of fashion, and its claim to airspace could soon — unless the evidence was compelling — be displaced by some novel issue of the moment.

There are many other television-backed services, such as the parallel one for adult illiterates, that are inevitable victims of the same cycle of limited television time, the need for novelty. Yet here we have a resource which reaches millions,

253

which creates an implicit curriculum for childminders, and which is always needed.

The best way forward would be the creation of an Open College — based on television, radio, literature, local groups. It could follow the model of the Open University,[9] but at a much more modest and practical level. A support service for childminders is just one of the elements that might be built into it. Clearly there are many more training, educational and social needs which could be met by an Open College based on people's immediate and practical needs.

So a charter for childminders ends with hopes for an Open College, which is a long trek from Dawnwatch. It is tempting to stop there. But there could be just one more piece missing from the childcare jigsaw.

15 A Minister for Children

Die Politik ist keine Wissenschaft,
(Politics is hardly an exact Science)
> Bismarck speaking in the Prussian Chamber,
> 18 December 1863

Necessitas non habet legum,
(Necessity has no law) attributed to Publius
Syrius, first century BC

The missing piece is a 'Minister for Children'. We live at a marvellous, awesome and unremarked time. In twenty industrial societies — for the first time in the history of man — we expect our child to live, and we no longer arm ourselves against his or her expected, feared, probable and early death. Only a hundred years ago it was not uncommon to bear a child, christen it James, see it die; then bear another child, christen it James and see it die; then bear another child and christen it James. . . . We have all wandered round old graveyards on Sunday evenings, and glimpsed on the gravestone markings that infinite human sadness from which we are so newly released. For much of the rest of the world this is still one of the cruel but basic gambles in life. Hopefully our present privilege is their future too.

And this fresh and now confident expectation of life invests elysian value in children. Never before have we given such hostages to the future. And suddenly we find that our priorities, plans and undertakings for children do not match our emerging hopes. At the very meanest, we struggle with new aspirations in the mesh of old laws. That is why we are, almost overnight, concerned with baby battering; tug-of-love

255

cases; children's safety on roads, in the home; children's rights in school, in hospital, in prison; children's vulnerability or responsibility in the overlapping worlds of sexuality, education, delinquency, the media, employment. Tomorrow morning's papers will be – and will necessarily be – full of such stories, doubts, and cries for change.

Perhaps a Minister for Children could help. We can do only so much in the back streets of Fartown, Brixton, Trafford, Nottingham. More could be done, and done differently, through the Palace of Westminster. Think of the antiquated, ignorant and useless law on childminding whose circumlocutions we have pursued through so many cities. Children – the one-quarter of our population who do not vote – need to be inked in on the political agenda. And, carrying futurity as they do, they could and should be very high on that list. A political tribune representing their often separate, unique and specific interest could at least co-ordinate present services and, with imagination, create preventative legislation. Of all this childminding has been one part, a homely, overlooked, practical and symbolic instance.

Without something like a Minister for Children, to whom is a report like this addressed? Not just rewriting the law is needed: but a social vision, expressed in policy and in the community, which recognizes the condition of childhood, and seeks to plan for its best present and better future. Without this last but missing piece of the jigsaw, we are left with that unfocused concern that deteriorates into everyday indifference. Childminding is only one – paradoxically simple and complex – emblem of such a state.

Yet, in a modest way, this research and action has illustrated or suggested some of the reasons behind the indifference to a quite specific aspect of early childhood which could – given imagination, will, and small resources – be utterly changed. Ponder some of the factors.

There has been prejudice against the working mother, or single working father. There has been reluctance to recognize that both are increasing, and are part of the intrinsic weave of the world we have created. Deeper than that there has been a serene ignorance amongst decision-takers or the makers of public debate as to how the harder-pressed parents of small children have to cope on a Monday morning. And underneath all lies one strong, instinctive disinclination which we largely share, and that is practical doubt before challenging the territory or the responsibility of the family. We certainly think that the family is the quintessential distributor and basic multiplier of love, care, and education; and that the greatest happiness of the greatest number is, in social policy, most likely to be attained by focusing resources on and through the family. And yet that has limits. This research has touched on child abuse and wife battering within the family; on marital break-up, and on the rise of single-parent families. It has illustrated inevitable, necessary or choice-based decisions to work when the child is young. It is no challenge to the family to offer evidence that its structure is changing, that working parents of the young in cultures where the implicit support of the extended family is less easy to take for granted are utterly crucial. We think positively about children, and the cyclical effect on the next generation; or we continue to ignore, and most surely reap recurring crops of dragons' teeth. Children, as the old myths once told us, *are* indeed society's seed corn.

Nor is the family threatened by a Minister for Children. Our piecemeal, episodic and sometimes (as with childminding) ill-contrived planning for the unenfranchised quarter of the population, endlessly illustrates that there are limits to what even the best-equipped family can do; but that much perceivable loss, stunting and suffering could be prevented by the conscious acts of society as a whole. No family yesterday could have removed the curse of cholera on every generation of childhood, no more than any family today can by itself make the urban environment safe for all its children. Man remains, as Aristotle saw him, essentially a social being. The private areas of freedom come after, and not before that insight.

But, as with childminding, only after many children have, unnecessarily, paid the price of our neglect.

257

Notes

Chapter 1 December Dawnwatch

The dawnwatchers included Barrie Knight, Brian Jackson, Anne Garvey, Julia McGawley and Sonia Jackson.

Chapter 2 Thinking

1 Hadow Report, HMSO, 1933.
2 Tim Horton, *Nil Growth and the Nursery Programme* NUT, 1975. The author says of costly nursery school buildings standing idle, either because they are open only during professional hours (9 a.m. to 3 p.m., five days a week, thirty-nine weeks of the year) or because — not being statutory — they are vulnerable to economic cuts.
   'The nation can surely not afford these buildings to stand like Martello Towers.'
3 Margaret Bone, *Day Care for Pre-School Children*, DHSS, 1975.
4 Horton, op. cit.
5 Bridget Plowden, 'Low Cost Day Care Facilities', a paper presented to a DHSS seminar in 1976. A DHSS figure released at the same time puts the number even higher — 335,000. No figures are very reliable in this field, since records from such an informal network of voluntary groups are very hard indeed both to collect and analyse. There is also an element of double counting. Our own daughter, Ellen, has in one week attended three separate playgroups, and that pattern must be common — especially amongst professional women who use playgroups a lot and either seek more relief from their child than a one-morning playgroup can give, or more stimulation for their child, or both.
   However, even if there is a large margin of error, for whatever reason, the speedy rise and present scale of this parent-provided provision is quite beyond doubt.
6 Department of Health and Social Security, *The Family in Society: Preparation for Parenthood*, HMSO, 1974. Despite the excellent paragraph quoted, this government publication — surveying the day-care needs of young children — and based on discussions with sixty-two statutory bodies, continues true to form and nowhere discusses childminders. Someone looking at the British scene from abroad would come away from it with an utterly misleading impression, as from all the major official literature until now.
7 Our attention was first drawn to this Circular by William van der

Eyken's book, *The Pre-School Years*, Penguin, 1974.

8 Central Advisory Council for Education (England), *Children and their Primary Schools*: The Plowden Report, HMSO, 1967 in many ways a pioneering and humane document, displays this same social remoteness: 'The day nursery is the proper place for those children who have to be away from before the age of three.'

What, one asks, does it mean by '*those* children'? It can hardly mean *their* children.

Tessa Blackstone puts the point opportunely in *First Schools of the Future*, Fabian Society, 1972:

> Would it be advisable for a small proportion of underprivileged children to remain outside the first schools in non-educational institutions, which could well become stigmatized because of their exclusive clientele of the most disadvantaged children in our society? Such children should be able to mix with their more fortunate peers and have the opportunity to benefit from trained teachers in these important years.

I would agree with the perception (if not always the language or logic here). My attention was drawn to this, as to other interesting points, by listening to my colleague, Jack Straw, arguing the pre-school case — always against hopeless odds — on political committees.

9 Barbara Tizard notes in a private paper from the Thomas Coram Research Unit, 'Provision for the under fives in ethnic minorities', 1976 that: 'a child who attends a half-day nursery school from his third to his fifth birthday will have spent only 4 per cent of the waking hours of his first five years at school'.

And we are, of course, a very long way from the situation where even a minority of children enjoy that provision.

10 Just how unusual is illustrated by the *History of Childhood*, edited by Lloyd de Mause, Souvenir Press, 1974, probably the definitive study of childhood experience in western societies over recorded history. It is a salutary analysis of children as burdens (infanticide), as saleable objects (slaves, oblation), as bothersome (swaddling, whipping), as sexual toys, or cheap labour, or creatures on whom adults could act out their violent fantasies. This scale of historical or cross-cultural perspective is conspicuously missing from the present debate in Western Europe, the United States, Canada, Australia and New Zealand about the nature of early childhood and what social provision is required. Peter Laslett in *The World We Have Lost*, Methuen, 1965 speaks of past child care in prosperous, literate, recordable Western societies as being a matter of 'semi-obliteration'. It is, of course, like little-marked grass graves, fading back into the landscape. With Norman chainmail, or the medieval three-field rotating crop system, or Henry's new-style Welsh castles, or Stockton and Darlington's early engines, we know every chink, acre, portcullis or cog. But only very recently, and only in parts of the world, are we learning to value children *in* themselves more than things *outside* ourselves.

Chapter 3 Exploring

1 Report by Christine Day, *Company Day Nurseries*. Institute of Personnel Management, 1975.

2 This was published as *0-5: Report on the Care of Pre-School Children*, by Simon Yudkin, Allen & Unwin, 1967. A pioneering document in its time, despite the negative legislation it prompted. But note again the Dickensian hangover. Unregistered childminders are said to 'constitute the sort of scandal that baby-farming in the mid-Victorian era provided for that generation'.

3 The negative attitude from above towards day care in the West Indian community is not easy to disentangle. Certainly the community does produce conspicuous examples of poor and damaging day care, and explanations of different cultural patterns in early childhood or settled marriage do not, I think, explain or excuse the sadness one sees. And certainly too there is a racial element; too-quick readiness to blame the black victim, and 'explain' the impoverishment of childhood primarily through the neglect of parenthood. I suspect the same applies to black or Puerto Rican minorities in the United States, to the children of 'guest workers' in Germany, or to the labouring and labelled poor in almost any industrial nation.

And in all such nations there is a specially negative charge in the legal history of day care — stemming from the first attempts of our forebears to clam up and control the vile exploitations of child labour and child life, which the first phases of the Industrial Revolution bred.

In their time they were hopeful measures, but they cast a dark shadow behind childminding today. I think of Buttercup's tra-la-la in *HMS Pinafore*, with which this study opens, or further back to 1862, with the creation of the Ladies Sanitary Reform Association of Manchester and Salford; when women were employed to visit working-class homes and teach the rudiments of hygiene and child-rearing. By 1890, Manchester Corporation was convinced (after twenty-eight years of the obvious!) and picked up the salary bill themselves. Much of this, I think, is in the almost imperceptible cultural pattern behind the Manchester chapters here.

Further afield, Florence Nightingale was placing majestic pressure on Buckinghamshire to follow suit. And nationally there followed the Infant Protection Act of 1892 a new lease of life for the nearly forgotten Life Assurance Act of 1774; the Prevention of Cruelty to Children Act of 1904; and then the Children's Act of 1908. Amongst many provisions there (not always carried to fruition) was the appointment of the 'Infant Protection Visitors', who enjoyed powerful police-like rights to enter 'premises where children are nursed and maintained'.

There is a lost historical study here. But in this research one felt its shadow, especially in Manchester, more generally in the legisla-

tive background to childminding, and — with special poignancy —
as one element in the difficult and struggling situation of mothers
and minders in the West Indian community. How curiously and
heavily the past lies over all of us; even as arrivals in a new land and
bearing a travelling historical burden.

Chapter 4 Childminding in Huddersfield

1 The Huddersfield area survey was done with the assistance of
students on Peter Lund's course at Huddersfield Polytechnic as
part of their field training. One of them in particular, Judi Thorpe,
made a major contribution, writing up her work as a degree thesis,
and later joining the team to organize courses for the very childminders we researched. We were fortunate too in that John and
Elizabeth Newsom's Child Development Research Unit at Nottingham University placed an outstanding postgraduate student, Kum
Kum Bhavnani, with the research team for a term.
2 Ron Barrowclough, *Social Atlas of Kirklees*, Occasional Paper no 3,
Dept. of Geography, Huddersfield Polytechnic — with the Batley
Community Project.

Chapter 5 Under five in Fartown

1 G. Stewart Prince, 'Mental health problems in pre-school West
Indian children', *Maternal and Child Care*, vol. III, no 26, 1967.

Chapter 7 Cornflake kids

1 We did this in co-operation with the BBC TV programme 'Man
Alive'. With the producer, Sue Boyd, we made an hour-long docu-
mentary on childminding in Manchester, beginning with the factory. This very fine programme was, on our side, part of our tactic
of 'open research' — the producer wrote of the experience in the
Listener, 25 July 1974. In its time it did a vast amount to draw
attention to the question of unresourced childminding, and helped
modulate public opinion more in favour of the positive approaches
that we were then just partly uncovering. But without BBC support
I doubt if we would have been able to obtain permission to carry
out this very small but unique packing-line research. Kelloggs could
very reasonably have said that from their point of view we would
only disturb production, and possibly give rise to unfavourable
publicity. We are therefore grateful to the Kellogg executives who,
after much discussion, gave us permission on the far-sighted grounds
that this allowed us to explore questions which were not confined
to Kelloggs alone, but to all employers of young mothers.

2 The Manchester research was carried out by Julia McGawley, who also drafted the first reports on it. It was very demanding and often lonely work since unfortunately we had not, at that stage, discovered a community of concern in Manchester, nor found the support or interest we had hoped for in the university, the colleges or the local authority. Much of that was to come later, when we moved on to an action/research phase, but meanwhile the seminal knowledge proved very hard and uncomfortable to win.

Chapter 8 Old Trafford

1 Report on Hulme V. prepared by W.K. Wilson, Manchester Corporation Director of Works, November 1973.
2 *Mother and Infant Health Review*, vol. 3, no 4, p. 21.
3 As Julia McGawley completed working with us on this very hard research stint, Sue Owen (we received financial backing from the Save the Children Fund) took over the reins to set up an action project on the basis of the local research. Creating the drop-in centre, which had never been done before, was the first step. Soon we managed to set up a necklace of five such informal centres (see Chapter 12).

Chapter 9 Portrait gallery

1 As Ann Oakley shows in *The Sociology of Housework*, Martin Robertson, 1974 this is a problem for the working class in general. The housewives she interviewed often saw their pre-school children as a source of frustration — messy creatures who untidied the tidy house and interrupted the housework with their constant demands for food and attention. Middle-class women were more likely to resent the housework, but find child care pleasureable.

Chapter 10 Childminding: a classic case in the cycle of deprivation

1 Charles Dickens, *Our Mutual Friend*, chapter XVI. I am grateful to Norman Franklin for first drawing my attention to this.
2 Quoted in an excellent survey, *All Our Children*, by Jack Tizard, Peter Moss and Jane Perry, Maurice Temple Smith, 1976.
3 Simon Yudkin, *0-5, Report on the Care of Pre-School Children*, Allen & Unwin, 1967 — a fugitive but influential paper, followed up by Simon Yudkin and Anthea Holme in *Working Mothers and their Children*, Michael Joseph, 1969.
4 Letter from the Department of Health and Social Security to the National Educational Research and Development Trust, 3 August 1976.

5 Scottish data from Jack Straw, special adviser to the Secretary of State at the Department of Health and Social Security, 29 March 1976. Northern Ireland information from Northern Ireland Council of Social Service, 3 May 1976, and Chief Social Work Adviser, Dundonald House, Belfast, 22 April 1976.

6 *Registration of childminders*

No of children per registered minder on average

1949	6·28
1950	6·35
1951	7·49
1952	7·46
1953	7·42
1954	7·79
1955	7·83
1956	7·90
1957	7·94
1958	7·89
1959	7·76
1960	7·76
1961	7·86
1962	7·99
1963	8·00
1964	8·00
1965	8·00
1966	8·31
1967	8·47
1968	8·13
1969	8·13

Effect of the 1968 Act

1970	3·31
1971	no data
1972	3·08
1973	3·02

7 Source: Central Statistical Office, 1973. But of course this increase is insignificant by comparison with the increase in the number of officially minded children — by nearly 500 per cent.

8 Source: 1971 census 1 per cent sample summary tables. (We must again recall the *caveat* of the field research in earlier chapters. The census here excludes many groups of women — single, widowed, divorced — who are exactly the ones to use childminders.)

9 *The Illegal Childminders: A Report on the growth of unregistered childminding and the West Indian Community* by Sonia Jackson, Association of Multi Racial Playgroups, 1972. Calculations on the number of West Indian children were then based on the 1961 census, which gave the West Indian population as 454,100 (317,900 born overseas and 136,200 born in Britain).

These figures were projected to 572,000 in 1971 (using E.J.B. Rose's massive survey, *Colour and Citizenship*) Oxford University Press, 1969. Figures for birth rates, family size and birth rate were derived later from *Questions and Answers on Race Relations and Immigration* Runnymede Trust, 1973.

10 G. Stewart Prince, 'Mental health problems in pre-school West Indian children', *Maternal and Child Care*, Vol. III, no. 26, 1967.

11 See Catriona Hood, T.E. Oppe, I.B. Pless and Evelyn Apte, *Children of West Indian Immigrants*, Institute of Race Relations, 1970, for an excellent survey of the situation then of West Indian mothers and their children. There is much valuable evidence too in Margaret Pollak's *Today's Three Year Olds in London*, Heinemann, 1973. And though not medical research, Augustine John's *Race in the Inner City*, Runnymede Trust, 1970, most sensitively documents the same range of questions.

12 *Action Registers One*, April 1974, *Two*, 1 November 1975, and *Three*, 1 November National Educational Research and Development Trust, 1976. The first and second *Action Registers* were edited by Sonia Jackson; the most recent edition was prepared by Barrie Knight and San Last. These documents were crucial to the concept of 'open research'. They simply asked official and voluntary bodies to record what they were doing in response to the unfolding research findings. This was enough to accelerate change. For instance, *Action Register One* was only able to publish response from six London boroughs and one other local authority. By *Action Register Three*, sixty-four local authorities were taking a positive, instead of negative, attitude to childminding.

13 Sources: Liverpool — communication from Training Officer, Social Services Department, 17 May 1974; Leicester — *Action Register Three*.

14 *Child of a Working Parent in Telford*: research and action report to the Telford Development Corporation from the National Educational Research and Development Trust, 1977.

15 *A Look at Childminding*, by Margaret Bristow and Jim Standing, County of Cornwall, Research and Development Study No.9, 1974.

16 The survey, by Margaret Bone, is in *Low Cost Day Care Provision for the Under Fives*, Department of Health and Social Security and Department of Education and Science. June 1976. The book also contains a brief presentation of our basic case for childminding as a possible breakthrough point in the cycle of deprivation.

17 Source: *Low Cost Day Care Provision for the Under Fives*, Department of Health and Social Security and Department of Education and Science, June 1976.

18 Source: *Company Day Nurseries*, by Christine Day, Institute of Personnel Management, 1975.

19 Source: *Childminding: Action Register Three*, ed. Barrie Knight and San Last, National Educational Research and Development

Trust, 1976.

20 As a prosperous middle-class family engaged on an exacting research project, we had no happier relationship than with the childminders who cared for our small children whilst we dawnwatched or pursued wisps of elusive statistics. Ellen today lights up at every chance to visit her first illegal childminder, Sylvia Howell, and — like a child in a Victorian nursery tale — calls her simply and lovingly 'my nanna'.

21 The evidence is extensively reviewed in A.M. Clarke and A.D.B. Clarke, *Early Experience: Myth and Evidence*, Open Books, 1976.

22 Family Day Care, United States Department of Health, Education and Welfare, Office of Child Development, 1973.

23 Figure from the Women's Bureau, quoted by the Child Welfare League of America in 'Day Care in the 1970s', by William L. Pierce, *Child Welfare*, vol. I, no 3, 1971.

24 *Windows on Day Care* by Mary Dublin Keyserling, National Council of Jewish Women, 1972.

25 Data on this section, apart from my own visits to many of the countries mentioned, is drawn from an excellent enquiry of European embassies in *All Our Children*, by Jack Tizard, Peter Moss, and Jane Perry, Temple Smith, 1976; *A Fair Start* by Tessa Blackstone, RSE Studies in Education, Penguin, 1971; *Two Worlds of Childhood: USA and USSR*, by Urie Bronfenbrenner, Allen & Unwin, 1971; *Windows on Day Care*, op. cit., *Current Trends in European Pre-School Research*, by Karl-Gustaf Stukat, Council of Europe and National Foundation for Educational Research, 1976; *Equality of Treatment between Men and Women Workers*, Commission of the European Communities, 1975, and several papers from the Child Welfare League of America, principally *Guidelines for Day Care Service*, 1972; *Day Care in the 1970s*. 1971; *Profiting from Day Care*, 1972; and *Changing Education* (supplement to the *American Teacher*, November 1971). A very useful overview, backed with full bibliographies is *Research on Early Childhood Education: an international survey*, edited by Maurice Chazan, SSRC, 1977. This looks at seven countries — Australia, Belgium, West Germany, Israel, Holland, Scandinavia and the USSR.

Chapter 12 Research into action

1 Credit for the funding of this pioneer project must go to the Gulbenkian Foundation and to the Chase Trust. The role of Richard Mills of Gulbenkian in winning this support for the National Elfrida Rathbone Society was especially important. It is not very often that one finds trusts supporting necessarily very speculative schemes, and then accepting and creatively using negative results, though this of course is what the task of trusts might largely be.

2 I was immensely helped in this evaluation (which could have been

so depressing) by Jenni Gunby, a very gifted visitor on sabbatical from New Zealand. She had worked with us years previously when we were setting up, at the National Extension College, the pilot experiments arguing the eventually successful case for an Open University. That innovative work also then went through a difficult passage; both times this touch of skill and inspiration from the other side of the world made a lasting mark.

3 Brian Jackson, *Changing Childminders*, National Elfrida Rathbone Society, 1976.

4 Much of our work here and elsewhere (especially with the West Indian community) would not have been possible without the sustained help and encouragement of Anthony Wilson from the Barrow and Geraldine Cadbury Trust.

Chapter 13 A tale of four cities

1 I say 'we' quite a lot in this section. But the 'we' was very much Hazel Wigmore, the quite oustanding director of the Centre, whose marriage of common sense and commitment, of endless energy and eternal tact, made it all hold together. As described, it can look straightforward, but my experience of this style of social intervention is that, unless it is run in a thoroughly workmanlike fashion, it could deteriorate into the sad state of a fireworks party on a drenchingly wet evening. It was Hazel, backed up by Judi Thorpe and Mary Crossley, who perfectly judged and maintained the elements of service, style and humble nuts-and-bolts administration.

2 The funding which led to this experiment in Huddersfield came from the Social Science Research Council. The Wates Foundation then agreed to meet one salary to help the carry-over into action research. This in turn encouraged the Save the Children Fund to attach a childminding adviser to the centre. Special help for work with unregistered minders came from the Sembal Trust, and work with adults who could not read or write came from the Adult Literacy Resource Agency. We then took advantage of the government's job-creation programme (an endeavour to create short-term work experience) to bring unemployed teachers and unemployed school-leavers onto the staff for a limited time. Lastly, we were backed throughout by the local authority, which supported our application to the Home Office under the Urban Aid Programme for further help. But a substantial part of the revenue was simply raised by the activities. Structured like this, the centre drew resources into a city that needed them, without having to lean at all seriously on the municipal budget.

3 All the Manchester work was directed by Sue Owen. Her salary was met by the Save the Children Fund and other staff came through the government's job-creation programme. Other costs were met by money we raised ourselves in any way we could, but again it was

amazing how very little money really was required in order to bring about striking improvements in the quality of child care.

4 In the *Observer*, September/October 1974.

5 We were only able to operate so well from Bradford because of the imagination and generosity of Eric Robinson, principal of Bradford College, who frankly argued that the facilities of his own college were often underused, and we might as well exploit them in order to make the research and action techniques nationally available. The National Conference in Bradford was very much the work of Barrie Knight and San Last, as was the third *Action Register* (the first two were compiled by Sonia Jackson).

6 A succeeding report analyses the result of this considerable broadcasting experiment. Much credit in the BBC is deserved by Neil Barnes who carried the argument for the programmes into that maze of corridors and offices which somehow houses the BBC's decision-brain; and to David Allen, who not only directed the series, but enthusiastically turned it into an effective social project. And all of us who took part in this extension of broadcasting into early childhood are conscious of the 'let's up and go' vivacity of Anne Morris who, in the midst of this raid (and of racing the first Beaujolais of the season in by light aircraft from France to England), astonishingly, most suddenly, and much to our grief, died.

7 The BBC announced that over 700 viewing groups had been set up to watch and discuss the programmes, bringing together childminders who might otherwise never have met each other. Numbers of registered childminders rose by 20 per cent during the six months that the programmes were broadcast.

Chapter 14 A charter for childminders

1 This notion has been most forcefully and brilliantly argued in Britain by Mia Kellmer Pringle, director of the National Children's Bureau.

2 Details of how senseless double standards operate in London are to be found in *Childminding in London*, ed. by Luise Nandy, London Council of Social Service, 1977.

3 *The Groveway Project: an Experiment in Salaried Childminding*, by Phyllis Willmott and Linda Challis. Institute of Community Studies and Shankl and Cox Partnership, 1977.

4 Among the benefits of the scheme, the authors note that it offers stable substitute family care in an environment not too dissimilar from the child's own background. Many day nurseries, staffed by middle-class professionals, see themselves defending 'proper' standards against the alien culture that surrounds them. (We've met some that symbolically strip and bath children on arrival, dressing them for the day in nursery clothes on the pretext of washing their own). When the class difference becomes a cultural one — black

children, white staff — the gulf is still harder to bridge. But recruiting day-nursery staff from ethnic minority groups is difficult (a problem discussed at length in the Community Relations Commission pamphlet, *Caring for Under-fives in a Multi-racial Society*, 1977). Salaried childminders are much more likely to reflect the racial mix of the local community — five of the Groveway minders were West Indian.

5   The debate about day care has been curiously divorced from thinking about child care in general. More enlightened local authorities have long since closed their residential nurseries, yet advocates of expanded day care continue to think of buildings and institutions — day nurseries or centres. As Phyllis Willmott and Linda Challis point out, childminding is not a poor substitute for nursery care. It offers many advantages both to parents and children: individual home care to the very young, disturbed or handicapped child, a family setting, flexibility in hours, convenience. And for an over-burdened single parent the link with an older, more knowledgeable person in the community can act as a lifeline.

6   The cost of day care is of course negligible compared with the £80 a week it costs to keep a child in local authority care when the family breaks down. The families served by the Groveway experiment — and by the childminders of Huddersfield, Manchester, Nottingham and Bradford — are precisely those most vulnerable to losing their children. Evidence drawn together by Robert Holman in his pamphlet, *Inequality in Child Care*, Poverty Pamphlet 26, Child Poverty Action Group, 1976, demonstrates the crucial importance of day care for poor parents, those in bad housing, and above all single parents (whose children account for 60 per cent of long-term admissions into care). Leaving aside the suffering caused by separation of children and parents, the ineffectiveness of social-work help, the future social cost of maladjustment and delinquency, it must make financial sense to tackle the enormous shortfall in day-care facilities head on if we hope to reduce the figure of 99,000 (steadily rising) children in care. This can only be done *fast* if we build on existing strengths within inner-city communities.

7   Prominent at this pioneer workshop was a determined London childminder, Monica Artis, who all alone had tried to carry childminders in her area into union membership. Until then we'd only been able to know and support her work through correspondence. Within the National Union of Public Employees, Alan Fisher, then General Secretary, and Reg Race, then Research Officer, were extremely helpful in making the idea of childminders as union members credible.

8   We draw this sharp distinction between union membership and forming the National Association (which sprang from the last programme of the BBC television series *Other People's Children*) partly from previous experience in bringing about a National Association of Careers Teachers. There all the members had achieved

union status, like other teachers, and this had a basic and beneficial effect on their salaries and similar questions. Nevertheless, it was not until the parallel professional association was formed (in the bar at a course held at King's College, Cambridge, by the Advisory Centre for Education) that they had the opportunity to meet, discuss, decide, share as careers teachers. We suspect the same professional interest within a vast union will come to apply to childminders.

9 We argue in the team as to who invented the name Open University. Most of us on this project, including Michael Young, Peter Laslett, Jenni Gunby, David Grugeon and Hilary Perraton, were involved in thinking out and acting out that earlier idea, then making it credible by twenty-six pilot experiments based, with BBC and IBA co-operation on the National Extension College. Michael Young 'planted the notion' on the Opposition of the day, led by Harold Wilson. Peter Laslett fed it into the official committees. I actually thought I dreamed up the name Open University in a boarding house in Sheringham, Norfolk. Sonia says she made it up as a title for an article by Michael in the magazine *Where*, which she was editing at the time. Barrie says we all made it up in the saloon bar of the Panton Arms in Cambridge. Whatever the truth, it is time we moved from an Open University to an even more important (and larger) Open College. The case is set out in the *Guardian*, 23 and 30 September, 1975.

Bibliography

Of making many books there is no end, and much study is a weariness of the flesh.   Ecclesiastes 12:12

Akram, Mohammed, *Far Upon the Mountain*, British Council of Churches, 1972.

Atkin, J. (ed.), *Do You Care? − the Community, the Minder and the Child*, Seminar report, Nottingham University School of Education, 1977.

Barrowclough, R., *Social Atlas of Kirklees*, Huddersfield Polytechnic, 1975.

Bell, Lorna, *Underprivileged Underfives*, Ward Lock, 1976.

Blackstone, T., *A Fair Start*, Allen Lane, 1971.

Blackstone, T., *First Schools of the Future*, Fabian Pamphlet 304, Fabian Society, 1972.

Blakeley, Madeleine, *Nahda's Family*, Adam & Charles Black, 1977.

Board of Education, *Report on Children under five years of age in Public Elementary Schools*, Parliamentary Papers, 1905.

Board of Education, *Report of a Consultative Committee on the School Attendance of Children below the age of Five*, Parliamentary Papers, 1908.

Bone, Margaret, *Day Care for Pre-School Children*, Office of Population Censuses and Surveys, 1975.

Bosanquet, N., *Race and Unemployment*, Runnymede Trust, 1973.

Bowlby, J., *Child Care and the Growth of Love*, Penguin, 1953.

Bowlby, J., *Maternal Care and Mental Health*, World Health Organization, 1956.

Bristow, M. and Standing, J., *A Look at Childminding*, County of Cornwall, Research and Development Study, No. 9, 1974.

Bronfenbrenner, Urie, *Two Worlds of Childhood*, Allen & Unwin, 1970.

Brook, Ray, *The Story of Huddersfield*, Macgibbon & Kee, 1968.

Brownlee, Maudette, *Comparative Psychological Development of Children with Group and Family Infant Day Care experience and Children reared at Home*, Medical and Health Assocation of New York, 1977.

Bruner, J., Reports to the SSRC from the Oxford Pre-School Research Group, unpublished, 1977.

Burgin, T. and Edson, P., *Spring Grove*, Institute of Race Relations, 1967.

Census, 1961, England and Wales, HMSO.

Census, 1971, England and Wales, HMSO.

Central Advisory Council for Education (England), *Children and their Primary Schools*: The Plowden Report, HMSO, 1967.

Chazan, M. (ed.), *International Research in Early Childhood Education*, SSRC/NFER, 1978.

Child Welfare League of America, *Changing Education* (supplement to the *American Teacher*), November, 1971.

Child Welfare League of America, *Expansion of Day Care in the United States*, Washington, 1972.

Child Welfare League of America, *Profiting from Day Care*, Washington, 1972.

Child Welfare League of America, *Guidelines for Day Care Service*, Washington, 1972.

Clarke, A.M. and Clarke, A.D.B., *Early Experience: Myth and Evidence*, Open Books, 1976.

Coad, Bernard, *How the West Indian Child is made educationally sub-normal in the British School System*, New Beacon Books, 1971.

Commission of the European Communities, *The Employment of Women*, Brussels, 1974.

Commission of the European Communities, *Equality of Treatment between Men and Women*, Brussels, 1975.

Committee on Child Health Services, *Fit for the Future*: The Court Report, HMSO, 1976.

Community Relations Commission, *Who Minds? A Study of Working Mothers and Childminding in Ethnic Minority Communities*, CRC, 1975.

Community Relations Commission, *Caring for Under-fives in a Multiracial Society*, CRC, 1977.

Cooke, J., *Nurseries and Creches in Colleges*, National Union of Students, 1976.

Day, Christine, *Company Day Nurseries*, Institute of Personnel Management, 1975.

Dennis, Wayne, *Children of the Creche*, Appleton-Century Crofts, 1973.

Department of Health and Social Security, *Report of the Committee on One Parent Families*: The Finer Report, HMSO, 1974.

Department of Health and Social Security, *The Family in Society: Preparation for Parenthood*, HMSO, 1974.

Department of Health and Social Security, *Low Cost Day Care Provision for the Under Fives*, HMSO, 1976.

Department of Health and Social Security, *Priorities for Health and Personal Social Services in England: A Consultative Document*, HMSO, 1976.

Dickens, Charles, *Our Mutual Friend*, 1864-5.

Eyken, Willem van der, *The Pre-School Years*, Penguin, 1974.

Fitzherbert, Katrin, *West Indian Children in London*, Bell, 1967.

Fitzherbert, Katrin, *Child Care Services and the Teacher*, Temple Smith, 1977.

Fonda, N. and Moss, P., *Mothers in Employment*, Brunel University and Thomas Coram Research Unit, 1976.

Freeman, Harold Jnr., *Families in Infant and Group Day Care Programmes*, Medical and Health Association of New York, 1977.

Gathorne-Hardy, J., *The Rise and Fall of the English Nanny*, Arrow Books, 1974.

Golden, Mark, *Overview: New York Infant Day Care Study*, Medical and Health Association of New York, 1977.

Goody, Esther, 'The varieties of fostering', *New Society*, 5 August 1971.

Gregory, E., 'Childminding in Paddington', *The Medical Officer*, vol. cxxii, no. 10, 1969.

Halsey, A.H., *Educational Priority: EPA Problems and Policies*, HMSO, 1972.

Holman, R., *Inequality in Child Care*, Poverty Pamphlet 26, Child Poverty Action Group, 1976

Hood, C., Oppé, T.E., Pless, I.B. and Apte, E., *Children of West Indian Immigrants*, Institute of Race Relations, 1970.

Horton, T., *Nil Growth and the Nursery Programme*, National Union of Teachers, 1975.

Income Data Ltd, *Child Care at Work*, Study 129, 1976.

Jackson, Brian, 'The Childminders', *New Society*, 29 November 1973.

Jackson, Brian, 'Childminding – a breakthrough in the cycle of deprivation', in *Low Cost Day Care Provision for the Under Fives*, DHSS, 1976.

Jackson, Brian, *Changing Childminders*, National Elfrida Rathbone Society, 1976.

Jackson, Brian and Rae, Ruby, *Priority Area Playgroup Project*, Advisory Centre for Education, 1968.

Jackson, Brian and Rae, Ruby, *Priority*, Association of Multi-Racial Playgroups, 1970.

Jackson, Brian and Jones, Joan, *One Thousand Children*, Advisory Centre for Education, 1970.

Jackson, Sonia, *The Illegal Childminders: A Report on the growth of unregistered childminding and the West Indian Community*, Association of Multi-Racial Playgroups, 1972.

Jackson, Sonia (ed.), *Childminding: Action Register One*, National Educational Research and Development Trust, 1974.

Jackson, Sonia, (ed.) *Childminding: Action Register Two*, National Educational Research and Development Trust, 1975.

Jackson, Sonia, 'The childminding research and development unit', *Health Visitor*, May 1975.

Jackson, Sonia, *The Educational Implications of Unsatisfactory Childminding*, paper given to the Developmental Sciences Trust, National Educational Research and Development Trust, 1975.

Jackson, Sonia, 'Unsatisfactory childminding', *New Community*, vol. IV, no. 2.

Jackson, Sonia, 'A new policy for childminders', *Social Work Today*, 4 January 1977.

Jackson, Sonia, Moseley, J. and Wheeler B., *Other People's Children*, ed. D. Allen, BBC, 1976.

John, A., *Race in the Inner City*, Runnymede Trust, 1970.

Kent, J. and P., *Nursery Schools for All*, Ward Lock, 1970.

Keyserling, M.D., *Windows on Day Care*, National Council of Jewish Women, New York, 1972.

Klein, V., *Britain's Married Women Workers*, Routledge & Kegan Paul, 1965.

Knight, Barrie (ed.), *First National Conference on Childminding*, National Educational Research and Development Trust, 1975.

Knight, Barrie and Last, San (ed.), *Childminding: Action Register Three*, National Educational Research and Development Trust, 1976.

Knight, Delphine, *At Work Together*, Pre-School Playgroups Association, 1976.

Labour Party Under Fives Working Party, *Social and Educational Provision for the Under Fives in Britain*, 1976.

Laslett, P., *The World We Have Lost*, Methuen, 1965.

Ludwig, M. and Ion, M., 'Studies of childminding', unpublished theses, University of London Institute of Education.

Mause, Lloyd de, *History of Childhood*, Souvenir Press, 1974.

Mayall, B. and Petrie, P., *Minder, Mother and Child*, University of London Institute of Education, 1977.

Ministry of Health, Health Services and Public Health Act 1968, Section 60, Amendments to the Nurseries and Childminders Act, 1948.

Ministry of Health, *Day Care Facilities for Children Under Five*, Circular 37/68, October 1977.

Nandy, Luise (ed.), *Childminding in London*, London Council of Social Service, 1977.

National Children's Bureau, *Coping Alone*, NFER, 1976.

National Children's Bureau, *Growing Up in a One Parent Family*, NFER, 1976.

National Educational Research and Development Trust, *Ministerial Responsibilities for Young Children*, 1976.

National Educational Research and Development Trust, *The Cycle of Deprivation*, NERDT, 1976.

National Educational Research and Development Trust, *The Nottingham Amnesty for Childminders*, NERDT, 1976.

National Educational Research and Development Trust, *The Child Care Switchboard Experiment: A Preliminary Note*, NERDT, 1977.

National Educational Research and Development Trust, *The National Children's Centre: An Introductory Note*, NERDT, 1977.

Nye, F. and Hoffman, L., *The Employed Mother in America*, Rand McNally, 1963.

Oakley, Ann, *The Sociology of Housework*, Martin Robertson, 1974.

Organization for Economic Co-operation and Development, *The 1974-75 Recession and the Employment of Women*, Paris, 1977.

Packman, J., *The Child's Generation*, Basil Blackwell, 1975.

Packman, J., *Child Care Needs and Numbers*, Allen & Unwin, 1969.

Parry, M. and Archer, H., *Pre-School Education*, Schools Council and Macmillan, 1974.

Pierce, William J., 'Day care in the 1970's', *Child Welfare*, vol. I, no. 3, 1971.

Pirsig, Robert M., *Zen and the Art of Motorcycle Maintenance*, Bodley Head, 1974.

Plowden, Bridget, 'Low Cost Day Care Facilities', in *Low Cost Day Care Provision for the Under Fives*, DHSS, 1976.

Policare, Henry J., *A Comparison of Psychological Experience of Infants in Group and Family Day Care*, Medical and Health Association of New York, 1977.

Pollak, M., *Today's Three Year Olds in London*, Heinemann, 1973.

Prince, G. Stewart, 'Mental health problems in pre-school West Indian children" *Maternal and Child Care*, vol. III, no. 26, 1967.

Pringle, M.L. Kellmer, *The Needs of Children*, Hutchinson, 1974.

Rogers, Everett M. and Shoemaker, F.F., *Communication of Innovations*, Free Press, 1971.

Rose, E.J.B., *Colour and Citizenship*, Institute of Race Relations and Oxford University Press, 1969.

Rosenbluth, Lucille, *Nutrition Provided to Infants in Group and Family Day Care*, Medical and Health Association of New York, 1977.

Runnymede Trust, *Questions and Answers on Race Relations and Immigration*, 1973.

Rutter, M., *Maternal Deprivation Reassessed*, Penguin, 1972.

Rutter, M. and Madge, N., *Cycles of Disadvantage*, Heinemann, 1976.

Rutter, M., Yule, W. and Berger, M., 'Children of West Indian migrants', *New Society*, 14 March 1974.

Schaffer, Rudolph, *Mothering*, Fontana, 1977.

Scott, Rachel, *A Wedding Man is Nicer than Cats, Miss*, David & Charles, 1971.

Spock, B., *The Pocket Book of Baby and Child Care*, Pocket Books, 1946.

Stapleton, P., 'Culture clashes and the childminder: problems relating to African families and the provision of day care', *Social Work Today*, July 1976.

Steiner, Gilbert, Y., *The Children's Cause*, Brookings Institution, 1976.

Stroud, Eric and Moody, V., 'One hundred mothers: a survey of West Indians in Britain', *Maternal and Child Care*, vol. III, no. 26, 1967.

Stukat, K.G., *Current Trends in European Pre-School Research*, Council of Europe and NFER, 1976.

Tizard, B., *Early Childhood Education: a Review and Discussion of Current Research in Britain*, NFER, 1975.

Tizard, B., 'Provision for the under fives in ethnic minorities', unpublished paper, Thomas Coram Research Unit, London University, 1976.

Tizard, J., 'Ten comments on low cost day care for the under fives', *Low Cost Day Care Provision for the Under Fives*, DHSS, 1976.

Tizard, J., 'Issues in early childhood education', *Child Development Society Newsletter*, no. 24, 1975.

Tizard, J., Moss, P., and Perry, J., *All Our Children*, Temple Smith, 1976.

United States Department of Health, Education and Welfare, *Family Day Care*, Office of Child Development, 1973.

Watkin, Brian, *Documents on Health and Social Services*, Methuen, 1975.

Wedge, P., and Prosser, H., *Born to Fail?*, National Children's Bureau and Arrow Books, 1973.

Willmott, Phyllis, 'Notes from Paris', *Social Work Today*, July 1976.

Willmott, Phyllis and Challis, L., *The Groveway Project: an evaluation of a salaried childminder scheme*, DOE, 1977.

Woodhead, M., *Intervening in Disadvantage*, NFER, 1976.

Yudkin, S., *0-5: Report on the Care of Pre-School Children*, Allen & Unwin, 1967.

Yudkin, S. and Holme, A., *Working Mothers and their Children*, Michael Joseph, 1969.

Index

277